With Her Machete in Her Hand

Chicana Matters Series
Deena J. González and Antonia Castañeda, Editors

With Her Machete in Her Hand

Reading Chicana Lesbians

BY CATRIÓNA RUEDA ESQUIBEL

University of Texas Press   *Austin*

First edition, 2006

Requests for permission to reproduce material from this work should be
sent to:
Permissions
University of Texas Press
P.O. Box 7819
Austin, TX 78713-7819
www.utexas.edu/utpress/about/bpermission.html

⊗ The paper used in this book meets the minimum requirements of
ANSI/NISO Z39.48-1992 (R1997) (Permanence of Paper).

Library of Congress Cataloging-in-Publication Data

Esquibel, Catrióna Rueda, 1965–
    With her machete in her hand : reading Chicana lesbians / by Catrióna
Rueda Esquibel. — 1st ed.
        p.   cm. — (Chicana matters series)
    Includes bibliographical references and index.
    ISBN 0-292-70971-4 (alk. paper) — ISBN 0-292-71275-8 (pbk. : alk.
paper)
    1. Lesbians' writings, American—History and criticism.   2. American
literature—Mexican American authors—History and criticism.   3. American literature—Women authors—History and criticism.   4. Mexican
American lesbians—Intellectual life.   5. Mexican American women—Intellectual life.   6. Women and literature—United States.   7. Mexican
American women in literature.   8. Mexican Americans in literature.
9. Lesbians in literature.   I. Title.   II. Series.
    PS153.L46E85   2006

                                                            2005009217

IN MEMORIAM,
Gloria Evangelina Anzaldúa
(1942–2004)

WITHDRAWN

La mujermacho alzó su machete
Allá en San Juan Puñacuato.
Los dedos de don Rafo saltaron
Y se le escurrió su coraje.

De la gente se oye decir
Que ya un hombre no vale nada
y hasta los huevos le estorban
a los machos de San Juan Puñacuato.
—GLORIA ANZALDÚA

Con su pluma en su mano
con paciencia y sin temor
escribió muchas verdades
y respeto nos ganó.
—TISH HINOJOSA

Contents

Acknowledgments

This book is the result of my partnership with Luz Calvo. I thank her for her collegiality, her love, her questioning of my logic and my language but never my capability or integrity. Her arms stretch me, her food nourishes me, her rooms shelter me, and she inspires every poem.

I want to thank my parents, Eleanor Marina Rueda Esquibel and José/Joseph Alfonso Esquibel. My mother, the artist, taught me the importance of the image, and my father, the storyteller, taught me the value of oral tradition. I also dedicate my work to the memory of Librada Tafoya Esquibel and Guadalupe Sanavia Rueda, amazing women from *México de aquí y de allá* who were proud of this oddest of granddaughters.

I am profoundly grateful to the authors who shared generously their time, their work, and their words, through interviews, public lectures, and even an unpublished manuscript. Specifically, I would like to thank Emma Pérez for early manuscripts of *Gulf Dreams* (1994), *1848* (2000), and *Blood Memory, or, Forgetting the Alamo* (2003) and our many conversations, both face-to-face and online; Terri de la Peña for an interview in San Francisco the weekend of the L.A. uprising as well as for some home truths as the book went to press; Cherríe Moraga, her personal assistant, Erin Raber, and her publisher, West End Press, for directing me to a copy of *Watsonville* before its 2002 publication. Cherríe Moraga has also been most generous in discussing her work in public forums such as "Transformations of Queer Ethnicities: A Conversation with Norma Alarcón and Cherríe Moraga" (1996). Sheila Ortiz Taylor spent a glorious summer day sharing memories, writing experiences, and twenty years of being "discovered" by young scholars. While I do not discuss her new novel, *Xtranjera* (the third Arden Benbow novel) in this book, it has nevertheless profoundly affected my work. Karleen Pendleton Jiménez shared "Not Everyone Turns Pink under the Sun." In early 2004 I shared chapter 5 with Gloria Anzaldúa, and I am grateful for her thoughts and feedback.

During the dissertation stage, I received exceptional attention and feedback on a rigorous writing schedule from Teresa de Lauretis, who "demands always a little more than my art can provide." Donna Haraway and James Clifford believed in my project and gave consistent support and feedback.

All along the way, editorial assistance was provided by Luz Calvo and Nancy San Martín. Marie Deer coached me for two summers, kept me on deadlines, and gave me a place to store my worries so I could concentrate on writing. Heo Min Sook, the best research assistant ever, has worked tirelessly on research, permissions, and bibliographies.

Pete Cruz and Carter Q. Serrett opened their home to me wholeheartedly for two years. They played (and made) magic, when I couldn't write, wouldn't write, and would rather do anything in the world other than write. For their love and support, I thank Nancy San Martin and Julie Marsh, Joanie Mayer, and also my sister, Christine Esquibel Wright, my nephews, Steven Vega, Cisco Vega, and Chip Wright, and my niece, María "Libradita" Wright.

The members and alumnae of the Research Cluster for the Study of Women of Color in Collaboration and Conflict have provided collegiality, mentoring, creative and critical opportunities, writing groups, *communidad*, and lifelines. Special thanks to Keta Miranda, Michelle Habell-Pallán, Luz Calvo, Deborah R. Vargas, Maylei Blackwell, and Nancy San Martín and to our faculty sponsor, Angela Y. Davis.

I have received encouragement and support from my colleagues in Women's Studies at the Ohio State University — especially Ruby Tapia and Rebecca Wanzo — and constant help from the staff: Ada Draughon, Linda O'Brien, and Melinda Bogarty.

My students, who now range from California to Texas to Iowa to Ohio, have drawn me out in independent studies, seminars, and many conversations. Former students have become colleagues, and I wish to thank Irene Mata, Adela Licona, Hector Carbajal, Gina Díaz, Mieka Valdez, and the members of Women's Studies 620 in winter 2003: Beth, Deborah, Heather, Kristen, Lakesia, Megan, Melanie, Min, Susanne, and Yi.

During my graduate student years, my research was funded by a qualifying essay grant from the History of Consciousness Department at the University of California, Santa Cruz, and the Chicana Studies Dissertation Fellowship from the University of California, Santa Barbara. New Mexico State University provided a summer mini-grant for author interviews. The National Endowment for the Humanities provided an Extending the Reach grant for two summers of support. The Ford Foundation provided a postdoctoral fellowship for a full year of research and writing. The Ohio State University provided additional support through research funds, salary supplements, office space, and staff. The College of Ethnic Studies at San Francisco State University provided an artist's subvention grant for the beautiful cover painting by Alma Lopez.

A shorter version of chapter 4 was published in *Velvet Barrios*, edited by Alicia Gaspar de Alba (Palgrave/McMillan). Chapter 6 was published in *Signs* 29 (9). Chapter 7 was published in *Tortilleras*, edited by Lourdes Torres and Inmaculada Pertusa-Seva (Temple). My thanks to my publishers for allowing me to reprint them here.

The *corrido* epigraph by Gloria Anzaldúa on page vi is reprinted with permission of the Estate of Gloria Anzaldúa, from her short story "La historia de una marimarcho," © 1989. The epigraph by Tish Hinojosa is reprinted with the permission of Warner Music.

Permission to reprint copyrighted material has been graciously granted by Norma Alarcón, Jo Carrillo, Terri de la Peña, Shirley Flores-Muñoz, Rocky Gámez, Alicia Gaspar de Alba, Alma Lopez, Cherríe Moraga, and Monica Palacios and by Arte Público Press, Children's Book Press, Third Woman Press, and West End Press.

Prologue: A Chicana Lesbian Scholar's Tale

There is, let us say, a mystery at the heart of the fiction we are reading The reader — the detective — goes in search of clues. How does she know what is a clue and what is a simple object or event, innocent of significance?

The master detective assumes initially there is no such thing as an innocent object or event. She stops along the way interrogating lamp-posts and dead cats, incidentally making herself ridiculous to passersby. But gradually, through great patience and a little luck, she amasses enough by way of object and event that when spread out all across her bed, or her breakfast table, or even her living room carpet they begin to group themselves into little piles of similarity. Aha, says the detective at the end of much rumination, and sends out little notes inviting the well-dressed suspects into the drawing room for a scene of revelation and finally accusation.

—SHEILA ORTIZ TAYLOR, *SOUTHBOUND*

I have spent the past ten years as a private detective, investigating the stories, the authors, the journals and anthologies, scrutinizing notes on contributors, peering through dusty photographs of authors, jotting notes in my tattered little notebooks. Ashamed, yet excited, I waded knee-deep into stories, into drama.

One detective alone does not make a case. I encountered other detectives in those means streets, those university libraries, those women's centers. Our eyes would meet over the stacks, and each would tip her hat, acknowledging the contribution of the other, but wary of letting slip any new clues.

I never meant to become a detective, an archivist, or a theorist. I only liked the stories. Sure, doll, that's what they all say: "Honest, sister, I was just reading the stories." Right. All the time, they're packing into the Book Garden, Mama Bear's, Sisterhood, Old Wyve's Tales, A Different Light,[1] come to hear the latest piece by the latest Chicana dyke author, waiting to hear if her fantasies match theirs, wear the same clothes, battle the same demons. Then they all run home with their heads full of stories, scribbling in their own little notebooks. I've heard it all before. All scholars are closet writers. We couldn't help it if we tried. I can spend ten years in research, but until I put it in writing, who's to know?

So this is my story. I'll tell it to you over a cup of joe. No fog, no fedoras, just another tale from another girl dick. It won't have the narrative closure you've come to expect, or begin at the beginning. In the beginning was the word, don't you know that by now? So I'll start with the word, and make flesh out of the details. If you want more than that, you'll have to go to the source.

I remember when I first started coming around here, telling people I studied Chicana lesbian writing. Might as well be up front about it, scare off the homophobes right away, deal with the crushes later. Still some white male graduate student, peering down from his superior height, responded, "Really? I shouldn't think there was a dissertation in that." Or a job. Or a future. But I stuck to my guns. Just you wait, brother, *la revolución*, she's a-coming, and you medievalists will be the first against the wall.

It was years before someone started asking the right questions. Not just who are you studying? But *what* about Chicana lesbian writing? What are you arguing? What are you finding? Where are you going with all of this? Because the stakeouts alone don't make the case, doll. You've got to write it all up, put the pieces together for the reader, the audience, the judge, the jury.

So now you be the judge, as I tell you that all stories start in the past, in the memory, in the fantasy of what once was or will be or has been or is now . . .

It all started with a story. About a Chicana on vacation in the Yucatán.[2]

Ah, the guilty parties begin to stir, writer and readers both. Yes, that's the one. And whether you love it or you hate it, it all comes down to the same thing: it is Chicano fantasy writ large with a lesbian pen. And it made my (heterosexual) advisor furious.

And it made my (heterosexual) (feminist) friends furious. And me, well it made me curious, about what they were finding so upsetting, about what it meant that Ixtacihuátl, the Aztec Princess, had come to life and said to esa Chicana dyke, I want you baby, I want you to want me.

And some folks say she's butch, not into roles, or "classically lesbian." I say she shows that desire is *pocha*. That what Chicana lesbians want is to be loved, to be claimed, to go back to the very beginning.

From Ixta to Maya to Gloria to Josefa to Catalina to Xochitl to Juana to Concepción to the unnamed lover, to the unnamed beloved, to Chulita, to Esmeralda, to Esperanza, to Lucha, to René, to every butch fantasy, every hot *sirena*, every *sinvergüenza* has a story.[3] This city's full of stories, and so is 'Burque and San Pancho and Falfurrias.

From the butch who turns straight girls o-u-t to the femme who goes to the nightclub with her favorite dildo in her handbag.[4]

They've all got their stories, and most of them will get you in trouble. I've got the *chisme* on all of them, written down in this little notebook. Or the one in my office, in my study, in my filing cabinet, under my mattress, on my laptop.

I've met women of history, both real and imaginary; Chicana lesbians born before there was a border, gachupine nuns, cross-dressing *conquistadoras*,[5] heroes to claim or problematic figures to ponder over. Women living in the shadow of the Alamo, the shadow of a man, someplace not here.[6] Women wielding machetes, tarot cards, black orchids, size-nines,[7] words.

Recently, I was disciplined in an English department, where I would tell unbelieving Victorianists that I regularly encounter the artists I study. The authors I talk about, talk back. If they react defensively, it's because they're real women (and men) who have been disrespected, scapegoated, threatened, and vilified. Who began to write fearing for their lives but who nevertheless continue to write, and to nurture young writers.

I love being a critic because it gives me the opportunity to give their work the attention it deserves. I get to be the reader who recognizes the allusions to Aztec Princesses, to corridos, to lesbian bookstores and coffee shops. I get to be the reader to whom the author doesn't have to prove she is queer enough, Chicana enough, lesbian enough, Mexican enough, feminist enough. (Enough is enough!)

My job is to link the stories with the clever remarks, to teach the significance of the work, whether in print or in the classroom. My job is to gather lost stories and tell them to new generations of women and men who never knew what came before. Who never knew that Sheila Ortiz Taylor published *Faultline*, "the first Chicana lesbian novel," in 1982.[8] My job is to remind old-school nationalist *machistas* that influence doesn't only flow in one direction, that queer Chicana art and fiction is important not only for what it says about queer Chicanas but also for what it says about Chicano/a culture, about American society.

And so to you, my judge and jury, my teachers and my students, you artists and authors and performers, I will introduce my cases and lay before you the facts and fictions.

With Her Machete in Her Hand

Introduction: History

Chicana lesbians have been appearing in print for over thirty years. They have been created by heterosexual Chicanas and Chicanos, by lesbian Chicanas, and by other writers whose works fall both within and outside Chicano/a literature. Yet Chicana lesbian writing has yet to be studied as a distinct field — as a body of work with genealogies, with imagined communities of writers and readers, with definable characteristics, themes, paradigms, and contradictions.

In this study, I begin to map out the terrain of Chicana lesbian fictions. In defining Chicana lesbian fictions as drama, novels, and short stories by Chicana/o authors that depict lesbian characters or lesbian desire, I realize that I am emphasizing one genealogy over others. By situating these works within Chicana/Chicano studies, I acknowledge the relationship between writings by queer Chicanas and Chicana/Chicano literature in general. Other valid approaches would be to examine these writings within the realms of Latina lesbian fiction, writings by lesbians of color, lesbian literature, or women's literature, and I try to acknowledge each of these genealogies at different points in my study.

The objects of my study are plays, short stories, and novels that feature Chicana lesbians: these texts are written primarily by lesbian and bisexual Chicanas, but there are also a number of texts produced by straight and gay male Chicanos, Chicanas who don't identify as lesbian, U.S. Latina, Latin American, and Anglo-American writers. All of these contribute to the image of the Chicana lesbian as she is constructed by literature, and make up a formidable collection of writings dating from 1971 to the present. My chronology itself is part of a larger argument: I don't believe in "firsts," that is, in naming one author or text as the "the first Chicana lesbian" author or text. In my view, to enact this naming invariably erases an author or text that came earlier, as a means of propping up the borders of identity. Thus, while I do start my chronology of Chicana lesbian writing with Estela Portillo's 1971 play, *The Day of the Swallows*, I don't claim it as the first Chicana lesbian text: obviously, such an argument could be contested on the grounds that Portillo herself was not a lesbian. In addition, while the main character, Doña Josefa, is explicitly queer, one can locate earlier literary characters and historical figures who we can read under the sign of Queer/Chicana: Zelda, the "neighborhood tough girl" in José Antonio Villareal's 1959 *Pocho*,[1] the seventeenth-century *criolla* nun Sor Juana Inés de la Cruz, and the sixteenth-century cross-dressing *conquistadora* Catalina de Erauso, to name only a few. My interest is not in policing the boundaries of who writes Chicana lesbian fiction and what makes a text belong in this grouping but rather in beginning the discussion of what Chicana lesbian fiction accomplishes.

Among Chicana lesbian writers, two have gained recognition in Chicano/a literary, academic, and feminist communities: Cherríe Moraga and Gloria Anzaldúa. As editors of the 1981 groundbreaking anthology, *This Bridge Called My Back: Writings by Radical Women of Color*, they ushered in an era of Chicana lesbian writing.[2] *This Bridge* was an early publication that prominently featured writings by openly lesbian Chicanas and Latinas. The essays of Anzaldúa and Moraga, those in this collection as well as those published subsequently, participated in the creation of Chicana lesbian identities through writing. Moraga has written six books and coedited three anthologies. In addition to four books, Anzaldúa wrote a number of short stories.

The work of Moraga and Anzaldúa is rarely perceived as being situated within a genealogy of Chicana lesbian writing. Instead they are decontextualized: Moraga is figured as the representative and/or definitive Chicana lesbian, and thus as a unique phenomenon; and Anzaldúa's theories and models of mestizaje, borderlands, and identity, as mapped out in *Borderlands/La Frontera* (1987), are discussed quite apart from her lesbianism. This has resulted in a containment of queer identities and queer cultural production within Chicano/a critical work. That is, either Chicana lesbians are embodied in one figure or their lesbianism is erased in discussions of their work. In my work I strive to recognize the contributions made by both Gloria Anzaldúa and Cherríe Moraga while at the same time reading their work in a larger context of Chicana lesbian writing.

I take as my starting point that Chicana lesbians are central to understanding Chicana/o communities, theories, and feminisms. Such an approach challenges any implication of heteronormativity as an essential characteristic of Chicana/o culture, as well as the assumption of heterosexuality as the starting point for Chicana feminism. It's crucial to recognize that the first articulations of feminist goals and struggles within the Chicano/a movement were marked by a homophobic backlash in which all Chicana feminists were subject to lesbian-baiting, at both personal and professional levels. Both heterosexual and lesbian Chicanas were injured in this "purge." My goal is not to dismiss the work of heterosexual Chicanas — particularly those whose careers were ended in spite of their "good" sexuality — but rather to point out the significance of lesbianism in these "primal scenes" of Chicana identity.[3]

Methodology

When I first began planning this book, I envisioned organizing it in terms of conversations between texts in order to investigate how Chicana lesbians in working-class rural communities work against, say, the masculinist focus of works like Rudolfo Anaya's *Bless Me, Ultima* (1972). My goal was to show how Chicana lesbian writing, firmly rooted in Chicano/a literature, takes up, reformulates, and queers existing paradigms. I was interested in showing Chicana lesbian writing as part of a continuum.

However, I felt that the structure of such an argument would reaffirm certain canonical texts while positioning Chicana lesbian writing as a recent phenomenon that merely reacts to or against canonical texts. Since Chicano literary criticism already foregrounds traditional works by male writers and minimizes the contributions of Chicana writers as newcomers or cultural and literary novices, I wanted to avoid reinforcing such structures of power. Even though Chicana feminist criticism has demonstrated the inherent sexism in the "newcomer" discourse (in addition to the ways in which such discourses exclude people of color from scholarship in the canon of American literature), it, too, has deployed similarly problematic strategies that marginalize Chicana lesbian texts within Chicana literature.

As a Chicana lesbian of L.A./Sonoran and northern New Mexican mestizo and Pueblo heritage, I am well aware of how problematic Chicana/o identity can be. I refuse the Chicano nationalist discourse that New Mexican *hispanos* have false consciousness and claim only a white European Spanish heritage. I see the anti-Semitism behind such statements as "Northern New Mexico societies are closed because they were founded by Crypto-Jews." At the same time, I have a lively appreciation for ways in which the story of the Mexican *conversos* disrupts narratives of traditional Catholicism in *nuevomejicano* communities (as were recently mobilized in a church-led protest against the art of Alma López).[4]

My methodology in this book is derived piecemeal from the scholars and movements that have shaped my own scholarship. Following Teresa de Lauretis, I work from the notion that lesbian writing is not a linear succession of traditions but rather a complex genealogy: One can focus on a particular line within that genealogy, but doing so generally excludes competing lines, fragments, dead ends.

Hayden White's theory of metahistory and emplotment (1973) is tremendously influential to the ways that I read these texts. White argues that history, because of its reliance on the narrative form, is subject to the same rules as "fictional" narrative, that narrative history is emplotted along the lines of romance, tragedy, comedy, and satire, and that historical narrative can be discussed through the use of the literary tropes of metaphor, metonymy, synecdoche, and irony.

It might at first appear backwards to use White's theories of history as narrative as a way of reading literature. My explanation lies in the work of Emma Pérez, who, in *The Decolonial Imaginary*, uses metahistory to discuss the roles of Chicanas in history:

> I am, in a sense, exposing how historians have participated in a politics of historical writing in which erasure — the erasure of race, gender, sexualities, and especially differences — was not intentional, but rather a symptom of the type of narrative emplotment unconsciously chosen by the historians. (1999, 27)

In its simplest form, my study is an exploration into themes of literary, historical, and visual representations of Chicanas, with particular focus on Chicana lesbians as subjects, objects, players, and characters within these topics. Specifically, each chapter is a case study taking up a mode through which Chicana literature represents Chicana lesbian life: La Llorona, the Aztec Princess, Sor Juana Inés de la Cruz, girlhood friendships, rural communities and history, and Chicana activism. In my case studies, I attempt to provide several examples of the ways in which the texts take up these themes and to what ends.

Schooled as I have been in the research cluster for the study of women of color in collaboration and conflict at the University of California, Santa Cruz, I turn to June Jordan and Audre Lorde, whose words continue to problematize any easy identity politics, recognizing that there is some degree of choice and action.

And even as I despair of identity politics — because identity is given and principals of justice/equality/freedom cut across given gender and given racial definitions of being, and because I will call you my brother, I will call you my sister, on the basis of what you *do* for justice, what you *do* for equality, what you *do* for freedom and *not* on the basis of who you are, even so I look with admiration and respect upon the new, bisexual politics of sexuality. (Jordan 1992, 193; original emphasis)

Jordan argues that identity is not de facto essential but manifested through action. At the same time, some identities are bestowed. In Ana Castillo's novel *So Far from God* (1993), the middle daughter, Fe, can choose to be "white" and "Spanish" and to live the American Dream, but ultimately, she is still caught in a system that treats her as "Mexican," female, expendable. Her silence will not protect her.[5]

We can choose, like Audre Lorde, to declare the multiplicity of identities that modify and confound any unified identities: "Because I am a Black lesbian feminist, warrior, poet, mother doing my work — come to ask you, are you doing yours?"[6]

In this, I wish to distinguish my work from, for example, the early trend in Chicano studies that refused to acknowledge such writers as John Rechy or Sheila Ortiz Taylor because they did not do the work of cultural nationalism, instead "putting sexuality before racial identity" (a value judgment that recent scholars have done much to question). Rather, like the writings of Pat Parker and Hilda Hidalgo that structure my argument about politics in my final chapter, I believe it is important to go beyond the limits of identity. In her poem "Where will you be?" Parker warns, "It won't matter/if you're/Butch, or Fem/Not into roles/Monogamous/Non Monogamous" when they come for the queers—"And they will come" (1978, 78, 75). Hidalgo, in her oral history, "El ser yo no es un lujo/Being Myself Is No Luxury" (1987), sees a sign that says "No coloreds, no mexicans, no dogs will be served on these premises." Rather than choose to argue that as a Puertorriqueña she is neither "colored" nor "mexican," she chooses to fight.

The Chicana lesbian characters, and the writers behind them, have chosen to fight, each with her *pluma*,[7] with her pen in her hand, for her place in Chicano/a culture and U.S. history.

Structural Overview

The dominant theme to emerge from this study is one of histories of Chicana lesbians written through fiction. Lacking historical proof of Chicana lesbian existence, Chicana writers have created one, indeed, created many, through their fiction. Chapters 3 and 4 begin with women in the histories of conquest, through the pervasive images of La Llorona and the Aztec Princess, respectively. Chapters 5, 6, and 7 focus on narrative strategies that create Chicana lesbian histories in colonial New Spain, in the rural Southwest, and in the coming-of-age story. Chapter 8, with its emphasis on politics and representation, discusses Chicana lesbians as contemporary agents and activists of history; and the final chapter, which shares the title of this book, discusses the articulation of Chicana lesbian heroes in discourses that have been defined as epic, male, and heteronormative.

Chapters 3 and 4 are devoted to representations of "the" indigenous woman, "La India" in Chicana lesbian fictions, by way of an extended discussion of the archetypes of Native American women in the Chicana/Chicano sexual imagination. Specifically, I discuss the figures of La Llorona, and Ixtacihuatl, the Aztec Princess. I discuss how Chicana lesbian authors portray, challenge, and change these figures through their representations.

In the fifth chapter, I examine fictional depictions of Sor Juana Inés de la Cruz. I am interested in what I call the ambivalent identification with Sor Juana. Many Chicana, Mexicana, and Latina writers have identified with Sor Juana as "the first feminist of the Americas" and as a woman of letters. Sor Juana occupied a specific privileged race/class position in the Spanish colony of New Spain. Politically progressive authors who choose to identify with her must also find a way to bring her closer to contemporary feminist and women of color politics. I focus on representations of Sor Juana in the fiction of Alicia Gaspar de Alba, in the drama of Estela Portillo Trambley and Carmelita Tropicana, in the cinema of María Luisa Bemberg, and in Octavio Paz's biography, *The Traps of Faith*, which, along with Sor Juana's selected writings, has served as the mainstream introduction to Sor Juana.

The sixth chapter begins with girlhood and adolescence, a time in which the Chicana becomes aware of her sexuality. *Las chamacas* are perceived as asexual, since they are not heterosexually active, at the same time that they are discouraged from recognizing or exploring their sexuality by mothers, family, community, and religion. I focus on the ways in which intense emotional attachments between girlhood friends are eroticized. Female friendships are initially encouraged in early adolescence, but as the girls mature, they are urged to give less emphasis to homosocial relations in favor of normative heterosexual relationships.

In chapter 7, I begin with an exploration of Chicana lesbian characters in rural communities, and the creation of Chicana lesbian histories through fiction. I focus on short stories by Gloria Anzaldúa, Jo Carrillo, and Rocky Gámez that use various narrative strategies—*corridos*, oral history, and lesbian pulp fiction—to represent the history of the Southwest as a Mexican history and to depict the rural community, which the Chicano/a movement often romanticized as the essential Chicano/a community, as always-already queer.

Chapter 8 turns to the politics of Chicana lesbian representation and Chicana lesbian representation of politics. I focus on the politics represented in two plays: *Heroes and Saints* (1992) and *Watsonville: Some Place Not Here* (1996). These works depict injustices committed against Chicano/a communities by a greater (and faceless) U.S. society. These are not historical stories of colonization but rather contemporary stories, showing the unfinished conquest, the nameless structural regimes that view people, women of color, Chicanas, as commodities, as unending sources of cheap labor, disenfranchised by poverty, by conditions of employment, by lack of documentation.

In my concluding chapter, I discuss the title of this book, *With Her Machete in Her Hand*, in relation to Americo Paredes's 1959 study, *"With His Pistol in His Hand": A Border Ballad and Its Hero*, and Tish Hinojosa's borderlands *corrido*, "Con su pluma en su mano" (1995).

CHAPTER 1
Chicana Lesbian Fictions

Publishing

The issue of visibility of Chicana (and in many of the cases below, Latina) lesbians is full of ambiguity. Lesbian writers have not always chosen to differentiate themselves from their heterosexual colleagues, either in their writings or in their public statements about their identities. Anthologies of Chicana writing of the past twenty-five years can be evaluated as falling into three categories: "nonlesbian," "lesbian-friendly," and "lesbian." "Nonlesbian" refers to those collections in which the authors and the tone are predominantly heterosexual. While lesbian authors may appear, their work is unmarked as lesbian, compartmentalized, or tokenized. Examples are *Woman of Her Word* (1983, 1987), edited by Evangelina Vigil; *Las mujeres hablan* (1988), edited by Tey Diana Rebolledo, Erlinda Gonzales-Berry, and Teresa Márquez; and *Infinite Divisions* (1993), edited by Rebolledo and Eliana Rivero.

Woman of Her Word was originally published as a special double issue of *Revista Chicano-Riqueña*[1] devoted to the writings of Latinas. It contains fifty-four pieces, mainly poetry, by twenty-four authors, and eleven works by visual artists. Neither the poetry nor the prose includes lesbian themes or content, and none of the authors or artists identifies herself as a lesbian. Yet the contributors include several authors who are now "out lesbians," among them the Cubana Achy Obejas and the Puertorriqueña Luz María Umpierre, or others such as Ana Castillo, who consistently deals with homoerotic desire in her writings. This lesbian absence is unmarked, as is the essential, structured heterosexual theme of the anthology, *Woman of Her Word* was a groundbreaking collection, a serious recognition by a major Chicano/Latino journal that women's writing is significant. And yet not only was lesbian writing *not* represented, its absence was not even remarked.[2]

Unfortunately, even later anthologies continue this trend. *Las mujeres hablan: An Anthology of Nuevo Mexicana Writers* (1988) was in part a feminist response to the 1987 publication of *Voces: An Anthology of Nuevo Mexicano Writers*, edited by Rudolfo Anaya, in which Chicana writers were perceived to have been underrepresented.[3] *Las mujeres hablan* features forty-four authors and artists, including Gina Montoya and Juanita M. Sánchez, both of whom later contributed to the *Chicana Lesbians* (1991) anthology. This anthology, striving for a broad cross section of *nuevomejicana* writers, provided an expanded model of women's literature, including recipes, artwork, and dichos, as well as poetry and prose. Emphasizing traditions and oral forms passed down from mother to daughter, *Las mujeres hablan* also included many writers from the same families. Unlike *Woman of Her Word*, which was organized by genre, *Las mujeres hablan* is divided thematically into sections, including "La Niñez Rescatada," "Nuestras Familias," "Nuestros Vecinos," and "Nuestros Paisajes,"[4] which are presented as traditional ways of dividing up women's worlds and women's lives. Like *Woman of Her Word*, there are no explicitly lesbian writings in the collection,[5] nor do any of the lesbian authors identify themselves as such.[6] The title phrase, "Las mujeres hablan," was consciously chosen by the editors as a refusal of the *dicho* "La mujer que sabe latín no tendrá ni marido ni buen fin": the woman who knows Latin — the educated woman — will not find a husband and will come to a bad end. The *dicho*, of course, equates spinsterhood with a bad end. Implicit in this collection of works is the notion that women *can* speak without fearing either of these eventualities. However, the implied undesirability of "spinsterhood" and thus the implications of compulsory heterosexuality are not addressed, either by the editors or the writings.

Infinite Divisions: An Anthology of Chicana Literature[7] is a large, broad-based, and historical survey of Chicana writing, no doubt intended as a textbook for literature courses. It features 175 works by forty-eight authors and spans the period from 1877 to 1993. In their thirty-page introduction to the volume, Rebolledo and Rivero discuss three major trends in current Chicana writing: the personal essay, "the redemption of the male relationship in the lives of Chicanas" (1993, 27), and "dealing more openly with sexuality," which covers menstrual imagery, heterosexuality, lesbian identity, and domestic and childhood sexual abuse. With respect to sexuality, they acknowledge the significance of the publication of the first anthology on Chicana and Latina sexuality, *The Sexuality of Latinas* (1989) and *Chicana Lesbians*. They make no mention of *Compañeras: Latina Lesbians*, although this may be because the majority of the writings in that collection are oral histories.

What I find particularly disturbing in Rebolledo and Rivero's discussion is the way in which they represent *The Sexuality of Latinas* (1989):

> The volume contains many audacious and even outrageous texts. It is a clear declaration that taboos are being tossed aside and that Chicana desire and sexuality will be articulated from various perspectives. (28)[8]

These two sentences seem to repudiate the collection at the same time that the editors are trying to acknowledge its significance. Their scandalized tone distances the editors, and *Infinite Divisions*, from the representation of *The Sexuality of Latinas*.

Furthermore, the editors manage to contain lesbianism in these two pages of the introduction. The selections by Cherríe Moraga and Gloria Anzaldúa downplay sexuality and seem to have been chosen mainly to conform with and enforce the thematic context of the collection, in particular the representation of archetypes, colonization, and motherhood. Of the formidable number of works in the collection, only three poems — "ever since" by Veronica Cunningham, "Making Tortillas" by Alicia Gaspar de Alba, and "Bearded Lady" by Bernice Zamora — deal with lesbian themes.[9]

In contrast, "lesbian-friendly" anthologies do contain writings that deal explicitly with lesbian themes. *Cuentos: Stories by Latinas* (1983), edited by Gómez, Moraga, and Romo-Carmona, and *The Sexuality of Latinas* (1989), edited by Alarcón, Castillo, and Moraga, figure prominently in Chicana and Latina literature, in particular for being two of the first works to focus on sexuality. Both collections have well-known Latina and Chicana lesbians among their editors, and both promote the works of lesser-known lesbian authors in both English and Spanish. Many of the stories had originally appeared in small alternative journals by women of color, such as the now-defunct *Conditions* and *Prisma;* others were new works or had originally been published outside the United States. While recognized as important to the development of

Chicana and Latina discourse, none of the stories has been addressed critically in Chicana literary studies.

The Sexuality of Latinas was originally published as the fourth volume of the now-defunct journal *Third Woman*. According to the editors' introduction, a special issue of the journal was envisioned in 1984 — one that would focus on Chicana and Latina lesbian writing. "However," they write, "such an issue has yet to materialize. In part this is due to the fact that very few professional writers — be they creative or critical — have actively pursued a lesbian political identity" (Alarcón, Castillo, and Moraga 1993, 8). Instead the special issue was broadened to focus on the sexuality of Latinas.

As examples of Chicana lesbian creative writers, the editors cite only Gloria Anzaldúa and Cherríe Moraga. In my bibliography of Chicana lesbian fictions,[10] I document the publication histories of other Chicana lesbian writers. By 1984 Sheila Ortiz Taylor had already published *Faultline*, her first novel featuring a Chicana lesbian protagonist, and in addition to Anzaldúa and Moraga, Rocky Gámez, Jo Carrillo, and Ortiz Taylor had all published short stories about Chicana lesbians. By 1989, when the "Sexuality of Latinas" issue was actually published, there were more than thirty stories by or about Chicana lesbians in print, in addition to an even larger number of essays and poems that were circulation.

The editors chose to "forgo a special lesbian issue" and instead decided to

> present [the lesbian's] voice as an integral part of the Latina experience — from the actively heterosexual, to the celibate, to the secretly sexual, to the politically visible lesbian. In this issue, then, which was started in the fall of 1986, the Latina lesbian is finally allowed to express the myriad aspects of her identity in relation to the same forces that have shaped her hermanas. (8)

"Lesbian" collections are the easiest to identify: *Compañeras: Latina Lesbians* (1987, 1994), edited by Juanita Ramos, and *Chicana Lesbians: The Girls Our Mothers Warned Us About*, edited by Carla Trujillo, are clearly by and about lesbians. However, though they are consistently invoked as important interventions into Chicana and Latina discourse, rarely have any of the works in either of these collections been studied seriously.

Compañeras, originally self-published by the Latina Lesbian History Project and then reissued by Routledge, features sixty-nine works by forty-seven authors and artists. The vast majority of the selections are personal essays, autobiographical vignettes, or oral histories. One memorable story by a Chicana author is Azucena Coronel's short story "Menudito," which depicts class and cultural differences in an interracial relationship while eroticizing traditional Mexican food. Below I discuss one of the oral histories, "El ser yo no es un lujo" by the Puertorriqueña Hilda Hidalgo, which both refuses and refigures the traditional "coming-out" story, mapping new directions for Latina lesbian identity.

Chicana Lesbians was published in 1991 by Third Woman Press. It features twenty-five authors in poetry, short stories, interviews, critical essays, and autobiographical vignettes. It includes previously unpublished writers, mainly from the San Francisco Bay area, as well as established writers such as Anzaldúa, Castillo, Moraga, and Yarbro-Bejarano. However, because *Chicana Lesbians* presents itself as the first anthology of Chicana lesbian writing, it unconsciously enacts an erasure of other Chicana lesbian authors who have been publishing since the early 1980s (Carrillo, Córdova, Gámez, Gaspar de Alba, and Ortiz Taylor) but who do not appear in the collection. Of the four short stories in the anthology, Cherríe Moraga's "La Ofrenda" and Monica Palacios's "La Llorona Loca" were previously published.[11] Terri de la Peña's contribution, "Beyond El Camino Real," is the first of her stories with explicit lesbian content to be published in a Chicana venue.[12] The editor, Carla Trujillo, describes the inspiration for the collection as coming from reading Ramos's *Compañeras*:

> At that time, *Compañeras* gave presence to the voices of Latina lesbians who, with the exception of Cherríe Moraga and Gloria Anzaldúa, had been largely unheard. Exuberant at its arrival, I anxiously read it from cover to cover. . . . As a Chicana lesbian, I wanted to see more about the intricacies and specifics of lesbianism and our culture, our family, mixed-race relationships, and more. (ix)

In Chicana lesbian literature, short stories, personal essays, and poems far outnumber longer creative works such as novels and plays. This is in part due to the fact that these shorter works can be produced in less time and can be published in a variety of venues: Chicana/o jour-

nals and anthologies, women's journals and anthologies, queer anthologies, collections of erotica, and lesbian journals and anthologies. Many
of the writers first publish short stories, which build up an audience,[13]
and then weave those stories into novels, or reprint them in their own
collections. In addition, many authors publish excerpts from novels in
progress to create momentum for the novel.

Criticism

To examine the ways in which Chicana lesbian literature is marginalized in mainstream Chicana literary criticism, I want to use Tey Diana
Rebolledo's *Women Singing in the Snow: A Cultural Analysis of Chicana
Literature* (1995) as a model. Because it is the "first [published] book-
length analysis of the Chicana literary tradition"[14] and because of
Rebolledo's prominence in Chicana literary criticism, it seems a suit-
ably representative work of mainstream Chicana criticism. Rebolledo's
larger project, developed in both *Women Singing in the Snow* and *Infinite
Divisions*, is the contextualization of Chicana writing in order to demonstrate that it is not merely a contemporary phenomenon but has traditions and a history. Thus she begins her study with nineteenth-century
Mexicana and Hispana writers—such as María Amparo Ruiz de Burton, María Christina Mena, and Josephina Niggli—and then moves
on to the early twentieth century—with the *nuevomejicana* writers Nina
Otero-Warren, Fabiola Cabeza de Baca, and Cleofas Jaramillo—and
then to women writers of the Chicano/a movement and recent trends
in Chicana writing.

In her introduction to the book, Rebolledo posits that Chicana critics writing on Chicana writers are "in the wilderness, the margins of
mainstream literature." She points out that most Chicana critics publish in small presses, whereas big-name Chicano critics, Calderón and
Saldívar, for example, publish with mainstream presses. She argues
that in their own work Chicano scholars marginalize the work of Chicana writers:

> The women (usually Cisneros and Anzaldúa) may be included as
> chronologically recent phenomena and tacked on toward the end of the
> book. That is not to say the critical discussion of their work is not use-
> ful, because it is, but as an addition, they are set apart from a contex-
> tual continuum. (1995, 3)

Rebolledo concludes her introduction by acknowledging the significant contributions of Yvonne Yarbro-Bejarano, "a critic whose work engages us all in further dialogue and understanding of lesbian issues" (9).

Rebolledo clearly wishes to recognize the achievements of Chicana lesbian writing; however, her analytic tools do not make it possible for her to articulate why the work is important and what it accomplishes. Discussions of Gloria Anzaldúa separate her writings from her lesbianism.[15] It is only in the ninth and final chapter of the book, "Mujeres Andariegas" (Wandering Women), that Chicana lesbian writers are discussed as writing Chicana lesbian literature. In the five pages devoted to the topic "Lesbian Topographies," many works are mentioned but not discussed: *The Sexuality of Latinas, Chicana Lesbians,* and Terri de la Peña's *Margins.* Rebolledo focuses on the best-known authors, examining "La historia de una marimacho" by Anzaldúa and Moraga's *Loving in the War Years.* She alludes to other works—Monica Palacios's retelling of the Llorona myth, "La Llorona Loca," the poetry of Angela Arrellano, and Alicia Gaspar de Alba's "Juana Inés"—but, again, these are not analyzed. Rebolledo then shifts her focus from Chicana lesbians and spends rather more time discussing other lesbian writers, specifically the Latin American novelist Sylvia Molloy and the mainstream American critic Bonnie Zimmerman. She concludes the section:

> For Zimmerman, critics who maintain a "consciously chosen position on the boundaries (and not one imposed by a hostile society) help keep lesbian and feminist criticism radical and provocative." This is intimately connected to Anzaldúa's vision of Mestiza consciousness in which she emphasizes that those positioned on the boundaries are often able to have a clearer vision of their surroundings. (1995, 202)

Rebolledo thus brings her argument back to a refiguration of Anzaldúa's *mestiza* consciousness without the lesbianism.

Rebolledo fails to locate Moraga, Anzaldúa, and Palacios in the same kind of "contextual continuum" that she demands Chicano critics accord Chicana authors. Nowhere do we see the early novels of Sheila Ortiz Taylor, the short stories of Rocky Gámez, the songs and drama of Naomi Littlebear Morena, or the work of any other Chicana lesbians who were writing well before the publication of *Loving in the War Years, Borderlands/La Frontera,* or, for that matter, *Chicana Lesbians.* Nor does Rebolledo address the issues of sexuality raised in the works of Ana Castillo, particularly in her novel *So Far from God,* which features lesbian characters. Instead, like the Chicano scholars she criticizes earlier, and for exactly the same reasons that she criticizes them, she depicts Chicana lesbian writing as a "chronologically recent phenomenon . . . tacked on toward the end of the book" (3). Although Rebolledo seems unable to discuss Chicana lesbian writing critically, she expresses a sincere desire to do so. Her gesture is to include Chicana lesbians within the realm of Chicana literature, to welcome them into the family gathering. It remains only a gesture, however, for once they arrive, no one knows quite what to say to them.

Fortunately, while this example may be representative of the ways in which Chicana lesbian writing is marginalized in Chicana/Chicano criticism, on the other side there are critics such as Norma Alarcón, Yvonne-Yarbro Bejarano, Mary Pat Brady, Sonia Saldívar Hull, and Emma Pérez, who consistently place Chicana lesbian subjectivity at the center of Chicana/o studies. Through her role in editing the journal *Third Woman*, Alarcón was active in the publication and distribution of Chicana feminist writings, including Chicana lesbian writers, and her critical work—"What kind of lover have you made me, mother," "Making Familia from Scratch," and "The Theoretical Subject of *This Bridge Called My Back*"—articulated the centrality of Chicana lesbians to Chicana feminisms.

Through her essays, Yvonne Yarbro-Bejarano has self-consciously constituted the field of Chicana lesbian criticism. Since 1986, when she began writing on Cherríe Moraga's first play, *Giving Up the Ghost,* her work has addressed the representation and construction of Chicana and Latina lesbian identities. Yarbro-Bejarano made an intervention into both feminist theory and Chicano/a literary theory by relocating Moraga's work in the context of Chicana writing, examining the plays' connections to Chicano/a writing, *teatro,* and other Chicana feminist drama. Her article "Deconstructing the Lesbian Body" examines the ways in which the lesbian subject, who is perceived as being only her body, her sexuality, is taken apart in Moraga's *Loving in the War Years.* Yarbro-Bejarano is quite pointed in her critique of the nationalist rhetoric that marginalizes and erases women within Chicano/a theater; however, she does not problematize that nationalism when it is refigured in Chicana writing. Starting in 1990, with her role in editing the exhibition catalog for *Chicano Art: Resistance and Affirmation,* Yarbro-Bejarano began moving her work from strict literary analysis into a cultural studies framework. Her essay "The Lesbian Body in Latina Cultural Production" also begins situating Chicana lesbian cultural production in a broader Latina context. Her more recent work has focused on the performance art of Monica Palacios, Carmelita Tropicana, and Marga Gómez, the photography of Laura Aguilar and Marcia Ochoa, and "A Chicana Femme's Tribute" to Chavela Vargas.

Since 1991 Emma Pérez has emerged as a significant voice in Chicana cultural studies. In her essay "Sexuality and Discourse," first published in *Chicana Lesbians*, Pérez deploys psychoanalysis to theorize the social and sexual oppression of Chicanas. Her theoretical construction of Chicana lesbian *sitios y lenguas* is a fruitful one for discussion of Chicana lesbian literature, given that it translates as both "sites and discourses" and, more playfully, "places and tongues."[16] Pérez develops this theme further in "Irigaray's Female Symbolic in the Making of Chicana Lesbian *Sitios y Lenguas*," in which she deploys Gayatri Spivak's notion of strategic essentialism to discuss the invention of a new "cultural vocabulary" by Chicana and Mexicana lesbians, which "mak[es] up words and poems with transgressive connotations."

In 1998 Carla Trujillo published her second anthology, *Living Chicana Theory*. This collection brings together both new works and many previously published essays by Chicana and Chicana lesbian creative writers and scholars from different disciplines, putting them in conversation with one another. Not all of the pieces are formal essays: there are performance pieces and written versions of oral presentations. Deena González contributes a critique of silences in Chicano/a studies, Alicia Gaspar de Alba develops her construction of Sor Juana Inés de la Cruz as a Chicana lesbian figure, Yvonne Yarbro-Bejarano discusses the photographs of Laura Aguilar, and Trujillo examines the figure of La Virgen de Guadalupe in Chicana lesbian art and literature.

A Community of Writers

In the introduction to *Chicana Lesbians* Trujillo describes her feelings upon reading Juanita Ramos's 1987 anthology, *Compañeras*:

> As a Chicana lesbian, I wanted to see more about the intricacies and specifics of lesbianism and our culture, our family, mixed-race relationships, and more. *Compañeras* had only teased me. Not only did I want more, I needed more. (1991b, ix)

In building my arguments about Chicana lesbian fictions, I am developing the notion of a community of writers. Drawing from Benedict Anderson's (1991) discussion of an imagined community constituted through discourse, I examine these texts as coming from a community of writers who see themselves as producing Chicana lesbian fictions.

Rather than argue for a strict, linear tradition of Chicana lesbian fiction, I am interested in the interrelationships of the texts and their authors. This is an important distinction, especially since, from my epigraph from Sheila Ortiz Taylor's *Southbound* to my final discussion of Cherríe Moraga's *Watsonville*, one might infer that I am arguing toward a linear progression, from earliest texts to most contemporary. Indeed, I have been disciplined enough to feel compelled to discuss the texts in chronological order—as I do in chapter 2—but it is also this tendency in my own work against which I struggle. It is not my goal to leave the reader with a sense that contemporary Chicana lesbian writing is somehow the culmination of all that came before. Instead, I am arguing throughout that there are many different ways to read these texts alongside one another.

There are countless queer Chicana lesbian subjects walking around, but the circle of published authors has been relatively small. Most of the authors know each other's work, even if they do not know one another personally. In addition, they are often called upon to review one another's books, or to contribute stories for anthologies. The stories themselves echo themes, sometimes deliberately, sometimes unconsciously, as the author takes up questions posed by her colleagues.

What I see developing is an ongoing conversation about Chicana lesbian identity and experience. This can even occur in the writings of one author. Terri de la Peña, for example, creates a community of Chicana lesbians on L.A.'s west side in her novels and short stories. Protagonists from one story will have cameos in another, and the evil ex from one story may find true love in the next. De la Peña emphasizes the role of community at the end of *Margins* and *The Latin Satins*, both of which feature a community coming together, in a lesbian bookstore or a lesbian bar, to appreciate and support its members, writers, singers, and performers.

Lest this argument appear esoteric, let me give concrete examples of Chicana lesbian writers reading Chicana lesbian writing. In 1992 de la Peña reviewed *Send My Roots Rain,* a lesbian novel featuring Carole

Rio, a Chicana-Riqueña protagonist by the Cubana author Ibis Gomez-Vega. De la Peña took special notice of the fact that Carole was alienated from the land, to which she should have been connected: "Not even her proximity to Mexico provokes a bond with the land; Carole remains a transplanted Easterner, fearful of the desert" (34). Gaspar de Alba reviewed *Chicana Lesbians* (1991) for *Signs* in 1993. Also in 1993, the Latina lesbian 'zine *este no tiene nombre* published Rose Cosme's review of de la Peña's *Margins* and Donají's interview with de la Peña ("A Closer Look") in the same issue (2 [2], winter 1993). In her essay, titled "One Chicana's View of *Margins*," Cosme takes exception to what she sees as

> [t]he real story or hidden text in *Margins*[:] . . . [its] acceptance of [the protagonist's] own mother's racism. The Melendez family who embraces a Mexican tradition and culture creates a fine line between who is an acceptable Mexican and who is not. (7)

Cosme critiques the racism within Chicano/a communities and expresses the wish that de la Peña's character would have spoken out against her mother's racist attitudes. While this review is clearly "balanced" by the very positive Donají interview with de la Peña, the next issue of *este no tiene nombre* includes a spirited defense of *Margins*, both by de la Peña and by the critic Ellie Hernández.

Hernández pushes readers to move from arguing about racism within Chicano/a communities to calling into question the racist structures that thrive off such divisiveness. "We are colonized in the deepest sense: racially, sexually, psychologically and, yes, intellectually. *Margins* draws attention to the self-loathing so characteristic of a conquered people . . . with the simplicity and integrity of a first novel" (1993, 7). De la Peña's piece, "Still on the *Margins*," begins, "It seems some lesbians, including some Latina lesbians, wish I had written another book. Others welcome *Margins* as the novel they had been awaiting" (1993b, 6). De la Peña describes the characters' differing attitudes about race as realistic. At the same time, she wants to push the argument beyond a disagreement into a "will to write" and challenges "other Chicanas and Latinas to channel their energies into producing their own much-needed contributions to Chicana and Latina lesbian literature" (1993b, 6).

In the spring issue of *esto no tiene nombre*, the editors, Margarita Castilla, Vanessa Cruz, tatiana de la tierra, Patricia Pereira-Pujol, and Lori Cardona, explain:

> In the last issue we made the difficult choice of publishing an unfavorable review of *Margins*. On the one hand, we wanted to support the efforts of an emerging Latina writer, one of the few that are getting published. On the other hand, we felt that the review was not a malicious attack but a Chicana's effort to put in writing some of her thoughts about an important work. Therefore in accordance with our editorial policy, we went ahead and published it. We got some flack for it, but we are very happy that some very articulate women, including Terri de la Peña, took the time to respond to it.
>
> This is what we want *esto* to be: an open forum, a place where we air things out, where we get down to business and speak to each other, with respect, the truths about our own lives. It is difficult, but maybe we will have to let some things go in order to make it happen. (Castilla et al. 4)

Another example of public conversation between writers occurred in 1995 when Emma Pérez reviewed de la Peña's second novel, *The Latin Satins*, for the *Lesbian Review of Books*. Pérez's argument focuses on the Tejana singer Selena, and her performance of Chicana sexuality, and she discusses the characters of *Latin Satins* as "Selena's Sisters," that is, as Chicana performance artists performing gender and sexuality. She draws attention to the characters' reactions against bisexuality and sadomasochism in the lesbian community:

> If de la Peña is demonstrating for us how [the characters] react against the expression of S/M politics in the community, then she succeeds. However, I sensed a moral ethic attempting to engineer the right kind of political lesbianism. . . . But these are personally charged controversies and only a minor contention within the novel. (1995a, 4)

De la Peña's subsequent review of Pérez's novel *Gulf Dreams* for *Sojourner* takes a critical view of Pérez's own structural and narrative strategies—"the novel's structure consists not of chapters but of paragraphs strung together"—especially the decision not to name the two main characters:

Yet while I recognize Pérez's strategy, I believe namelessness in this instance proves confusing. As any writer focusing on female characters realizes, repetitive "shes" and "hers" often result in a jumble of misplaced identities. In my own fiction, I tend to be almost ritualistic about choosing characters' names. I cannot expect other writers to share my practice but admit to being disappointed by Pérez's decision to leave her major characters nameless. I wish I could refer to them by name rather than as "the narrator" and "the object of her desire." Ana Castillo adheres to a similar strategy in some of the stories in *Loverboys*, her recent collection. To each her own, though I hope unnamed characters do not become a staple in Chicana fiction. What better way to say "we are here" than to bestow melodious Spanish and/or indigenous names on our fictional characters to make them more memorable. (1996, 6)[17]

Thus I am not arguing for some idealized utopic notion of a community of writers but rather for a space in which the authors debate the identities, languages, and spaces of Chicana lesbianism. There is constant contestation about what it means to be a Chicana lesbian: Being the only Chicana in a white lesbian community, being part of a larger Latina lesbian or lesbian of color community, being the only dyke in a Chicana/o community, developing a crush on a girlhood friend, the erotics of loss,[18] the refusal of normative gender roles, butch/femme relationships, non-butch/femme relationships, growing up in the barrio, growing up on the ranch, relationships with mothers and grandmothers, girl gangs, religious visions, healing ceremonies, motherhood, interracial relationships, Chicana-Chicana relationships, Chicana lesbians as vampires, as academics, as nuns, as bad girls. The list goes on. These conversations are irreconcilable, and to some extent, that is their point.

CHAPTER 2

The Mystery of the Weeping Woman

During my second year as a Ph.D. student, I was a teaching assistant in my first-ever Chicano/a studies class, and I was alternately dubious, furious, and inspired. One of the lectures by Shirley Flores-Muñoz, the instructor, was titled "Post-Colonial Myth, or, A Message from the Past: La Llorona, La Malinche, La Virgen de Guadalupe." I remember the lecture clearly. Flores-Muñoz described hearing about La Llorona and the way the story stayed with her:

> La Llorona was said to be a woman who neglected her children, party-ing and dancing into the night, a mother who either abandoned her children or killed them by drowning them in a river. La Llorona was barred from entering heaven until she recovered her children from the river; it is said that she wanders the rivers at night weeping and wail-ing for them.
>
> As a child, the legend of la Llorona reinforced my fears about living up to the expectations that were placed on me by my family and society. Yet when I grew up, I wondered about this poor woman. (1997, 165)

Flores-Muñoz linked the tradition of La Llorona stories with the vio-lence of the conquest: the indigenous men murdered, the indigenous women mourning. She talked about reevaluating the three Mexican mothers: La Llorona as the survivor, not the murderer; La Malinche as finding a way to work for the lives of her people; and La Madre Virgen and the need to make peace with her impossible standard. That lecture was a real experience of Llorona storytelling: the students were hanging on Flores-Muñoz's every word but also arguing against her deconstruction of La Llorona, her excavation of conquest, patriarchy, and rape.

When I began my own research, I discovered that Chicana lesbian literature, too, is haunted by this mysterious woman of sadness. She walks the waterways. Her cries echo in the night, striking fear into the hearts of children.

Mythic Mexican Mothers

Chicana feminist scholarship has long been concerned with the iconography of Mexican womanhood, and Flores-Muñoz's theorizations are part of on ongoing dialogue. Discussions have focused on three key figures, La Malinche, La Virgen de Guadalupe, and La Llorona, all of whom are closely tied to the Spanish conquest of Mexico, to colonialism and mestizaje. These mythical Mexican mothers form a maternal trinity in the Mexican and Mexican American cultures. Although each of these figures has been viewed differently during different historical periods, today they are commonly figured as the sexual mother, the virgin mother, and the murderous mother, respectively. Yet, as Gloria Anzaldúa (1993a, 108) argues, Chicana writers and artists consistently "reread" them through their work.

La Malinche

> No, Malinche was not a lesbian, in so far as the records of her sexuality suggest, but we can make her one if we choose. (D. González 1991)

Variously described in the historical record as Malintzín, Malinalli, and Doña Marina, the first of this trinity is best known as La Malinche. This Indian woman has figured as the original/originating mother of the mestizo peoples of the Americas and thus as a symbol of the rape, conquest, and colonization of the native peoples under Spain. Born to an Aztec cacique family, La Malinche was sold to Mayan traders as a child, who sold her again on the Yucatán coast. She "knew the language of Coatzacoalcos, which is that of Mexico, and she knew the Tabascan language also" and was able to serve as translator for Hernán Cortez: "without Doña Marina we could not have understood the language of New Spain and Mexico" (Díaz del Castillo 1963, 86–87). A key instrument in the downfall of the Aztec empire in 1519, La Malinche has been figured as a traitor to her people since the end of the colonial period.[1] The stigma of *malinchismo/vendidismo* has been repeatedly used to keep Chicanas "in their place."

This Mexican nationalist strategy was appropriated by Chicano nationalists in the 1960s. Chicana feminists in particular were identified with La Malinche. Adelaida Del Castillo's 1977 study, "Malintzín Tenépal: A Preliminary Look into a New Perspective," identifies discourses of La Malinche while contributing to them and is a significant intervention into the Chicano nationalist representation of La Malinche. Del Castillo identifies three key strategies in (Mexican/Chicano) representations of La Malinche:

> (1) [La Malinche] is oftentimes presented very simply . . . as . . . part of the necessary back-drop to Cortés' triumphant conquest . . . [;]
> (2) her portrayal assumes synonymity with destruction when she is singled out as the sole cause of the fall of the "patria" and becomes the scapegoat for all Mexican perdition . . . [;] (3) romanticists . . . [depict] Doña Marina as the misguided and exploited victim of the tragic love affair . . . [with] Hernán Cortés. (124)

Through her own "mystical interpretation of a historical role," Del Castillo proposes an alternative representation—that La Malinche "not be portrayed as negative, insignificant or foolish, but instead be perceived as a woman who was able to act beyond her prescribed societal function, namely that of being a mere concubine and servant, and perforce as one who was willing to make great sacrifices for what she believed to be a philanthropic [objective]" (126). Thus Del Castillo proposes a fourth strategy of representation for La Malinche: she is a product of her time, culture, and religious conversion, acting in good faith.

Norma Alarcón, in her essays "Chicana's Feminist Literature: A Re-vision through Malintzin/or Malintzin: Putting Flesh Back on the Object" (1983) and "Traddutora, Traditora: A Paradigmatic Figure of Chicana Feminism" (1989b), proposes a fifth view of La Malinche. She views la Malinche as a pragmatist in a patriarchal culture who chooses to become a speaking subject (*la lengua*).

Chicana lesbian authors have recognized a connection between La Malinche as victim of patriarchy and the nationalist representation of feminists and lesbians as Malinches. Visible in the 1969 statement "La

Chicana does not wish to be liberated" is the pressure brought to bear against and among Chicanas to minimize sexism within *el movimiento* in view of the larger picture: liberation of the Chicano/a community.[2] Lesbian-baiting was a particularly effective form of silencing feminist women.

> The Chicanas who voiced their discontent with the organizations and with male leadership were often labeled "women's libbers" and "lesbians." This served to isolate and discredit them, a method practiced both covertly and overtly. (S. López 1977, 26; cited in Moraga 1983, 112)

Sonia López identifies the effectiveness of lesbian-baiting (although she doesn't name it as such) when she elaborates: "A saying, 'Las Chicanas con pantalones,' was often used to ridicule and tease Chicana activists" (27).

The nationalist logic equated feminism with usurping the dominant male role and thus with both lesbianism and La Malinche.

> You have the straight brothers and sisters quoting that now famous line about the women's movement being a white woman's trip filled to the armpits with bulldaggers and castrating bitches and of course no self-respecting 100% Mexican will have jack shit to do with that unless you don't mind being called a vendida, sellout. . . . The only way out is to walk hand in hand with your man and together battle the white devils of oppression. (Morena 1980, 346)

In her play *Survivors: A Lesbian Rock Opera* (1980), Naomi Littlebear Morena creates a Chicana protagonist, Clara, who refuses to accept the "Woman of Color" role assigned to her in her white feminist community. Clara argues that feminists, like Chicano nationalists, erase her lesbianism in favor of their preconceived notions of her identity and role.

In works such as Cherríe Moraga's "A Long Line of Vendidas" and Gloria Anzaldúa's *Borderlands/La Frontera*, the connection between Malinche and lesbians is pursued as a means of turning patriarchal *machista* logic on its head:

> Not me sold out my people but they me. *Malinalli Tenepat* or *Malintzín* has become known as la Chingada—the fucked one. . . . Because of the

color of my skin they betrayed me. The dark-skinned woman has been silenced, gagged, caged, bound into servitude with marriage, bludgeoned for 300 years, sterilized and castrated in the twentieth century. (Anzaldúa 1987, 44)

Moraga pursues the metaphor further, ironically reclaiming the reviled, or, in the words of Michele Cliff (1980), "claiming an identity they taught me to despise":

The woman who defies her role as subservient to her husband, father, brother or son by taking control of her own sexual destiny is purported to be a "traitor to her race" by contribution to the "genocide" of her people — whether or not she has children. In short, even if the defiant woman is *not* a lesbian, she is purported to be one; for like the lesbian in the Chicano/a imagination, she is una *malinchista*. Like the Malinche of Mexican history, she is corrupted by foreign influences [that] threaten to destroy her people. (Moraga 1983, 113; original emphasis)

Thus the title of Moraga's essay "A Long Line of Vendidas" challenges the interpellation of Chicana lesbian as Malinche. Reversing the taunt of five-year-olds, "I know you are but what am I?" Moraga demands, "I know I am, but what are you?" To call the Chicana lesbian *una malinchista* is a priori to critique Chicano/a culture's misogyny.

These arguments are carried still further in the work of Emma Pérez. In "Sexuality and Discourse" (1991), Pérez reexamines the formation of Mexican and Chicano male identity through La Malinche, expanding on the psychoanalytic concepts of Oedipus and castration. She argues that the Mexican/Chicano male must disparage the indigenous mother in order to identify with the Spanish conquistador father. Implicit in Pérez's argument is the Chicana lesbian daughter's duty to recuperate La Malinche, to save her mother from history, or at least to memorialize her struggle. Deena González develops the same idea explicitly in "Malinche as Lesbian" (1991). Thus Anzaldúa, Moraga, Pérez, Morena, and González can be said to propose a sixth model of La Malinche: Malinche as lesbian and thus a challenge to patriarchal logic. These six models demonstrate the roles of La Malinche in the Chicana/Chicano imaginary, and the last one especially demonstrates her significance to Chicana lesbian writing.

La Virgen de Guadalupe

La Malinche does not reign alone as the mother of Mexican and Chicano/a people. Her "good" counterpart is La Virgen de Guadalupe. La Virgen is tied to the cultural conquest, *la otra conquista*. She is a syncretic mixture of religious figures, combining the "old" mother goddesses of indigenous Mexico (Teotenantzín, Coatlaxopeuh, Cihuacoatl) with the new Catholic Virgin Mary. Catholicism began to enjoy real success in the Americas only after the 1531 apparition of "una azteca, vestida en ropa de india" (an Aztec woman, dressed in the garments of an Indian) (Anzaldúa 1987). She appeared to the Indian Juan Diego, a recent convert to Catholicism, on the hill of Tepayac, a site sacred to Tonantsi, an Azteca-Mexica earth goddess.

Like La Malinche, La Virgen de Guadalupe has gone through several reformations. During the Independence period, her image was carried as a battle standard by *criollos, indios,* and mestizos against the Spanish *peninsulares*. Her image was also prominent in the Mexican Revolution. Yet, as Guillermo Gómez-Peña (1996a, 175) has pointed out, Guadalupe is the signifier for contradictory signifieds: "a fundamentalist Catholic movement operating out of fear of modernity and change," yet protector of the undocumented farmworkers; a symbol of the PRI, to "guard our identity, our national character, and our sovereignty," yet a loving mother who embraces all her children — low-riding cholos, Chicana lesbians, and student activists alike — with unconditional love. La Virgen is never stern or condemnatory but always loving and accepting.

The challenge La Virgen poses to Chicana feminists is her link to a patriarchal religion in which she has consistently been used to enforce women's self-abnegation, in a culturally approved *marianismo*: "the model for the ideal woman ... derived from the religious cult of the Virgin Mary" and based on humility and self-sacrifice (Macklin 1980, 129). La Virgen is an impossible ideal that no flesh-and-blood woman can live up to. But after the Chicana feminist daughter rebels against her mother, La Virgen, she comes to understand her. It is through their identification of La Virgen with a human woman — one's own grandmother, one's own mother, one's self — that Chicana artists in particular have made peace with her.

In doing so, however, they have not come to peace with the Catholic church, conservative Guadalupanos, or Mexican and Chicano patriarchy. Chicana artists'—especially Chicana lesbians'—icons of La Virgen are met with bomb scares, death threats, and defacement. By putting a human face on La Virgen, Chicana artists have assailed her position of the Virgin Mary, "alone of all her sex."

An analogy occurs in Chicano/a theater: El Teatro Campesino puts on a biannual Christmas performance of the apparitions of La Virgen de Guadalupe. As Yolanda Broyles-Gonzalez shows in her oral histories of the women of El Teatro Campesino, casting decisions consistently divided women by age, experience, and skin color. Actresses such as Socorro Valdez and Olivia Chumacero complained that La Virgen, who ought to have been the most important character in the play, was reduced to a figurehead by casting decisions that restricted the role to the youngest actresses. In the Guadalupe performance, experienced actresses were never cast as La Virgen, because "[t]hey see the Virgen of Guadalupe as a soft, demure, peaceful, saintly ingénue type" (Broyles-Gonzales 1986, 127–128). Coincidentally, casting for La Virgen was restricted to light-skinned actresses and excluded Indian-featured women. In particular, women who spoke up for themselves within the organization were quickly typecast. Valdez was told, "You don't look like La Virgen. Your teeth are too big." She replied, "¿Apoco estaba molacha La Virgen de Guadalupe? [You're telling me La Virgen had no teeth?] That is the stupidest thing I ever heard" (Valdez, in Broyles-Gonzalez 1986, 178). I provide this example to show how Chicanas' attempts to humanize icons is a particularly feminist challenge, often perceived as a threat.

Any challenge to the traditional iconography of la Virgen is interpreted as an assault on the values of Mexican/Chicano culture. When reactionary organizations proclaim "Lesbians insult La Virgen de Guadalupe," the identification of lesbians with Malinche (i.e., as cultural traitors) becomes clear.

If, as Carla Trujillo (1991) contends, Chicana lesbians are "the girls our mothers warned us about," then La Virgen de Guadalupe might be considered just such a mother, "warning" her daughters against lesbianism. Indeed, this is the reactionary formation. Yet Chicana feminists and Chicana lesbians emphasize the unconditional nature of La Virgen's maternal love. In La Madre's words, "I will give all my love and motherly compassion to those who seek my aid" (Guerrero 1987, 97).

La Llorona

Although the tale of La Llorona is occasionally conflated with La Malinche, or interpreted as a variation of La Malinche, there are convincing arguments that La Llorona is a distinct figure (Limón 1990; Tedlock 1996). Like La Malinche and La Virgen de Guadalupe, La Llorona is a syncretic figure, with both European and American aspects. In one sense, La Llorona is Medea, an abandoned woman slaying her children. Yet La Llorona's genealogy includes "another distinctive Indian legend, that of Cihuacoatl, the Aztec goddess who . . . appeared in the night crying out for dead children," and Cihuahuateo, the spirits of women who died in childbirth (Limón 1990, 408).

There are two distinct types of La Llorona stories. The first is the *encuentro*, which focuses on encounters with La Llorona. These are often first-person narratives, related by those who have seen La Llorona and lived to tell the tale. The second type, the *historia* of La Llorona, tells how an ordinary woman came to murder her children and why she continues to weep and search for them.

Once upon a time, there was a beautiful woman, virtuous and poor. She was discovered by a wealthy young man. They fell in love and were very happy together. They were blessed with beautiful children (two, more or less). One day the woman's lover abandoned her (or announced his marriage to a highborn woman, or announced he was taking the children away from her). In rage and despair she drowned him (or the children) in the nearby river. Forever after she has been doomed to haunt the riverbanks, looking for her lost lover (or her lost children).

The many variations of La Llorona stories, like the variations of Delgadina (see chap. 9), allow for the storyteller, the performer, to choose the version that best fits her purposes. Thus, like Toni Morrison's *Beloved,* the tale can be told as an indictment of a system of slavery that makes some women and their children the literal property of their male owners. It can also be told as a warning to poor women to choose partners of their own social status. It can be a lament for the generations of indigenous Mexicans killed during the conquest, of the constant danger to single mothers, as a condemnation of female sexuality, as an anti-abortion warning.

La Llorona is an exemplum of a bad mother; in at least one version, she is an irresponsible mother who just wants a good time. One night while she was out having a good time, her children came to grief.

Although she did not actively murder her children, she was clearly responsible for their deaths and was condemned to wander the earth in search of the children she had not watched in life. In another version, La Llorona is "said to have drowned her children in exchange for eternal life," an exchange that turns out to be a cruel hoax, as she is condemned "for eternity to wander riverbanks and ditches crying out for her children" (Gaspar de Alba 1998a, 163 n. 43).

Folklorists have argued that the only thing the various La Llorona stories have in common is that they are stories about La Llorona. This tautology illustrates the fact that, for instance, there are a number of contradictory explanations for La Llorona's ghostly wanderings.

"IT WAS NOT A STORY TO PASS ON"

The tale of La Llorona is frequently told to excite and frighten children into obedience. In Denise Chávez's second novel, *Face of an Angel*, however, the narrator, Soveida, tells a story of La Llorona and emphasizes that she did not learn the tale from her mother, Dolores:

> When I was young, Dolores never told me stories of La Llorona, the mythical woman who wandered by the river's edge, mourning her children she herself had drowned. It was only later that I came to hear about the woman spurned and scorned by her lover. Unable to live without him, she killed their children, whom she loved most in the world. La Llorona was a sexual phantom, a wailing woman who wandered the riverbanks late at night, a mysterious, haunted spirit of lost love. (1995, 49)

Perhaps Soveida's mother refused to frighten her own daughter with the tale of a murderous mother. Dolores was herself an abandoned woman (*una dejada*), so perhaps she rejected the idea that such a woman would turn her anger against her own child.

Similarly, in Ana Castillo's *So Far from God*, Sofia (*otra dejada*) refuses to pass on the story:

> Mostly she just knew what her father had told her, that La Llorona was a bad woman who had left her husband and home, drowned her babies to run off and have a sinful life, and God punished her for eternity, and [Sofia] refused to repeat this nightmare to her daughters.
> Sofia had not left her children, much less drowned them to run off with nobody. On the contrary, she had been left to raise them by her-

self. And all her life, there had always been at least one woman around like her, left alone, abandoned, divorced, or widowed, to raise her children, and none of them had ever tried to kill their babies. (1993, 161)

Because of their own experiences as single mothers, as *dejadas*, and as women who know well the sexual double standard, both Dolores and Sofia refuse La Llorona's tale, and thus they refuse the patriarchal logic of La Llorona.

Sandra Cisneros goes even further in refusing to pass on the tale of La Llorona in her short story, "Woman Hollering Creek." The protagonist is rescued from a no-win situation through the collective work of women for women. Cleófilas—a young bride from Monclova, Coahuila, now on "el otro lado"—is battered by her husband. Restricted to her house, she feels she has no one to turn to—"Unless one counts the neighbor ladies. Soledad [Loneliness] on one side, Dolores [Sadness] on the other. Or the creek [suicide]" (1991b, 51). Cleófilas remembers her father's words to her on the day of her wedding: "I am your father, I will never abandon you" (43). She reflects on "[h]ow when a man and a woman love each other, sometimes that love sours. But a parent's love for a child, a child's for its parents, is another thing entirely" (43).

As her husband's violence escalates, Cleófilas notices that the news is always full of violence against women: "This one's a cadaver, this one unconscious, this one beaten blue. Her ex husband, her husband, her lover . . . " (52). As Mary Pat Brady (2002, 134) argues, Cleófilas's "chilling inventory of commonplace violence accompanies [her] commonplace activity . . . symbolizing [her] immersion in abuse and isolation. The repetitive language emphasizes her powerlessness to escape the next attack."

Pregnant with her second child, Cleófilas must beg her husband's permission to go for prenatal care. The radiologist notices her bruises, contacts another woman, and arranges her escape. Cleófilas is helped by a sisterhood of women, showing that she has more choices than Soledad, Dolores, and the creek. Felice (Happiness), the truck-driving Tejana who delivers Cleófilas and her family to the San Antonio bus station, is a woman unlike any Cleófilas has ever known.

The fact that she drove a pickup. A pickup, mind you, but when Cleófilas asked if it was her husband's, she said she didn't have a husband. The pickup was hers. She herself had chosen it. She herself was paying for it. (55)

Cisneros's story emphasizes that the story of La Llorona, of a mother murdering her child, masks the everyday stories of mother, wives, and girlfriends murdered, battered, or killed in self-defense. It reasserts the mother-child bond as stronger than the bond of heterosexual love while also holding out the possibility for woman-to-woman bonds. According to Sonia Saldívar-Hull, Felice "is a feminist in practice and could even be figured as a Chicana lesbian," at any rate "either as [a] lesbian or as a heterosexual woman-identified-woman who . . . rejects homophobic, misogynistic Chicano community roles that naturalize heterosexuality" (2000, 106–107, 123).

"LA LLORONA LOCA"

In Monica Palacios's comedic performance of the *historia* of La Llorona, the tale comes directly from her mother:

> Growing up, my mother would tell me scary stories of the Latino folklore character known as La Llorona Loca—the crazy crier. According to my mother, ". . . this woman drowned her children—apparently woke up on the wrong side of the bed—a little pissed off." (1990b, 174)

The narrator's mother seems to suggest a warning to her daughter: be careful, esa, because I, too, might wake up on the wrong side of the bed one morning. You don't want to mess with me when I'm a little pissed off, because you don't know what I'm capable of. In the mother's version, the story is one of senseless violence and remorse, told for a child's benefit without the distraction of tragic love affairs.

In telling her own "true" story of La Llorona, Palacios does the opposite of her mother. She focuses entirely on the tragic love affair. Searching for a deeper truth than her mother's frightening tale, Palacios claims to have searched the "La Llorona archives" at the University of California, Los Angeles, until she found the real story of La Llorona. In this version, the woman who became La Llorona has a name, though not necessarily a proper one: Caliente.

> As beautiful as she was, she had never married. . . . One glorious day, a stranger rode into town, looking for a woman. The stranger galloped down the main drag when all of a sudden, the stranger caught the eye of Caliente. . . . Their eyes locked. Caliente walked toward the

stranger. The stranger took off her hat—that's right—I said *her* hat!
Her black curly locks fell down to her leather chaps. The stranger,
who was looking mighty fine and very voluptuous to Caliente said,
"[I]f you want something good, you will ride with me and you will be
my woman, *mi mujer*!" (145; original emphasis)

Alas for Caliente, La Stranger was not as faithful as she was passionate. After an unspecified period of bliss, La Stranger "took Caliente to
their favorite spot by the river. 'My vida, I am like the river, I am the
happiest when I am moving.'" In simpler terms, La Stranger confesses
to having an affair and Caliente, in a jealous rage, drowns La Stranger
in the river.

> Realizing that she had done this horrible, horrible act, [Caliente]
> started to cry uncontrollably until she fainted into the river and died.
> I'm sorry to bring you down, folks, but that's life. (146)

Palacios effectively turns this tragic tale into lesbian camp. To do so,
she specifically removes any reference to (innocent) murdered children. Caliente murders her (unfaithful) lover instead of directing her
violence toward someone else. Yet by avoiding any reference to children, Palacios also removes the more disturbing elements of the story.
Palacios's "La Llorona loca" may be a warning to unfaithful lovers, but
it lacks the powerful danger of the murderous mother. La Llorona has
been replaced by Caliente, a "Mexican spitfire" of a jealous lover.

Unlike the abandoned mothers in *Face of an Angel* and *So Far from God*,
Palacios's narrator identifies with Llorona, not as a mother, but as a
wronged woman, a sexual woman. In this way, she is able to render La
Llorona as a lesbian: a woman of great love and thus capable of great
violence.

LESBIAN MOTHERS AND CHILD MURDER

I would suggest that this separation between Llorona as murderous
mother and Llorona as lesbian is in some way connected to the status of
lesbian mothers. Lesbians with children are always in danger of losing
custody of them. Reactionary descriptions of feminism making women
"leave their husbands, kill their children, practice witchcraft and become lesbians" illustrate how lesbians are imagined as a threat both to
the construction "motherhood" and to their own children.

In an op-ed piece in the summer 1992 issue of *esto no tiene nombre*, Yvevacha challenges Latina lesbians to claim all members of their community, not only the good role models. In particular, she is drawing the reader's attention to Ana María Cardona, who was sentenced to death for the murder of her son. "After making it very clear that Cardona was a lesbian, the press always went on to ask 'How could a mother do this to her child?'" Yvevacha reports:

> The lesbian community in Miami stood by silently while Ana was sentenced to death and her lover Olivia González [a codefendant turned State's witness] got a couple of years in jail. Where was the outrage? Everyone treated this case as if it had been the first situation of horrid child abuse ever to be known of in Florida. We accepted the inequities of our judicial system, thereby giving credence to the anti-lesbian attitudes of the larger community. (1992, 21)

Echoing Pat Parker's poem, "Where will you be?" Yvevacha charges that the Miami lesbian community and Latina lesbians in particular have distanced themselves from Ana Cardona. She emphasizes the need to "change attitudes about motherhood within our community" and also demands, "If you think a mother and her children are in distress," you have a responsibility to reach out and help that women and those children before abuse happens. "Don't turn the other way when you see a woman in distress and then be ready to say what a criminal so-and-so is. That criminal could be you" (21).

Thus Yvevacha demands that we Latina lesbians identify with Ana Cardona, that we put aside a desire for only positive representation and instead work on behalf of our sister, that we not identify ourselves against her. Her challenge, "that criminal could be you," provides insight into a particularly challenging drama, Cherríe Moraga's *Mexican Medea or The Hungry Woman.*

MEXICAN MEDEA

> I discovered the mutilated women of our indigenous American history of story: La Llorona, Coyolxauhqui, Coatlicue. I worship them in my attempt to portray them in all their locura. (Moraga [1995] 2001a, x)

Cherríe Moraga was commissioned to write a play on La Llorona called *Mexican Medea* by the Berkeley Repertory Theater. First staged in April 1995, Moraga's La Llorona–Medea depicts a lesbian mother who slays her own child. Moraga challenges the rules of representation (i.e., that we should strive to depict our culture in a positive light) by combining the murderous mother with the outcast of Aztlán.

The conviction of Ana María Cardona provides a key to understanding the drive of this piece. It is similar to the case of Margaret Garner, who was used by abolitionists to call for the end of the institution of slavery that makes logical such violence and by supporters of slavery to argue that such an abhorrent act illustrates the inferiority of the black race. For Moraga to claim La Llorona is the opposite of what the characters Dolores and Sofia do: they choose not to retell this story because of the way it portrays women. At the same time, in both novels, their daughters either hear the stories from their peers or encounter La Llorona herself.

Moraga could have decided to portray La Llorona in a positive light, as Gloria Anzaldúa does in her children's book, *Prietita y La Llorona* (see below). Or, like Christa Wolf, she could have chosen to depict Medea as the woman unjustly blamed for her children's death. Instead, Moraga goes back to Euripides to articulate how Medea's revenge is tied to Jason's breaking of a sacred contract between them. Then Moraga moves the fifth-century B.C.E. drama forward to "the early part of the second decade of the twenty-first century" after the people have risen up and the former United States is divided into city-states by peoples of color (6). Like Gomez-Peña's "News from Aztlán Liberado," Moraga's futuristic fantasy shows that the old order has changed. She is unable to accept this utopic Aztlán, however; she sees past the revolution to the counterrevolution, to the reestablishment of patriarchy, and the purging of the queers, the inevitable result of nationalist victory.

Ironically, in Aztlán Liberado, indigenous blood quantum persists as the legitimate claim to the land. Medea possesses the appropriate blood quantum (as does her son) to claim land in Aztlán. Her ex-husband, Jason, does not and can only possess the land through Medea or through their son.

In the 1986 version of Moraga's *Giving Up the Ghost*, Amalia, the older femme Mexicana character, tells of a dream:

I had a dream once . . .

You and I . . . were indias, baking something
Maybe bread, maybe clay pots . . .
We were very happy.

> And then . . . suddenly . . . the dream changes.
> The mood is dark, clouded.
> I am in my hut . . . alone.
> I remember being crouched down in terror.
> In our village, something . . . (*remembering*)
> Some terrible taboo has been broken . . .
> Suddenly, there is a furious pounding at my door.
> "Let me in! Let me in!" And it is *your* voice . . .
> But I am unable to move when I realize it is you who has gone against
>   the code del pueblo. (52; original emphasis)

Amalia's vision is acted out in the 1994 revision of *Giving Up the Ghost* and becomes central to *Mexican Medea*. Medea (an older femme Chicana) and her female lover, Luna, have broken the taboo: Medea not only betrays her heterosexual marriage for this butch woman's passion, she chooses exile, ostracism, living in the borderlands over maintaining her position in the center. Ten years later, however, she is tired of her marginal existence and angry about being deprived of her birthright, her legitimate place in Aztlán. She renegotiates with Jasón, seducing him as part of the bargain, to be reinstated as his wife. After the fact, Jasón changes the terms, limiting Medea to a dependent status without giving her the legitimizing title "wife." To prevent his victory, Medea is driven to poison her son, Chac Mool.

Such is one version of the tale. As Moraga says, she strives to represent Medea in "all her locura." At the same time, almost inevitably, Medea is not the character we identify most with. The lesbian subjectivity of the play is split between the femme Medea and the butch Luna. With the seduction of Jasón, Medea loses her legitimate claim as the lesbian and Luna becomes the central figure. Luna is the character who truly connects with Chac Mool, teaching him about his *herencia* (which is growing blue corn), teaching him that his strength need not be at someone else's expense. Ultimately, Medea is incapable of learning the same thing and betrays her love for Luna.

Finally, the play refuses/confuses the outcome, as we see that Medea is not in prison for the murder, as it first appeared, but in a mental institution. Chac Mool comes to take her home, thus suggesting that Medea never really killed him but certainly did some kind of violence to their relationship that has landed her in this institution.

Moraga's play is balanced between understanding Medea's position and turning away from her to choose instead the "innocent" subjects,

Luna and Chac Mool, both of whom stay true to themselves. Moraga plumbs the depths of La Llorona and Medea in this play, but she ultimately turns away from "the criminal [who] could be you," instead focusing on Luna, the visible butch lesbian whose sexuality makes her a priori a criminal.[3]

ENCUENTROS

Encounters with La Llorona range from tales of La Llorona stealing children to those of Llorona seducing men. She merges with other bogeyman characters, such as El Cucuy and the Chupacabra, and with other siren figures from other myths, such as mermaids, ondines, and selkies. I am less interested in the seduction stories, because, as Saldívar-Hull (2000, 119), "it was the males, after all, who were the ones threatened by La Llorona." I find the encounters with children particularly interesting, especially when told from a lesbian perspective, with lesbian subtexts, or with possible lesbian endings.

WEEPING WOMAN

Alma Luz Villanueva weaves a complicated series of stories around La Llorona, grandmothers, mothers, and daughters in her collection, *Weeping Woman: La Llorona and Other Stories*. "La Llorona," here Isidra, a grandmother, tells her granddaughter, Luna, *la historia* of La Llorona as rain falls steadily in San Francisco:

> "All my life, in Mexico . . . when it rained too long, we could hear
> her, La Llorona, crying for her children down by the river. Crying
> and lamenting, with her beautiful black shawl over her head. Not for
> protection from the rain, no but because she was either too beautiful or
> perhaps too ugly to behold."
> . . . "Why was she crying, Mamacita?"
> "For her children, Niña. When the great flood came, and the terrible men from the great ocean came, she turned her children into fish."
> Isidra paused to wet her dry lips. "It was the only way to save them,"
> the old woman added, seeing the terror on her granddaughter's face.
> (1994c, 2)

Isidra's tale is intricately tied to the Spanish conquest, "when the terrible men from the great ocean came," and La Llorona's children include all the indigenous peoples who were killed during and after the sixteenth century.

In Isidra's version, the metamorphosis is not permanent: the children were sometimes able to revert to their original human form.

> They would come to her if her sorrow was so great. Then, she'd take the black shawl from her head, making sure no human being was nearby to witness her magic, and scooping it into the river like a net, her children would appear one by one. (2)

In Isidra's version, then, La Llorona did not kill her own children but merely transformed them to protect them. La Llorona is still a dangerous figure, certainly to the men who would hurt her children, but certainly also to the children themselves. Like young Luna, they may be frightened and horrified at being "saved" in this manner.

Isidra clearly identifies with La Llorona. Her memory drifts back to the bright Sonoran sun:

> [A]nd Isidra thought of her three children who'd survived their infancy. The ones who'd lived long enough to hear about la Llorona. And then only one survived to adulthood. Luna's mother. May [Luna] not be like her mother, the old woman prayed for the child silently. I have no daughter, she added with her familiar sense of perpetual grief. Just the little fish the river took away, and I have no magic. No, not anymore. (3)

In the context of the short story itself, Luna is the daughter of a bad mother, a promiscuous woman who brings men into the house for violent sexual encounters, who batters her own mother, and who fails to protect her daughter from molestation or to comfort her afterward. Isidra, the grandmother, is good-natured but powerless: she is elderly and frail, an immigrant, and poor. She is horrified at what her daughter has become but loves and cherishes her granddaughter. Luna hears her grandmother weeping in the night. At the end of the story, Isidra and Luna take a bus to the beach where they encounter La Llorona: "There was a dark figure moving along the beach, slowly. Her shawl covered her head. She looked tall and strong as she came toward them, weeping and singing" (7).

Here the story abruptly ends. One possible reading is that Isidra drowns Luna in the ocean to free her from the dangers of her environment ("the terrible men"). However, the text also contains clues that suggest that Luna survives the encounter: "Years later, Luna would re-member her grandmother's touch was like dry, loose feathers. Comfort without pain. Strange, irrational—*a silent comfort*" (7; original empha-sis). Another possible reading, then, is that Isidra drowns herself in the ocean, unable to sit by and watch as Luna is violated in her mother's world.

The rest of the collection contains stories of young girls, women, and boys suffering the violence of rape, patriarchy, racism, and war. Grown men look at women and children like prey, like commodities. Although the female characters have different names, we can glimpse occasion-ally one who looks like an older Luna or her mother. A seashell motif is woven through the other twenty-two stories. In each, a protagonist draws strength from the seashell, which helps her to escape, to survive, to endure.

The final four stories in the collection return to the protagonist Luna. Each of these stories is an alternate ending for Luna, or rather, a differ-ent version of who Luna would become: "El Alma/The Soul, One," "El Alma/The Soul, Two," "El Alma/The Soul, Three," and "El Alma/The Soul, Four." All four of the stories remember that night on the beach with Isidra and La Llorona and tell us that Luna was given a seashell to protect her. And all four reach closure with Luna returning to the beach on her fiftieth birthday.

In "El Alma/The Soul, One," it is four days until Luna's birthday. She looks back on her life: "Fifty years old, two marriages, two chil-dren, a grandchild, my new lover," a student who committed suicide. "Mother, daughter, wife woman. Did I fail at everything?" (139, 142). She wonders how her grandmother would have judged her. Her sister self in "El Alma/The Soul, Two," looks back on her life, how she was raped by her mother's lover when she was an adolescent, her time in and out of institutions. In this story Luna is struggling with her own sense of failure: "I've failed everyone and I have nothing." And again Llorona's laughter washes over her like a song.

In "El Alma/The Soul, Three," it is the day before Luna's fiftieth birthday, and she is on a very different beach. In Denmark, she looks out on the North Sea, remembering. Isidra left her not only words and stories but also a knife, a butcher knife, to keep in her bed to protect her from the violence in her home. On the same night that Luna in "Two" was raped, Luna in "Three" stabs to death her would-be rapist. Her mother testified at Luna's trial, at the cost of her parental rights, and

Luna was acquitted and adopted. Now a successful doctor, a lesbian with a life partner, Luna knows her grandmother would be proud of her. She also thinks of her mother. In her final incarnation, "El Alma/ The Soul, Four," Luna is a professional poet. In her memory she pictures her grandmother Isidra giving her first poetry reading.

Together, these five stories encompass the two types of La Llorona tale mentioned above: the *historia* and the *encuentro*. Villanueva's four endings to Luna's story argue that there is not only one ending to the story of La Llorona. In the same manner, the four "alma" stories break apart the monogamous heterosexual narrative so important to the concept of La Llorona by showing us a mature heterosexual woman with a young male lover, a mature lesbian with a lifelong female lover, and two other women whose sexuality is not explicitly articulated. Thus Villanueva (like Palacios) opens up lesbian endings to the Llorona story and at the same time (like Cisneros) marks the violence against women masked by the traditional La Llorona tales.

PRIETITA Y LA LLORONA

Gloria Anzaldúa also avoids the disturbing aspects of La Llorona. Her bilingual children's book, *Prietita y La Llorona*, is an *encuentro* showing another side to La Llorona. The protagonist, Prietita is searching for an herb to cure her ailing mother. Her friend and teacher, the *curandera*, has provided her with a drawing so that she will be able to recognize the plant.

> At first Prietita stayed close to the fence, but as she searched for the rue plant she wandered deeper into the woods. Suddenly, she thought she heard a crying sound, and she remembered her grandmother's stories of La Llorona — the ghost woman dressed in white. Her grandmother said that La Llorona appeared at night by rivers or lagoons, crying for her lost children and looking for other children to steal.
>
> Prietita shivered. She turned around and looked for the fence, but it was nowhere in sight. She was lost. (Anzaldúa 1995, 10)

Initially, Prietita's fear of La Llorona makes her uneasy in her surroundings. She asks assistance from the various animals she encounters but is unable to locate the plant. As it grows dark, Prietita becomes discouraged. "Again Prietita heard a faint crying sound. . . . This time she was sure it was a woman crying. She wanted to run away, but she forced herself to walk toward the sound" (22). She finds La Llorona and, though fearful, asks her for help finding the herb. La Llorona silently leads the girl to the plant and then guides her back through the woods to the fence. After La Llorona disappears, Prietita's friends and family come looking for her. When she tells them she was guided by La Llorona, her cousin cries out, "But everyone knows she takes children away. She doesn't bring them back." "Perhaps," the *curandera* responds, "she is not what others think she is" (29).

Anzaldúa's story presents a test of Prietita's courage and her willingness to "look beneath the surface . . . to discover the truths that may be hidden" (author's note 32). Like Palacios, Anzaldúa describes her fascination with La Llorona and her desire for more information:

> When I was a little girl growing up in South Texas . . . , my mamagrande used to tell me scary stories about La Llorona. . . . All the children were afraid of La Llorona—I was afraid too, but even at that age I wondered if there was another side to her. (Author's note 32)

Like Villanueva and Palacios, Anzaldúa is refashioning the image of La Llorona to complicate this most frightening mother in the Chicano/a imaginary. Clearly, Anzaldúa hopes to encourage young Chicanas and Chicanos to view this mythic figure with an open mind: the story itself suggests that courage and open-mindedness lead to maturity. In fact, unlike the earlier examples of mothers who chose *not* to tell their daughters of La Llorona, Anzaldúa is telling her symbolic daughters (i.e., young Chicanas) a new story, a different kind of story of La Llorona. Whereas the "old" story gives a woman a choice between "Soledad, Dolores, and the arroyo," the new story shows La Llorona helping the young Chicana find necessary medicine on ancestral lands, medicine vital for her mother's survival. Through their portrayals, the authors lay to rest childhood fears, while La Llorona channels her power away from violence against her children and toward protection of those children or anger correctly aimed at the faithless lover.

Whereas La Llorona represents the Mexican maternal, another popular figure, the Aztec Princess, focuses on the Mexican/Chicana/indigenous woman as sexual, passive, historical, and contemporary. Chicana lesbian appropriation of this figure is the subject of the next chapter.

CHAPTER 3

Black Velvet Fantasies: "The" Aztec Princess in the Chicana/o Sexual Imagination

What I need to explore will not be found in the feminist lesbian bedroom, but more likely in the mostly heterosexual bedrooms of South Texas, L.A., or even Sonora, México.

— CHERRÍE MORAGA, "PLAYED BETWEEN WHITE HANDS"

Cherríe Moraga lays claim to an economy of desire shared, not along the lines of sexual orientation, but through a cultural imaginary that crosses the border between the United States and Mexico. Moraga's provocation inspires me to explore Chicana lesbian representations, to articulate the connections between these representations and certain sexual spectacles that circulate through the Chicano/a and Mexican communities of "South Texas, L.A., or even Sonora, México."

In this chapter I examine the genealogy of the Aztec Princess — "the" Indian woman[1] — in Chicana and Chicano literature and visual culture. This mythic figure has taken on a specific sexual significance, a performance of race and gender that represents sex and the feminine. I trace this genealogy from Mexican art to Chicano/a popular culture, to new renderings that both invoke and play with a Chicano nationalist construction of gender. Finally, I explore the way in which this Aztec Princess figure circulates in two short stories — by Terri de la Peña and by Alicia Gaspar de Alba — to challenge the idea of passive female sexuality.

The Aztec Princess, Ixtacihuatl

La Malinche, La Virgen de Guadalupe, and La Llorona are representations of La India in Chicana/o art and literature, and as maternal figures, they stand together. The fourth figure is Ixtacihuatl, the Aztec Princess, a sexual figure but not a maternal one. Ixtacihuatl circulates widely in Chicana/o popular culture but has gone largely unmentioned in Chicana/o cultural criticism. I believe that her story—the Legend of the Volcanoes—and, more important, her representation fuel the Chicana/Chicano sexual imagination. Like the stories of Pocahontas and La Malinche, this legend owes much of its current form to the nineteenth-century constructions of national identity—a nationalism that is consolidated through the creation and circulation of a Mexican mythology.

Rafael Pérez-Torres retells the Legend of the Volcanoes:

In Mexican legend, Ixtacihuatl is a princess who falls in love with Popocatépetl, a warrior from a rival tribe. Upon hearing of his death in battle, reported erroneously to her, Ixtacihuatl kills herself out of sorrow. Popocatépetl returns victorious from his military exploits only to find his beloved dead. He takes her up in his arms and carries her to the mountains where he stretches her out and hunches beside her, guarding her body by the fires he burns eternally for her. Thus are explained the volcanoes Ixtacihuatl and Popocatépetl, that loom above the Valley of Mexico [Mexico City]. (1995, 191)[2]

Pérez-Torres has argued that for the first wave of Chicano/a poets, "the 'recollection' of Mexican and (less commonly) Mayan myths and images . . . employs pre-Cortesian cultures and values as a foil, as a rejection of the most pernicious influences of the Enlightenment and capitalism[,] . . . as a dream for contemporary Chicano life" (173). At the same time, he complicates our readings of the deployment of such myths:

The idea of a Chicano mythic "memory" manifested in ethnopoetic expression represents less an unproblematic recuperation of indigenous culture than a complex cultural construction of self identity. From this view, the myths and legends that tend to infuse Chicano literary products cease to be collectable fragments of a non-European Other and become instead part of a larger cultural palette from which Chicano artists draw as they scrutinize the complex and continuous identities comprising the subject-position "Chicano/a." (176)

One reading of the Legend of the Volcanoes might contend that it buries Chicanas "beneath the weight of a subject-position meant to be self-sacrificing and reverent" (Pérez-Torres 1995, 192). My reading proposes a more ambivalent relationship to Ixtacihuatl, her fetishization, the romanticization of her dead, sensual, Indian body, and the equation of the earth itself with the feminine form.

Since the 1940s and 1950s this legend has circulated primarily through the calendar paintings of the Mexican artist Jesus Helguera. These paintings dramatize scenes from Mexican myth and history: romantic tales of the tragic love of the Aztec Princess Ixtacihuatl and her lover, Popocatépetl, of "amor indio." They form a visual link between modern Mexicanos (and by extension Chicanas/os) and the Aztec heroes of a bygone era. There is a familiarity with these two characters, an intimacy on the part of Mexicans and Chicanas/os, who frequently refer to them by the diminutives Ixta (or Ixtli or Mixtli) and Popo. Helguera often combined Maxfield Parrish sunsets with Indian princesses resembling Lucha Reyes and Dolores Del Rio and settings that owe more to Tinseltown than to Tenochtitlán. His paintings feature a muscular and active Aztec warrior carrying or mourning the scantily clad and voluptuous body of an Aztec princess. This image inscribes particular fantasies about essential Mexican identities: the male is cast in the subject position, a virile and potent warrior; the female is an object of (visual) pleasure, a voluptuous and receptive body. She is the desired body and, at the same time, a dead body, suggesting an erotic pleasure akin to necrophilia.

Why are these images so prevalent? What pleasures are derived from viewing the sleeping or dead body of the Aztec Princess? On the one hand, they may mark nostalgia for the lost ideal of pre-Columbian culture. Popo mourns his lost love, dead by her own hand before their wedding, and contemporary Chicanas/os mourn the lost "empire" of the Aztecs. At the same time, Ixta's body seems to represent a disavowal of colonial violence. The first part of that disavowal would state, I know very well that Indians died horrible deaths in the colonial institution of New-Spain-which-became-Mexico, yet I prefer to imagine Indian death as the romantic tale of tragic love, through the visually pleasing image of Ixta's body. The disassociation of Ixta's death from colonial violence is crucial to the success of both the image and the legend. Finally, the death of Ixta is a visual signifier of the constant reinvention of native Mexicans as extinct: they are represented as always already dead. As Norma Alarcón (1990, 374) has argued, "The historical founding moment of the construction of [national Mexican] mestizo subjectivity entails the rejection and denial of the dark Indian Mother as Indian . . . and [the denial of] the Indian position even as that position is visually stylized and represented in the making of the fatherland." Thus the construction of the nationalist subject as mestizo—and as the legitimate inheritor of Mexico—rests on this depiction of Aztecs as extinct and as wholly separate from contemporary indigenous populations and social movements.

Antonia Castañeda (1992) argues that not only does the study of the "American West" display U.S. expansionist policies, but in historical documents those policies lay claim not only to the land but also to the women who lived there. "The white colonizers' appropriation of the native woman—by representing her as sexually available to the colonizer and as oppressed within her own culture—[has been] pivotal to the ideology and the political agenda" (1992, 524). In her examination of the historiography of what is now the U.S. Southwest, Castañeda finds "two dichotomous images of women of color in the literature":[3]

> "Good" women of color are light-skinned, civilized (Christian), and virgins. They are "good" because they give aid or sacrifice themselves, so that white men may live; white men marry them. "Bad" women are dark-skinned, savage (non-Christian), and whores; white men do not marry them. (517)

The dichotomy that Castañeda describes certainly applies to Pocahontas and to the prenationalist representation of La Malinche.[4] Peter Hulme (1986, 193) argues that the figures of Pocahontas and Malinche raise "a particularly fascinating intersection—between the boundaries of race and class; and Pocahontas—like many similar figures—can in the end assume an ideologically potent mythic status despite her race only because she is an intelligent, pure and above all *noble* Indian" (original emphasis). Unlike Malinche and Pocahontas, however, "the" Aztec Princess does not choose a white man but an Aztec warrior, the muscular, virile Popocatépetl, who becomes an emblem of Mexican and Chicano masculinity.

I see these discourses—the mythic Mexican mothers and the Legend of the Volcanoes—as providing both a context and a complex genealogy for the representation of La India as she appears in the Chicana/o sexual imaginary in general. I employ both of these discourses to examine the image of "the" Aztec Princess in Chicana/o visual culture and Chicana lesbian fiction.

"Aztec" Calendars: Aztec Sex Goddess

Helguera's paintings have enjoyed enormous popularity among Mexicans and Chicanas/os and have been reproduced in a variety of mediums by both Chicano/a and Mexican artists. Many Chicana and Chicano artists have used the images as stages of Chicana/o identity. I want to examine these calendars for what they are representing, particularly with regard to the Indian woman, and how this representation has become a part of what I conceive as the Chicana/o sexual imagination.[5]

Tomás Ybarra-Frausto (1986, 21) discusses the Aztec imagery of these calendars as a significant source of inspiration for Chicano/a artists, who "emphasized forms of visual expression functioning as integral elements of the decorative scheme in the home environment." Specifically, Ybarra-Frausto discusses "two pervasive graphic traditions . . . exemplified by the *almanaque* (calendar) and the *estampa religiosa* (religious imagery)":

> Traditionally, the annual almanaque is given to favorite customers by local merchants. . . . Although created as advertisements, the almanaques exclude any specific product from the visual representation itself. Rather, the illustrations often feature Mexican genre scenes, interpretations of indigenous myths [such as] the Aztec warrior holding a dead maiden in his arm[,] . . . a pictorial representation of the myth of Ixtacihuátl[6] and Popocatépetl made famous by the Mexican calendar artist Jesús Helguera. These . . . illustrations are often saved and displayed as household icons. (21)

These calendars are available in the United States at restaurants, hair salons, gift shops, "mexicatessens," *botánicas,* and car repair shops as well as from Chicana/o art galleries. Not only are the Helguera calendars themselves pervasive, but their themes are re-created by other artists.[7] Ybarra-Frausto's reference to the calendars as "integral elements of the decorative scheme in the home environment" provides entry into a theorization of the calendars *as* environment. Indeed, Chicano/a artists such as Lawrence Yañez and Pattsi Valdez use Helguera's images to create an ambience of Chicanísmo. For example, in his 1988 serigraph *Cocina jaiteca,* Yañez depicts a modern Mexican American kitchen. The walls of the kitchen are bare but for three "icons": a crucifix, an image of La Virgen de Guadalupe, and a calendar of Popo and Ixta. Similarly, in the set design for Gregory Nava's 1994 film, *Mi familia,* Pattsi Valdez reproduced Helguera's *Leyenda de los volcanes* on the walls of the family restaurant. In both of these instances the images of Ixta and Popo evoke Chicano/a cultural traditions and fantasies as a way of setting a Chicano/a mood. The imagery of Ixta and Popo frequently appears in the background, as part the representation of Chicano/a lived space, of the everyday environment.[8] Likewise, Ixta and Popo remain "largely unremarked and untheorized."[9]

In *Amor indio* (Fig. 1) Popo and Ixta are seated together on a boulder. The sky behind them is dark with clouds. Popo is seated facing right, with his feet braced against the stone table and his knees supporting Ixta's back. Ixta sits with her body facing to the left, her head tilted back against Popo's arms. Both figures are scantily clad but decorated with jewelry. Popo wears a feathered headdress of narrow quills in red and gold. Large gold earrings hang from his ears, and around his neck he wears two strings of beads and one of animal claws or teeth alternating with beads. His red cloak is knotted high on his right shoulder, but his chest and legs are bare and well muscled. A quiver of arrows hangs against his cloak. Ixta's head is tilted back, her eyes closed, her lips parted. Her limbs are slack, pale, and rounded, with no muscle definition. Her white sheath of a dress leaves her arms and shoulders bare and clings to her breasts, revealing her erect nipples. Her hair, adorned with flowers, falls down her back and onto Popo's legs. She wears a string of beads and another of seeds, as well as three bracelets: two of gold and one of stones. An animal skin is draped across her lap, and she holds a small bouquet of wildflowers between her fingers. A small fawn is in her lap. On the ground before the two figures are Popo's bow and a slain bird of prey.

It is not clear whether *Amor indio* is depicting a scene that takes place before or after the death of the Aztec Princess. Is Ixta basking in Popo's embrace, or does he cradle her dead body? While the title suggests to me that this is a love scene, with a living princess, I think that the ambiguity is itself intrinsic to the image. The contrast between the masculine and feminine figures is striking: Popo is hard, the hunter, the slayer;

Figure 1. *Amor indio,* by Jesus Helguera. Courtesy of Calendarios Landín, Inc., San Antonio, Texas.

Ixta is soft, the nurturer. Popo's headdress and jewelry speak of birds and animals slain; Ixta wears flowers, seeds, and stones. His muscles bespeak action; her limbs suggest repose. He has killed the raptor; she cradles the fawn.

All of these images combine in an exclusively sexual representation of Ixta and, in a sense, of "the" Indian woman of Mexico. She is silent, passive, and always desirable. Such an image reinforces the passive sexuality of the Indian woman as put forth in the story of La Malinche as La Chingada. In this case, however, Ixta is reclaimed in the sense that she is the object of desire not of the white conqueror but of the brown warrior. Yet she is still always passive, receptive, sexualized.

Chicana feminism has frequently positioned itself against the image of the Aztec Princess, as in Angie Chabrám-Dernersesian's (1992, 81) discussion of the gender disparity in early Chicano/a studies: "Brave Aztec Chicano warriors . . . scout the cultural horizon accompanied by shapely Aztec Chicana princesses sporting the national denomination, Aztlán, on their [bosoms]." Chabrám argues that Chicana feminist writers, by articulating multiple Chicana (female) subjectivities, challenge the unitary Chicano (male) of movement ideology. She makes her point by contrasting these writers with "the calendar Aztec princess[es], who hung like ornaments on the laps of their mates in an untouched paradisiacal landscape" (89). Similarly, Ana Castillo's poetry strives for a representation of love beyond the structure of romance in "Ixtacihuátl Died in Vain."[10]

In between the evocation and the imitation of Helguera's work, Helguera the individual and originating artist is often forgotten. Though Helguera was not the first artist to depict Ixta and Popo, it is his images that are reproduced. In border cities such as Juárez and Tijuana, one can purchase copies of Helguera's work reproduced in oil and acrylic on canvas, black velvet, and ceramics. The cover of *Black Velvet: The Art We Love to Hate,* Jennifer Heath's 1994 book on black velvet paintings, features *Ixtacihuátl and Popocatépetl* by the Tijuana artist Tawa. Tawa's velvet painting is clearly derivative of Helguera's *Leyenda de los volcanes,* but Heath's discussion makes no mention of the Helguera original:

> One perennial favorite native motif is that of the Aztec warrior and maiden Ixtacihuátl and Popocatépetl, for whom Mexico's two famous volcanoes are named. Velvet artists stencil the couple in many swoony poses, but Tijuana painter Tawa follows this beautiful ancient legend of love lost and turned into nature, scene by scene, meticulously by hand, and his magnificent work commands great respect. (7)

Helguera's Ixta and Popo continue to be a popular theme for reproduction by young artists who regularly send in their sketches to *Teen*

Angel and *Low Rider* magazines, and their images appear frequently in murals, on customized cars, on Chicana/o bodies as tattoos, or as the models for Aztec dance costumes. The popular 1970s Chicano band Malo (second only to Santana), featured Helguera's *Amor indio* as the cover art for their album *The Best of Malo*.

I argue that Helguera's images come to stand in for both the Legend of the Volcanoes and the characters of Ixta and Popo: that is, viewers know the image whether or not they know the story, and the image clearly goes back to Helguera.

"To ace out a homeboy": Refiguring Chicano Masculinity

In 1974 Manuel Cruz — a Chicano artist already known for small sculptures of Aztec figures, pachucos, and the Brown Berets — completed a mural at the Ramona Gardens Housing Project in East Los Angeles. Although untitled, the mural is frequently referred to as "Homeboy" (Fig. 2) because of its caption: "To ace out a homeboy from another barrio is to kill la Raza. Y Viva la Raza." It depicts a car driving off to downtown L.A. Inside the car two figures are silhouetted. The passenger points a large gun out of the window. On the right side of the mural stands the Aztec warrior, Popocatépetl. In his arms he holds the body of a young man with blood streaming from a bullet wound in the chest.

This painting is a complex refiguring of Popocatépetl. He is larger than life, and his long cloak gives him a superhero quality. Ixta is absent from the painting, and in her place is a Chicano youth. Unlike Ixta — who sometimes appears to be sleeping — the young man is clearly dead. His body is stylized rather than sexualized. His jeans and plaid shirt are shapeless. He shows no skin, and there is no detailing of chest and thighs. For once, Popocatépetl neither looks down in grief nor up to the heavens in protest. His eyes gaze out at the viewer, presumably another homeboy, to whom the caption is directed.

Cruz employs Popo to stage a critique of popular representations of Chicano gangs as Aztec warriors. These would-be warriors, the mural suggests, are perpetuating violence against Chicanos: rather than continue the tradition of the Aztec warrior, they are in fact exterminating him.

Through the image of Popo with the young man's body in his arms, Cruz reappropriates a heterosexual image (Popo and Ixta) for a homo-

Figure 2. Untitled mural ("Homeboy"), by Mañuel Cruz.

social purpose (ending gang violence). There is no ambiguity about the homeboy's death precisely because there is no need to eroticize him. The young man is intended as a figure with whom the viewer should identify—and thus consider (his) own mortality—rather than one whom (he) should desire.

Popo in this case represents a new aspect of brotherhood: not the brotherhood of the gang, where you protect your own at the expense of others, but a brotherhood of La Raza, in which all Chicanos share the same heritage and the same future. Many Chicano nationalist representations of Aztec rely on the theme of the "double conquest" (by Spain *and* by the United States) as, for example, in Rudolfo "Corky" Gonzalez's epic poem "I Am Joaquín," Luis Jiménez's drawings *Mexican Allegory on Wheels* and *Cholo with Low Rider Van*, and Ana Castillo's poem "Our Tongue Was Nahuatl." The "double conquest" thus emphasizes the distance between the modern-day Chicano/a and the Aztec past. Cruz's mural, on the other hand, interpellates Chicanos, accusing Chicano gangs of collaborating in the genocide of their people. Cruz is deliberately operating within a masculine discourse, one that ignores the presence of girls in gangs and of women in Chicano/a communities. That is to some degree its appeal: Popo should be taken seriously precisely because he speaking as one warrior to another.

La historia de amor: Queering Aztec History

As Manuel Cruz moves Popo from a heterosexual economy to a homosocial one, the artist Joey Terrill goes further in *La historia de amor*

(Fig. 3). Terrill's calendar painting is a queer interpretation of Helguera's *Amor indio* to articulate a gay Chicano identity. Instead of Popo and Ixta, *La historia de amor* features two Aztec males in the same pose as Popo and Ixta in *Amor indio*. The volcanoes Ixtacihuátl and Popocatépetl loom in the background. However, the position of the human figures has been altered so as to conceal part of the volcano Ixtacihuátl, that is, to conceal what would be the woman's breasts.

The Aztec Princess has been replaced by an Aztec youth, wearing only a white loincloth (draped rather like briefs).[11] Like Ixta, he is loose-limbed but very muscular, reclining in the arms of his lover. His partner, Popocatépetl, cradles him. Popo is dressed and posed the same as Helguera's Popo in *Amor indio*, yet there is a certain "queeniness" about the feathered headdress, the profile, that was always present in *Amor indio*, where, perhaps, it passed unnoticed in the heterosexual economy of the painting. On its own, Terrill's painting produces "la historia de amor"—an unwritten history of gay Chicano love whose genealogy can be traced back to the Aztecs.

Terrill's painting enacts important cultural work, intervening in a realm of representation in which the gay male body was always-already Anglo and in an Anglo-centric AIDS education milieu. The painting uses a queer interpretation of the warrior and the princess to articulate a gay Chicano identity. Like Helguera's paintings today, Terrill's work does not circulate solely as art in Chicano/a communities. Rather, it circulates as the image on a calendar used for advertising. In this case, *La historia de amor* is the featured image of a 1995 calendar issued by VIVA, the Lesbian and Gay Latino Arts organization of Los Angeles. This calendar was funded by a grant to provide AIDS education in a culturally specific context.

The VIVA calendar is a brilliant semiotic and political move: because both heterosexual and queer Chicanas and Chicanos are familiar with the imagery of Ixta and Popo, they are drawn in by Terrill's image in a look-once, look-twice inscription of gay Chicanos. The caption reminds the viewer that AIDS is not merely a problem of "los otros" but one that affects Chicano/a communities. Finally, the message, "Support your brothers with HIV," draws on Manuel Cruz's reinterpretation of Popo as brother caring for brother. Like Cruz's mural, Popo has a message for today's warriors; instead of calling for an end to gang violence, Popo urges political and emotional support for Chicanos

Figure 3. *La historia de amor,* by Joey Terrill, © 1994. Courtesy of the artist.

with HIV. The VIVA calendar thus urges both gay and straight Aztec warriors to support their modern-day gay and straight HIV-positive warrior brothers.

In the VIVA calendar, the bilingual caption "Apoya tus hermanos con VIH/Support your brothers with HIV" appears below the painting. This caption serves to reinscribe the Ixta and Popo more specifically than does the title *La historia de amor*. While Terrill's painting focuses on the love relationship between the two men, it provides a culturally specific historicization of homosexuality. The caption, however, foregrounds the death of the Aztec Princess: the message about HIV marks it as an image of love, death, and mourning. Popo is once again holding his dead/dying lover.

The caption, like the advertisements on the calendars on which Helguera's paintings are reproduced, provides the material reason for the circulation of the image. Helguera's paintings on calendars were intended as commercial advertisements; Terrill's queer Aztec lovers appear only in the context of AIDS education.

Terrill's work draws attention to the "drag queen" qualities of the Aztec warrior, as well as the ways in which an overemphasis on the masculine body resonates with contemporary gay male representations. Terrill leads the intrepid scholar, not only to the nationalist images of Jesus Helguera, but also to the work of Saturnino Herrán, whose earlier depictions of the warrior and the princess and whose drawings of Aztec youth now resonate with the radical queer Latino performance of the twenty-first century.[12]

Chicana lesbian fictions, like other Chicana/o cultural productions are shaped and influenced by images and fantasies produced by U.S. mainstream culture, Mexican mainstream culture, and Chicano nationalism. Further, I believe the Chicana lesbian writings not only take up these images and fantasies, not only queer them, but in doing so, they work to queer the origin stories themselves.

Ixta: Homosocial and Homosexual Women on the Border

My visual world included . . . graffiti . . . ; bakery and market calendars of sexy Aztec princess Ixta draped over the lap of strong Aztec warrior Popo; the Lotería; tattoos of the Virgen de Guadalupe on men's backs; . . . and murals mostly depicting Emiliano Zapata, Francisco Villa, and Aztec warriors. (Lopez 1999b, n.p.)

In her digital print *Ixta* (1999; Fig. 4), Alma Lopez presents her portrayal of Popocatépetl and Ixtacihuátl. While her work clearly references the traditional Helguera image, like Cruz and Terrill, she creates complex new meanings.

Lopez describes the creation of *Ixta* as the "familiar myth, but with two princesas on the U.S./Mexico border." *Ixta* allows for more than one possible reading. There are layers of imagery as well as meaning. In the foreground is the corrugated tin of the U.S.-Mexico border near Tijuana, the wall bearing the signs of border peoples. The two women (Cristina Serna and Mirna Tapia) dominate the center of the scene, both in contemporary urban dress. Behind them are the lights of Los Angeles, and in the far background, Helguera's *Leyenda de los volcanes* (reversed).

Drawing from Catholic iconography, Lopez poses the active woman in the scene with her arms extended, approximating both a Jesus figure and La Virgen de Guadalupe. Her fallen compañera lies directly on top of the U.S.-Mexico border, representing, perhaps, the women who die in crossing, the women who were murdered in Juárez,[13] the borderlands as a site of violence against Chicanas/os and Mexicanos and specifically against women. Lopez contrasts the urban dress of the two women with the stylized garments of the warrior and the princess in the background. In fact, both women wear black, which conceals their bodies; the Aztec Princess wears white, which reveals the details of her body.

Like Manuel Cruz's Popo, the active woman in the scene seems to proclaim the injustice of her *compañera's* death. She demands an end to violence from her Chicano/a community. Lopez's Ixta itself blurs any border between homosocial and homosexual. *Ixta* was featured on the poster for "Sin Vergüenza y Con Pasión: the Third Annual Queer Latina/o Youth Conference," which was held at the University of California, Los Angeles, in 1999. Thus the context in which the image circulated (queer youth) and the depiction of "la leyenda de los volcanes" suggest that the two women are lovers, yet the legacy of Manuel Cruz's "Homeboy" mural allows them also to be read as queer *familia*.

Like *Historia de amor* and *Ixta*, Chicana lesbian fictions provide not only a view of queer Chicano/a culture but also a *queer* view of Chicano/a culture, a view of the queerness within Chicano/a culture — the spaces from which, in spite of a dominant heterosexist discourse, queer identities have sprung and in which they remain hidden by the dominant discourse.

In my work, I constantly come up against questions of essentialism, a notion of "the" real Chicana lesbian. Many of the authors whose writings I look at are dealing with these questions, giving voice to a unified

Figure 4. *Ixta,* by Alma Lopez, © 1999 (special thanks to Cristina Serna and Mirna Tapia). Courtesy of the artist.

Chicana lesbian or contesting the terms of the question itself by showing a multiplicity of Chicana lesbians. My goal is to take the latter road — to show a multiplicity of images as a way of saying that there is no "one" Chicana lesbian voice, even while I draw attention to the different ways in which all these stories may yet take up common themes, images, and fantasies. And yet the often unspoken basis of my argument is that there *is* such a thing as Chicana lesbian writing, however openly I might try to define it. While the mappings of identities might not boldly proclaim "Here are Chicana Lesbians," Chicana lesbians[14] exist, and seeing the world through their eyes provides others with different views and different worlds. Following Gayatri Spivak, Emma Pérez argues for strategic essentialism — the notion that even while we recognize that there is no unified Chicana lesbian identity, we nevertheless can choose to come together under the *sign* of Chicana lesbian (or, say, the banner *Lesbianas Unidas* at the Cinco de Mayo parade) and still embrace or contest the differences between us.

My goal is to draw attention to these literary arguments and their outcomes. At the same time, I find myself validating and praising those works that refuse easy answers. Ignoring the inherent contradictions in these stories would betray the goals of my work; however, I believe that recognizing an internal contradiction need not result in the dismissal of the work that the stories (and their authors) do.

Thus, to return the example of Joey Terrill's *Historia de amor,* even while the artwork questions heterosexist constructions of Chicano/a history, we can also see the way it follows nationalist discourse of Mexican identity, which names us, the mestizo children of Mexico, the legitimate heirs of the Aztec empire while the Mexican state continues to delegitimize and marginalize the indigenous communities of Latin

America, which go beyond national borders and which problematize the "legitimacy" of "our" inheritance. Similarly, we can see how the myth of the death of the Aztec Princess, reworked in Terrill's work and framed in the project of AIDS education, confirms a popular vision of "the AIDS victim" as always already dead and dying. To see these complexities and contradictions at play behind the image is not to dismiss Terrill's work. Rather, it increases our appreciation of the work that Terrill's image accomplishes, though we may be left uncomfortable by all the fantasies thus laid bare.

In literature, as in art, Chicanas and Chicanos have continued to draw on the imagery of Ixta and Popo. The depictions of La India in Terri de la Peña's "La Maya" and Alicia Gaspar de Alba's "Excerpts from the Sapphic Diaries of Sor Juana Inés de la Cruz" and "La Mariscal" draw from the visual iconography of Ixtacihuátl as well as from the Mexican mothers, La Malinche, La Virgen de Guadalupe, and La Llorona.

"La Maya": Desire for Authenticity

> I came for you, Adriana. And I want you to stay — para siempre. (de la Peña 1989, 7)

In her 1989 short story, "La Maya," Terri de la Peña recounts an erotic tale of a Chicana protagonist, Adriana Carranza, vacationing in the Yucatán Peninsula, apart from her Anglo lover, Liz:

> Adriana had noticed that the tropical climate heightened her sexuality. . . . She had . . . erotic dreams . . . about brown-skinned Mexicanas with glossy hair and compelling eyes. She wondered if being among her own people had made her more open to these fantasies. (2)

Adriana's fantasies articulate a notion of La India as difference at the same time that she symbolizes Mexico, and thus for the Chicana protagonist, authenticity. While masturbating on the beach, Adriana fantasizes "a naked Mayan woman beside her":

> La Maya's body seemed sturdy and powerful. . . . Adriana wanted to blend with esta mujer extraña, and she grabbed the thick ends of la Maya's flowing hair. Her cabello de india felt like a lifeline. (2)

When Adriana meets her tour guide, Pilar de Oro, who has "the grace of a prowling jaguar," she identifies her immediately with La Maya of her fantasies:

> Her penetrating eyes spoke of ageless mysteries. With a Mayan profile, she seemed to have stepped from the pages of a Mexican art book. . . . She even wore an embroidered huipil, a short version which revealed her strong legs. Adriana stared. La Maya had come to life. (3)

The representation of Pilar as the Aztec Princess equates ancient Mexico with sensuality. The embroidered *huipil* evokes Indian heritage and emphasizes Pilar's legs. In the legacy of the conquest, La India represents sexuality. This interpretation is confirmed by Adriana's reference to Pilar as simply "La Maya." During the tour, Adriana strikes up a conversation with Pilar and speaks to her in Spanish. Surprised, Pilar replies, "Muchas norteamericanas no les gusta hablar nuestro idioma." Adriana hastens to correct Pilar's reading of her as *una norteamericana*, declaring, "Soy Chicana. Me encanta hablar español" (4). In the middle of the night, a restless Adriana is lured to the pyramids by an elusive Pilar.

> [Adriana] ran towards the Temple of the Warriors and halted at the foot of its staircase. . . . [Pilar called,] "Aquí—aquí estoy." . . . Almost crawling, Adriana advanced up the ancient steps and arrived breathless. At the apex of the temple sat la Maya, a resplendent goddess enthroned upon the sculpture of the Rain God, Chac Mool. Her huipil lay forgotten beside her. La Maya's strong brown legs were spread to reveal her vulva, and her black mane was loose, covering her breasts like a feathery shield. (6)

The phrase "covering her breasts like a feathery shield" is again evocative of Helguera's calendars. Ixta's breasts are always shielded while at the same time they are a focus of attention. The feathers in Helguera's paintings usually signify Popo, not Ixta. Popo always wears a feathered headdress of red and gold, sometimes heavily plumed and sometimes of flat feathers. Ixta, in contrast, generally has flowers in her hair.

Throughout this sex scene, Pilar is not specified by her name but only as "la Maya":

La Maya leaned back on her primitive throne and opened her legs wider. Adriana crouched before her, hungrily tasting la Maya's musky nectar. . . . La Maya could hardly keep from sliding off the throne. At her tumultuous orgasms, she screamed Adriana's name, and her primeval cry reverberated amidst the temple's stone pillars. . . . Adriana slowly raised her head to find la Maya with her head thrown back, her legs still apart. Adriana could not see la Maya's face, but even in the darkness she sensed a difference. (7)

This difference is that "la Maya" has once again become Pilar, neither princess nor goddess.

De la Peña's language in these sex scenes is both conventional and hyperbolic. The use of overblown phrases such as "La Maya could hardly keep from sliding off the throne" and "her tumultuous orgasms" is unabashed in its reinforcement of the signs of La India: "her primitive throne," "her primeval cry reverberated amidst the temple's stone pillars."

This sexualization of the native woman is problematic because it participates in international practices of selling third world women to first world consumers. Feminist analysis of these practices focus on state-sanctioned prostitution propping up a faltering national economy. As Cynthia Enloe (1990, 36) argues, "Sex tourism is not an anomaly; it is one strand of the gendered tourism industry." Adriana does not perceive her desiring gaze as the gaze of the colonizer. The implication is that because she is lesbian and, more important, because she is Chicana, her desire for "la Maya" is represented as free of unequal power relations.

Yet the context of the Helguera calendars makes this more than just a simple exoticization. It is, in fact, one Chicana lesbian interpretation of Ixta and Popo: in this cast the warrior has been replaced by Adriana and the maiden by Pilar. One significant difference is that Pilar is here much more active, though no less sexual, than Ixta. In one sense, then, Pilar *is* Ixta come to life; she may be active and she may be queer, yet she remains confined by the frame of the calendar in which she represents a particular racialized sexuality.

Thus the desire of the scene, like the nostalgia evoked by Helguera's calendars and replicated in Chicana/o art, is also very clearly linked to a desire for authenticity, for a connection between the ancient Aztec and the contemporary Chicana/o. Adriana seems to articulate this desire, without necessarily recognizing it. At one point, the vacationing Chicana snaps pictures of Pilar on the steps of El Caracól. "I plan to show these slides to my students," she explains. "Chicano kids need to be aware of their history" (5). Unconsciously, perhaps, Adriana is conflating Pilar with Mayan architecture and thus with Chicano/a heritage.

Adriana desires Pilar—not simply as Pilar but as La Maya, La India, "the" native Mexican woman. Adriana wants to be accepted: the *pocha* embraced by the mythic Mexican mother. Pilar's first words to Adriana after her orgasm indicate the Chicana's success: "I came for you, Adriana. And I want you to stay—para siempre" (7). Pilar asks again at the end of their lovemaking, "'You will stay?' Adriana did not hesitate. 'Yes'" (8). Yet this acceptance that Adriana has won from Pilar is withdrawn the next morning when she wakes up alone. Pilar is off guiding another tour. When she returns she is cool and distant. The story ends that evening with Adriana searching the darkness and listening "for the haunting cry of la Maya" (9). Thus Adriana's fantasy figure of Pilar becomes linked to La Llorona, emphasizing Pilar's mythic maternal function.

De la Peña herself seems to see this story as tapping into the Chicana/o sexual imagination. In her second novel, *Latin Satins* (1994), her character Jessica Tamayo chooses "a thin volume of lesbian erotica" in which to indulge herself. When Jessica reads a story of "tropical moonlit nights [and] passionate sex among Mayan ruins" (1994, 92), it becomes clear that the purple paperback is actually *Intricate Passions* (1989), the anthology in which "La Maya" was first published.[15]

Though it contains humorous elements, "La Maya" is not deliberately satirical in its reworking of Ixta and Popo. Rather, it attempts to situate the Aztec Princess in a lesbian context while taking the image itself at face value. The Chicana narrator gazes at Pilar with unabashed desire. She does not see her own gaze as in any way objectifying or exoticizing the native woman. Indeed, because Adriana is Chicana, her gaze—like that of Popo—is perceived as innocent of power dynamics. At least in her own mind, hers is not the colonizer's gaze. Through her articulation, "Soy Chicana," she sees herself as *like* Pilar, as being among her own people, even while the terms in which her desire is expressed make it very clear that she believes herself *unlike* Pilar, and she very much wants to be accepted and to stay "para siempre."

"La Mariscal": Not Your Aztec Princess

In a black velvet painting on the wall, a voluptuous Indian maiden of-
fered her bronze breasts to an armored conquistador. (Gaspar de Alba
1993b, 46)

In her 1993 short story, "La Mariscal," Alicia Gaspar de Alba explores
the connection between La Malinche and Ixta in the Chicana/o sexual
imaginary. As in Helguera's paintings of Ixta and Popo—and the many
replications of those in Chicano/a and Mexican art—the "voluptuous
Indian maiden" represents an excessive sexuality. In the final scene of
"La Mariscal," this black velvet painting in the back room of a border
brothel highlights that Ixta is the other side of La Malinche. Both stereotypes focus on the sexuality of the Indian maiden, for two different
enterprises.

By casting an Anglo-American male sociologist as the main narrative figure in "La Mariscal," Gaspar de Alba engages the ways in which
historical texts (and other official forms of knowledge) have traditionally represented Native American and Mexican/Mexican American
women in sexualized terms. Yet the object of the scholar's desiring gaze
is a postmodern princess prostitute, aware of the roles intended for her
and able to manipulate them to her own advantage.

In Gaspar de Alba's short story, Jack Dublin, a Boston-born sociologist employed "at a University that fancied itself Harvard-on-the-
Border" (41), has crossed into Mexico to satisfy his "lust for a woman[,]
. . . the primal urge to feel her naked and vulnerable beneath him" (45).
The material reality of the "Combat Zone," the area of the border catering to American GIs, is such that the sexual services of Mexican
women are commodities to be purchased. As far as Jack is concerned,
all the women across the border—Aztec Princesses and "monkey-
faced" Mexican prostitutes—are for sale. The object of Jack's interest
is a woman who doesn't look like a "a working girl": "With her smooth
olive complexion, the bloom of peacock feathers in her blue-black
hair, her embroidered Mexican dress, she looked more like an Aztec
princess" (42).

This woman, Susana, seems uninterested in Dublin's advances and
tells him, "Look, señor, . . . I'm from Chihuahua, and I'm just waiting
for my sister. . . . I don't work here." By identifying herself as not from
the border zone, Susana argues that she is not for sale, not a border

Mexicana, and thus not a prostitute. Yet when she leaves the room for a moment the bartender confides, "Her name is Berta[,] . . . but she uses Susana with the Gringos" (46).

Susana/Berta plays with the roles that Jack desires of her. When he wants an Aztec Princess, she is coy, refusing, yet clearly reading his intent. He is pleased that "she wore no makeup and smelled of honeysuckle" (44), and while she waits for him to light her cigarette, he attempts to put her in her place:

> He hated the taste of tobacco in a woman's mouth. . . . He had to let her know that she was special, and special ladies didn't smoke, in his book. . . . "I don't mind the smoke" he said to Susana, . . . "It's the image that [bothers] me. I don't like to see a woman with a cigarette in her mouth, much less an Aztec princess like you. (46)

For Jack, cigarettes are linked with women's sexuality, which is out of his control, linked to his wife in Boston who left him for her lesbian friends. He remembers "all those nights he'd waited for Barbara, only to have her sneak in just before sunrise, smelling of tobacco and a perfume she didn't own. It had taken him a long time to figure out what she was doing and then even more time to believe it" (44). It is clear that he finds solace in Mexican prostitutes precisely because, in his mind, they are unlike his ex-wife: their sexuality exists only for his convenience. Yet "tonight, he wanted to serve Susana, kneel before her and taste her native blood, swallow the Aztec seed of her, save her from the cage of The Red Canary" (45). The language of "primal" sexuality is deliberately overblown. Susana's refusals further incite Jack's desire. He wants the fantasy of a "pure" Aztec Princess even while he wants to purchase her sexual services.

Antonia Castañeda describes the racialized fantasies featuring Native American, Mexican, and Mexican American women as

> contradictory images of the "noble princess/savage squaw" and the "Spanish señorita/Mexican prostitute," respectively. The "noble princess" and the "Spanish señorita" . . . reject their own kind, native men, in favor of their white saviors. Marriage to the blue-eyed strangers saves them from the oppression of their own men and thus from the savagery of their race, culture, group, and nation. (1992, 518)[16]

Yet in Jack's fantasy the Aztec Princess is never wholly separate from the savage squaw, for it is her native blood that inflames his desire. It is this contradiction that Susana plays upon when she acknowledges his desire for the Aztec Princess. He is pleased to finally meet her in a back bedroom of the bar but dismayed to find "that his Aztec princess had applied lipstick and false eyelashes" (Gaspar de Alba 1993b, 46). Susana, knowing that he doesn't want her to smoke, is deliberately "finishing her cigarette" when Jack comes to her in the back room. "The room reeked of tobacco. She got up to close the door and rinsed her mouth out with brandy" (46). Instead of cleaning herself up for him, she has in fact "dirtied" herself, putting aside the mask of the Aztec princess and replacing it with the mask of the Mexican prostitute. The black velvet painting on the wall, of "a voluptuous Indian maiden offer[ing] her bronze breasts to an armored conquistador," is an exhibition of Jack's fantasy in which he plays Hernán Cortés to Susana's La Malinche.

Yet Susana/Berta has toyed with him to the end. "Jack tried to kiss her, but she turned her head. 'I don't kiss for money,' she said" (46). Susana's final words bring the story to an abrupt end. The Mexican female sexuality, which he sought to control, has eluded him. Susana/Berta will sell him the sexual act but nothing more: no Aztec Princess to be saved from her cage, she paints his fantasy in lipstick and false eyelashes against a black velvet backdrop and refuses to be rescued by Prince Charming's kiss.

While Chicana lesbian representations of La India cannot escape the frame of racialized sexuality depicted by "the" Aztec Princess, they may stage strategic relationships to it. "La Mariscal" foregrounds the heteronormative representation of Ixtacihuátl/Malinche *as* representation, balanced by an ostensibly "real" Indian/Chicana/Mexicana. Berta can assume the role of "Susana" pragmatically and so deftly that, despite his social scientist's intuition, Jack cannot truly perceive the performance until it is painted in garish lipstick and black velvet.

Whereas the myth of "the" Aztec Princess romanticizes and effaces the sexual violence perpetrated against native women of the Americas, "the scene" of prostitution, contrasted as it to the colonial sexual fantasy, ironizes the Anglo male academic and the wish fulfillment in play in his construction of "the" Mexican woman. Gaspar de Alba highlights the material conditions faced by women like Berta, deromanticizes the position of the border subject, challenges the always already hetero-sexuality of Mexican and native women, and demonstrates how a Chicana feminist perspective changes both the context and the meaning of historical and cultural fantasies.

De la Peña's "La Maya" reappropriates the image of the Aztec Princess for lesbian identity. "La Maya" does so in a sex-positive fantasy of Chicana/Chicana desire. Finally, "La Mariscal" stages the Aztec Princess as a male fantasy, with which contemporary Chicanas and Mexicanas must contend.

I return now to the epigraph from Cherríe Moraga's "Played between White Hands." That essay is part of the ongoing debate that followed the April 1982 Barnard Sexuality Conference[17] concerning the sympathetic exploration of the topic of lesbian sadomasochism and the negative coverage of the conference in the feminist newspaper *off our backs*. Moraga is taking exception to a specific article[18] in which "through white feminist eyes Mirtha Quintanales and [Cherríe Moraga] are Latinas and nothing but Latinas." She continues, "We are *used* throughout the article as representatives of our culture . . . , our organizations . . . , our politics" (Moraga 1982, n.p.). On another level, Moraga is also taking issue with how both the pro-S&M and anti-S&M camps are eager to "play" women of color to their own advantage. Thus, in this article, she argues that though Latinas are invoked in the argument, the argument itself leaves Latina sexuality outside the door.

Moraga's words continue to resonate in my research, especially as I search for Chicana and Latina voices that articulate their own sexuality. How do Chicana lesbian writers see their work as representing a specific Chicana sexual imaginary? I am driven to explore these questions because in literature, in history, in cultural representations, the history of Chicanas, Chicana lesbians, and Chicanas/os is overshadowed by dominant paradigms of Anglo-American history, models of Manifest Destiny, concepts of land and women "there for the taking," the erasure of communities of peoples of color who predate Anglo-American immigration. My goal in outlining genealogies of Chicana sexual imagination is, in part, to move away from hegemonic narratives of lesbian identity derived from classical, European, and Anglo-American roots (Sappho, Barnes, Hall, Bannon) that erase or distort histories of working-class and people of color. Such hegemonic narratives enact a violence that is contested by the writings of Cherríe Moraga, Terri de la Peña, and Alicia Gaspar de Alba that I have discussed here. These narratives are further contested by the Chicana lesbian fictions that I take up in the next chapter.

Simultaneously, I want to refute the masculinist/ nationalist argument that homosexuality is a "white thing." Chicana lesbian sexuality takes on familiar images, forms, and narratives at the same time that it names a queerness that is always already there. Thus, to return to Moraga's words with which I opened this chapter, these stories show how these images, which may well be displayed in "the mostly heterosexual bedrooms of South Texas, L.A., or even Sonora, México," are employed by Chicana lesbian authors to represent a specifically queer Chicana imaginary.

CHAPTER 4

Sor Juana and the Search for (Queer) Cultural Heroes

Maybe, in the delirium of her deathbed, she imagined you — brown-skinned, poor, female, sitting in a college classroom, reading about her, choosing among books, picking up a pen. Then her spirit flew into the sky over Mexico, bursting into hundreds of fragments of brilliant light, and became a new constellation.

—AURORA LEVINS MORALES, *REMEDIOS*

Sor Juana Inés de la Cruz, seventeenth-century poet, scholar, and dramatist of New Spain, has frequently been claimed as a literary foremother to contemporary Mexicana, Chicana, and Latina writers. The Puertorriqueña poet and historian Aurora Levins Morales posits a direct relationship between Sor Juana and contemporary Latinas. In *Remedios*, a prose poetry history of Puerto Rican women, Levins Morales writes that today's Latina students partake of the same rituals as Sor Juana, "choosing among books, picking up a pen." "We" invoke "her" as our ancestress, culturally and symbolically, even though, unlike her, we are "brown-skinned [and] poor" as well as female. Of course, Sor Juana, a Catholic nun who bore no children, cannot literally be our ancestor, but figuratively we have been inclined to trace our literary heritage to this first feminist of the Americas as we pick up our pens.

Born Juana Ramírez de Asbaje, Sor Juana was a self-taught prodigy who won the attention of the court of New Spain. A favorite of the Vicereina Leonor Carreto, Marquesa de Mancera, Juana was examined by more than forty scholars in a failed attempt to find a gap in her education. Although she entered the convent of San Jerónimo in

Mexico City, she was by no means isolated from society. Two volumes of her work were published in Madrid during her lifetime, and one volume posthumously. She is best known for her defense of women in "Carta Atenagórica" (1690). For many Chicana writers, she represents the beginning of three hundred years of Mexicana creativity.

"An important cultural heroine who symbolizes the intellectual woman[,] . . . Sor Juana appears as a constant figure" in poetry, fiction, drama, film, art, and feminist theory by Chicana and Latina artists and authors (Rebolledo 1995, 58–59). She has been represented as a hero, a saint, a martyr, a feminist, a pawn, an individualist, a heterosexual in love with her confessor, a woman who completely denied her sexuality in favor of the life of the mind, and a lesbian who was "passionately attached to the Viceroy's wife" (Levins Morales 2001, 43).

I examine Sor Juana as a contradictory figure for Chicana writers and readers. On the one hand, she is lauded as the first feminist of the Americas and a foremother of Chicana feminism. On the other hand, she occupied a privileged racial and class position in the colonial hierarchies of New Spain. I discuss Octavio Paz's biography of Sor Juana, especially in relation to Alicia Gaspar de Alba's "interview" with Sor Juana, Estela Portillo's play *Sor Juana* (1983), María Luisa Bemberg's film *Yo, la peór de todas* (1990), and Alicia Gaspar de Alba's short stories and novel about Sor Juana.

This Lesbian Nun Who Is Not One: *The Traps of Faith*

Problematically for Chicana feminists, Octavio Paz's *Sor Juana, or The Traps of Faith* (1988), has served as the authoritative text on the seventeenth-century nun. Paz's early theoretical discussion, *The Labyrinth of Solitude* (1961), renders Chicano/a culture in explicitly masculinist, sexist, and homophobic terms.[1] That the only modern biography of Sor Juana Inés de la Cruz—the "first feminist of the Americas"—should be written by Paz seems to add insult to injury.

The Traps of Faith locates Sor Juana in the historical and cultural context of colonial New Spain, claiming her for the nation of Mexico. Paz attributes to Sor Juana a heterosexual orientation—in part, perhaps, to recuperate her from earlier homophobic biographers whose vulgar Freudianism painted her as having a "masculinity complex." In her "Interview with Sor Juana," Gaspar de Alba discusses the specter of "masculinity" in biographies of Sor Juana:

> Octavio Paz is not the only one of Sor Juana's critics and biographers to declare that there was nothing "abnormal" (to use their word) about Sor Juana; still, Paz is unique because instead of simply dismissing the possibility, he tries to prove that any traces of "masculinity" which may have surfaced in Sor Juana's character derive from a combination of psychic traumas: melancholia, subjection to the church, compensation for the absent father, penis envy, and perhaps even a courtly love affair (with a man, of course) gone awry. (1998b, 140)

It is true that Paz talks himself into circles to prove that Sor Juana could not have been a "lesbian" in the twentieth-century sense. At one point he contends, "Of course Sor Juana was bisexual, but what does that say? All but a handful of humanity is bisexual" (1988, 506). Paz's argument about Sor Juana's relationship with the Vicereina María Luisa Manrique de Lara suggests that if there was any "homosocial attachment" between the women, it is a result of the sexually segregated society in which Sor Juana lived:

> An excess of libido could not be directed toward an object of the opposite sex. A different object — a female friend — had to take its place. Transposition and sublimation: the loving friendship between Sor Juana and the Countess was the transposition; the sublimation was realized by means of the Neoplatonic concept of love — friendship between persons of the same sex. (1988, 217)

Implicit in this argument is the belief that "an object of the opposite sex" — that is, a man — is the (only) appropriate object of a woman's desire. Thus, Paz argues, if homosexuality is present, it is clearly "situational homosexuality." Certain women, it is known, when placed in a women-only environment (say, a women's prison), have been known to engage in homosexual activity. However, when they are out in the "real world," they engage in heterosexual activity. Thus if Sor Juana felt she was "in love" with the Vicereina, it is merely an attribute of circumstance. The notion of situational homosexuality is widely accepted, especially in sociological contexts,[2] but the very construction begs the question of whether it is, in Adrienne Rich's famous term, actually "compulsory heterosexuality." Paz's argument fails to acknowledge that in heteronormative society, women's "heterosexuality" is similarly socially constructed; that is to say, libido is not allowed to attach to persons of the same sex and thus is directed toward persons of the opposite sex.

Paz admits, "The hypothesis I have just outlined does not necessarily exclude the presence of Sapphic tendencies in the two friends. Neither does it include them. Any comment on this subject would be mere supposition; we lack facts and documents" (217).[3] He goes on to argue that no matter how passionate the relationship between the two women, it must have been chaste.[4]

Certainly it is inarguable that "lesbian" is a modern identity. However, work in the history of sexuality reveals amorous and/or sexual relationships between women, even between nuns, before Sor Juana's time,[5] and from Saint Augustine on, discussions of women's religious communities have been tied to warnings against carnal emotions and relationships between women.

The Tenth Muse Speaks for Herself:
The Politics of Locating *Criolla* Nun or *Nueva Mestiza*

Gaspar de Alba's "Interview with Sor Juana Inés de la Cruz" attempts to reclaim Sor Juana from her biographers and "to reconfigure [her] not as a Hispanic but as a Chicana lesbian feminist" (1998b, 143). She begins her reconfiguration of Sor Juana by evaluating her status in New Spain: "There is no sense in denying Sor Juana's membership in the educated class, nor in denying that Chicana lesbian feminists also share that privilege (regardless of our individual class backgrounds)" (143).

Gaspar de Alba here argues that, regardless of individual class backgrounds, Sor Juana and "Chicana lesbian feminists" are similar in that they are "educated." Of course, this argument privileges what Gaspar de Alba terms the "educated class" over Sor Juana's actual racial and class status in the pigmentocracy of New Spain. In fact, overlooking — or looking beyond — Sor Juana's status is a necessary step for Chicanas who would reclaim her. Sor Juana must be reclaimed on a basis other than racial identification. She can be recuperated for contemporary Chicanas as a Mexican, an intellectual, a feminist, a poet, a lesbian, or an agent for the subaltern classes only outside of race and class.

To posit an equivalence between "Sor Juana's membership in the educated class" and academic "Chicana lesbian feminists [who] share that
privilege (regardless of our individual class backgrounds)," Gaspar de
Alba must take on the contradictions of Sor Juana's status. In seventeenth-century New Spain, Sor Juana's membership in the elite class
(educated or not) was predetermined by her race, which allowed her a
certain mobility unavailable to, for example, her *mulata* slave, Juana
de San José.

Gaspar de Alba argues that Sor Juana

> [is] a model of the nueva ciudadana, that is, a woman of the Americas,
> product of colonization, employing her agency and her tongue to cre-
> ate an autonomous identity. . . . Moreover, because her experience is
> rooted in the soil of the so-called New World (despite her liaisons with
> the Spanish aristocracy), and because the bulk of her education takes
> place within the musty covers of European books, she is a product of
> cultural mestizaje. She is, in fact, a mestiza in Gloria Anzaldúa's sense
> of the word. (144)

The idea of Sor Juana Inés de la Cruz as the new mestiza must be situated within the development of theories of mestizaje. In "Chicana Feminism: In the Tracks of 'the' Native Woman," Norma Alarcón (1990, 374)
argues that the "assumption of mestizaje in the Mexican nation-making
process was intended to racially colligate a heterogeneous population
that was not European." However, she continues,

> [i]t is worthwhile to remember that the historical founding moment of
> the construction of mestizo subjectivity entails the rejection and denial
> of the dark Indian Mother as Indian . . . and to actually deny the In-
> dian position even as that position is visually stylized and represented
> in the making of the fatherland. Within these blatant contradictions,
> the overvaluation of Europeanness is constantly at work. (377)

This is an important point, that mestizo identity, as it has operated
in Mexico, is part of the nation-making process that upheld the Indian
woman as the ancestor of the mestizo nation even as it erased her. Such
is the mestizaje developed by José Vasconcelos ([1929] 1979). Indeed,
Vasconcelos took for granted the superiority of the European "race," to
which the mestizo could aspire:

Las razas inferiores . . . irán ascendiendo en una escala de mejoramiento étnico, cuyo tipo máximo no es precisamente el blanco, sino esa nueva raza a la que tendrá que aspirar el blanco con el objecto de conquistar la síntesis. (72)

Inferior races . . . would go on ascending a scale of ethnic improvement, whose maximum type is not precisely the white but that new race to which the white himself will aspire with the object of conquering the synthesis. (Trans. Jaén 1997, 32)

Vasconcelos argues for a futuristic utopia, a fifth race, always yet unborn, never realized but always in gestation (see Martínez-Echazábal 1990, 39).

In the 1960s and 1970s, Chicano nationalism took Vasconcelos's theory of mestizaje at face value, emphasizing the future synthesis while perpetuating the erasure of the native woman as described by Alarcón. An obvious example is the figure of the three-headed mestizo. This popular icon of the Chicano/a movement depicts the profile of a male Spaniard facing left, the profile of a male Indian facing right, and a male mestizo facing forward. The image synthesizes the Spanish and Indian figures into the mestizo as the realization of La Raza Cósmica by depicting a trinity of male figures, emblematizing the erasure of the native woman so necessary for this origin story.

In *Borderlands/La Frontera: The New Mestiza* (1987), Anzaldúa moves beyond Vasconcelos's model of mestizaje. Anzaldúa argues against the notion of "betterment of the race"; rather, she emphasizes the return of the repressed native woman, as neither an Indian Princess nor a personification of the land. Thus, instead of a simultaneous romanticization and erasure of the Indian, Anzaldúa proposes a reclamation of the subaltern and the abject. Anzaldúa argues, "To live in the Borderlands means you/are neither hispana india negra española/ni gabacha, eres mestiza, mulata, half-breed/caught in the crossfire between camps" (216). Anzaldúa's New Mestiza is not caught in rigid identities but "copes by developing a tolerance for contradictions, a tolerance for ambiguity" (101).

Gaspar de Alba herself develops "a tolerance for contradictions, a tolerance for ambiguity," when she claims Sor Juana, a member of the colonial court, as a New Mestiza. Specifically, she is invoking an argument of cultural mestizaje quite apart from racial mestizaje. Because both the colonizer and the colonized are formed through colonialism, even a first-generation *criolla* is significantly different from her peninsular counterparts.[6]

Gaspar de Alba builds her argument through reference to Aída Hurtado (1989), who argues that white women enjoy a privileged relationship to white men, and thus access to power, because they are capable of providing racially pure heirs (i.e., more white men). White women are thus seduced by patriarchy through their relationships with white men. Hurtado goes on to posit, "Women of color . . . are rejected by white men because they would reproduce racially mixed offspring who would threaten the white male privilege" (quoted in Gaspar de Alba 1998b, 141). Hurtado's model, like patriarchy, constructs woman of color asexual *by definition*.

In applying Hurtado's argument to New Spain, Gaspar de Alba focuses on Sor Juana's nonheterosexual status:

> Interestingly, Sor Juana both seduced and rejected white men. Certainly, her beauty, wit, and rhetoric seduced the nobles and aristocrats (not to mention their wives) who sought her company as much in the *galanteos de palacio* as in the *tertulias* she held in the convent; however, she also rejected white men for the same reasons that white men reject women of color: reproduction. Her rejection of what Adrienne Rich calls "compulsory heterosexuality" meant that she would be nobody's mother, wife or mistress. (1998b, 143)

This is the closest Gaspar de Alba will come to discussing Sor Juana's racial status directly.[7] In her argument, the woman's position is changed from object being seduced or rejected by white men to subject with the power to seduce and reject them. According to Hurtado, whereas white men reject women of color because the latter can produce only impure offspring, Sor Juana rejects both white men specifically and reproduction in general. By focusing on Sor Juana's rejection of the reproductive role for women, Gaspar de Alba demonstrates the manner in which heterocentrist constructions of women's racial positions collapse in a nonheterosexual context. Thus, while using Hurtado's model, Gaspar de Alba highlights the heterosexualization of women of color implicit in such constructs. Such a challenge to the heterosexual imperative is quite radical, as a comparison with Estela Portillo Trambley's *Sor Juana* demonstrates.

Estela Portillo Trambley's Redemption Narrative

Estela Portillo Trambley's 1983 play, *Sor Juana,* depicts the rise and fall of Sor Juana and addresses the role of the (always-already hetero-sexual) Chicana writer in relation to her community. In one sense, the play is a redemption narrative, as the brilliant and arrogant Sor Juana is brought to a true sense of Christian charity through her passionate attachment to her confessor, Father Antonio Núñez de Miranda. In the play, Father Antonio is priest to the poor, not to the court. Young Juana Inés leaves village life behind and is seduced by the artifice of the viceroy's court. She falls in love with a nobleman, and when his Spanish bride arrives to claim him, she takes refuge in the convent. She is chastised by Father Antonio for her pride, but in spite of her love for him, she continues to seek wider recognition of her genius. The church fathers punish her by cutting her off from Father Antonio. During a popular uprising, she sees one of her childhood friends (a slave) killed by the viceroy's soldiers. Appalled by her own participation in the structures of power, Sor Juana renounces her writings, sells her goods, and gives the money to the poor. She is reconciled with Father Antonio and nurses him until his death.

In another sense, the play is about political and racial consciousness. Described as "of peasant stock," Father Antonio spends his time minis-tering to the people of the barrio — mestizos, *mulatos,* and *zambos*[8] — and is more in sympathy with their uprisings than with the viceroy's govern-ment that subjugates them. He seeks to show Sor Juana that her social position has a human cost. By infusing political consciousness into the play, Portillo Trambley grapples with Chicana identity even as she at-tempts to reclaim this heroine of New Spain.

According to Rebolledo (1995, 59), "Portillo turns the traditional perspective of Sor Juana around by presenting her at the end of her life (after she had forsaken her quest for knowledge) and imbuing her with a contemporary 'social' conscience." I would argue that, apart from this social conscience, heterosexuality is the defining character-istic of Portillo Trambley's *Sor Juana.* Young Juana enters the convent when she finds that Bernardo, her lover, is betrothed to a peninsular noblewoman. Mature Juana renounces her worldly possessions in an attempt to win back the good favor of Father Antonio.

Bernardo is a fictional device: there is no historical evidence that

Juana ever had such a suitor. In spite of this lack of evidence, however, many of Sor Juana's biographers have proposed a romantic disappointment as the reason she entered the convent.[9] There is also no evidence that Sor Juana's feelings for Núñez de Miranda were romantic or sexual. She wrote no love poems to Nuñez de Miranda. She did, however, write love poems to the Condesa de Paredes. As Gaspar de Alba argues in "The Politics of Location," Sor Juana's biographers consistently try to prove her heterosexuality without evidence while at the same time arguing against her lesbianism in spite of the evidence.[10] For Portillo Trambley, heterosexuality provides the motivation for otherwise unexplainable events: her rejection of court life, her entry into the convent, and her renunciation of her writings.[11]

Portillo Trambley's a priori assumption of Sor Juana's heterosexuality is widely accepted. Tey Diana Rebolledo, for example, finds Sor Juana's heterosexual identity troubling but accepts it as the historical truth of the character:

> As disturbing as it seems to be for Portillo that Sor Juana made many of her life choices because of the impact of the men in her life, . . . nevertheless the play does emphasize Sor Juana's feminist independence, and the sexism and lack of opportunity for women in colonial Mexico. (1995, 59)

In her reading of Portillo Trambley, Rebolledo accepts the representation of Sor Juana as explicitly and exclusively heterosexual. In other words, she does not question the "truth" of Sor Juana's heterosexuality—which is, in terms of the play, strangely disturbing. In fact, she collapses the historical Sor Juana with Portillo's fictional character. Thus Rebolledo further buttresses the representation of Sor Juana as a disappointed heterosexual.

In spite of what I read as the heteronormative representation of Portillo Trambley's *Sor Juana,* the play is interesting precisely because Portillo attempts to imbue Sor Juana "with a contemporary 'social' conscience." Sor Juana's girlhood is characterized by her friendship with two of her family's slaves who are about her own age, Juana and her brother Andrés. Slave Juana—as she is listed in the cast of characters—is based on a historical figure, Juana de San José, a *mulata* slave given to Sor Juana by her mother when she entered the convent.[12] Slave Juana's brother Andrés, a fictional character, marries another slave, Camila. After many severe beatings from his new owner, Don Rafael Martín, Andrés attacks Don Martín and escapes to the mountains with Camila.

Sor Juana/Slave Juana

Portillo makes much of the similarity of the name Juana for both nun and slave while marking the difference in their racial and class positions. The pragmatic Slave Juana challenges Sor Juana's indifference to the material lives of the poor and her deliberate blindness about the political unrest:

> *Slave Juana*. You forgot Andrés was like your brother long ago.
> *Sor Juana*. I have not forgotten. But that was long ago. It's a different world.
> *Slave Juana*. You not love Andrés. You not care. Andrés and Camila go to mountain where people hide. Soon they will fight!
> *Sor Juana*. Fight? That is only fearful talk. It will not come to that.
> *Slave Juana*. You do not see because your nose in book all the time.
> (167–168)

In June 1692 there was a revolt in Mexico City because floods the previous year had reduced the maize crop. The mountain people came down to the city seeking grain. The crowds demanded food from the viceroy and the archbishop, and a riot ensued. In the second act of *Sor Juana*, Andrés and Camila take part in the uprising, and Camila, now pregnant, is shot in the stomach by a Spanish soldier. Andrés kills the soldier and takes refuge with his sister in the convent. Although Sor Juana conceals him, he is discovered by the soldiers. The second act ends with Sor Juana's soliloquy describing Andrés's death:

> They dragged you away from here and put a rope around your neck. Your eyes were dark with fear. I saw you dangling from the hanging tree. My eyes cannot erase it. My mind cannot erase it. A sovereign fact, this death of yours which was . . . a death of me. Oh, the raw concreteness of the world! The mind is not enough, is it? Oh, I have wept loudly in the dark and felt a copious guilt . . . And that dark, mysterious flow where no words exist — I found it, didn't I? Faith . . . (188; ellipses in original)

Andrés's death makes clear to Sor Juana something that Father Antonio had tried and failed to convince her of earlier: she owes her allegiance to the poor people she grew up with, not to the viceroy's court. She now understands that New Spain is extinguishing the life of the country just as brutally as Andrés's life has been extinguished by the soldiers. I suggest that Portillo Trambley employs Andrés's death—not represented onstage—to invoke the lynching of African Americans in the United States—the quintessential image of racial violence.

While the image of the soldiers shooting a pregnant Indian woman in the stomach may also appear to be a fabrication of the author, Portillo Trambley's account corresponds roughly to Octavio Paz's description of the uprising:

> On [Friday] June 6 there was a panic: a rumor spread that supplies had run out; people rushed to the granary, crowding the doors. The guards were unable to keep order, and one of them clubbed a pregnant Indian woman, who miscarried on the spot. She was gathered up by an indignant Indian woman, placed on a litter, and a carried in a procession to the place of the Archbishop by fifty women and about twenty men. . . . At the granary, Friday's events were repeated, and word flew that the guards had beaten another Indian woman. She was exhibited, nearly lifeless, and borne in a new procession to the Plaza Mayor and the residences of the Viceroy and Archbishop. (Paz 1988, 439–440)[13]

Shouting "insults and obscenities," the crowd threw stones at the balconies of the palace. Soldiers fired from the roofs. The crowd set fire to the palace and to the municipal building across the street. (Viceroy Galve and his wife had taken refuge at the monastery early Sunday.) Paz (1988, 42) also relates that Carlos Sigüenza y Góngora, a friend and contemporary of Sor Juana, maliciously attributed the uprising "not to oppression by the Spanish or the incompetence of the authorities or to the scarcity of maize, but to the malevolence and drunkenness of the Indians." Retribution was swift: "The sale of pulque was prohibited and instructions were given that no Indian could enter the city. . . . On June 10 the arrests began and on June 11 the executions: four Indians were condemned to death. . . . Their hands were cut off and exhibited in the plaza" (Paz 1988, 442).

This uprising and Sor Juana's speech close the second act of Portillo Trambley's play. The final act consists of Sor Juana's reconciliation with her confessor, Antonio Núñez de Miranda, and her care of him during his illness. The play concludes with this note: "Father Antonio Núñez de Miranda died February 17, 1695. Sor Juana Inés de la Cruz died April 17, 1695, two months to the day after the death of her beloved confessor" (195).

For Portillo Trambley, then, Sor Juana's renunciation of her writing and the sale of her books, curios, and artifacts are not a reaction to the repression of the church but a conversion, through which she gives up everything in order to devote herself to the poor and needy. This is Sor Juana's salvation, her racial/class consciousness, her realization that her participation in the court has endorsed its oppression of her people. This narrative seems in sharp contrast to the prevailing feminist attitude that it was Sor Juana's persecution by the church that led her to renounce her writing. According to Paz's source notes to his biography of Sor Juana, early biographies of Sor Juana may have suggested Portillo Trambley's view of Sor Juana's and Father Antonio's relationship:

> Genaro Fernández McGregor maintained that Núñez de Miranda, Sor Juana's confessor, was wiser, more generous, more upright than she: a saint. Fortunately, he says, Núñez de Miranda's superior qualities finally prevailed; Sor Juana renounced writing and she, too, undertook the path toward saintliness. (1988, 503)

However, in Portillo Trambley's narrative, Sor Juana's salvation proceeds not through religion so much as through her recognition of her duty to Mexico. Sor Juana says:

> They will say that all good things evaporated in Mexico with the coming of the rebellion, that I was forced to give up my possessions, my writing. They will make of me a martyr. I am not . . . I see [the truth] in the barrios each day. (191)[14]

The Life of Saint Hyacintha of Mariscotti

In Portillo Trambley's *Sor Juana* — as in the earlier biography she may have drawn from — the story of Sor Juana is emplotted according to a conversion narrative. The prototypical conversion stories are those of Saints Paul and Augustine, but a more direct parallel with Sor Juana can be found in the legend of Saint Hyacintha of Mariscotti. Hyacintha is distinguished first for her personal wealth, which she used to live comfortably in her convent for ten years, ignoring her vow of poverty. Her confessor, who had occasion to visit her during an illness, was appalled by this and exhorted her to change her ways. Hyacintha gave away all her property, slept on bare boards, and devoted herself to the poor. She is, in fact, a patron saint of the poor.

Like Portillo Trambley's *Sor Juana*, both *Yo, la peór de todas* and *Sor Juana's Second Dream* bear the mark of Saint Hyacintha, but María Luisa Bemberg and Gaspar de Alba are more critical and self-reflective in their deployment of this saint's legend than is Portillo Trambley. In Portillo Trambley's play, Juana is "saved" through her renunciation of worldly pursuits; in contrast, both Bemberg and Gaspar de Alba critique Sor Juana's confessor, showing how his wish to "save" Sor Juana demands her absolute subjugation and humiliation.

La peór de todas/The Worst of All and the Traps of Nation

Bemberg's film *Yo, la peór de todas* (1990) circulated widely among lesbian and gay film festivals and contributes to "lesbian" representations of Sor Juana. Questions (typically homophobic ones) about Sor Juana's sexuality have been evident in biographies of her. An early example is the work of Ludwig Pfandl (1946), whose vulgar psychoanalytic reading of Sor Juana's work produced the diagnosis of a masculinity complex.[15] Today, Octavio Paz (1988) is the definitive biographer of Sor Juana. Although *Yo, la peór de todas* is based on Paz's biography, Bemberg foregrounds Sor Juana's relationship with the Vicereina María Luisa Manrique de Lara—a relationship that Paz goes to great trouble to convince us is not "lesbian" in the contemporary sense.[16]

In *Yo, la peór de todas*, "Slave Juana" has been replaced with "Josefa," an indigenous servant who tends Sor Juana at the convent. When Sor Juana and Josefa return home to attend Sor Juana's mother at her deathbed, Josefa asks to be allowed to remain behind with her children and her grandchildren, in short to resume a life of her own instead of merely serving as a prop to Sor Juana's life. Sor Juana grants her request with the observation that she had never heard Josefa speak so many words before.

The decision to replace the *mulata* slave with an Indian slave seems part of the politics of representation in the film: *Yo, la peór de todas* represents New Spain as being made up of Spaniards, *criollos*, and Indians.[17] The Indians exist only at the margins of the story, as servants: Josefa comforts Sor Juana, and an Indian maid tends to the vicereina's son.

However, at times the *criollo* and Spanish characters in the film masquerade as Indians. In one scene, the viceroy and vicereina are entertained by two wrestling dwarfs dressed as Aztec warriors. In another, Vicereina María Luisa bestows a headdress of blue quetzal feathers on Sor Juana in recognition of the many poems Sor Juana has dedicated to her (and her husband). While she is initially struck speechless with emotion at the gift, Sor Juana is aware that she and the vicereina are being observed by men, so she attempts to ease the tension of the moment. She dons the feathered headdress and curtsies deeply before the vicereina, pronouncing herself "Moctezuma, prostrate at the feet of Cortés." In this instance, Sor Juana, the *criolla*, becomes the Aztec ruler Moctezuma conquered by the Spaniard Cortés, as Sor Juana the woman is conquered by her love for María Luisa.

Finally, when the viceroy is recalled to Spain—the Spanish crown replaced viceroys on a somewhat erratic schedule, so as to undermine the possibility of building a power base in New Spain—he delivers the message in person to Sor Juana, whom he knows will be at the mercy of the archbishop of New Spain once their protection is withdrawn. Sor Juana is more concerned with her personal loss of María Luisa's companionship than with the political loss of the vicereina's protection. The viceroy assures her that his wife "has fallen in love with Mexico." Sor Juana's reply—"Mexico will miss her"—acknowledges her own situatedness in María Luisa's love for Mexico, as well as the ways in which she symbolically takes on the role of Mexico to María Luisa's Spain.

Three Stories and a Novel: From Novice to Icon

Gaspar de Alba published three short stories depicting Sor Juana Inés de la Cruz as a lesbian: "Juana Inés" (1992b), "Excerpts from the Sapphic Diaries of Sor Juana Inés de la Cruz" (1992a), and "Cimarrona" (1994a). Rebolledo offers a brief discussion of Gaspar de Alba's "Juana Inés" in her study of representations of Sor Juana in Chicana literature:

> Alicia Gaspar de Alba has made the figure of Sor Juana even more revisionary in . . . a short story about the life of Sor Juana. Gaspar de Alba sees Sor Juana as a lesbian, and her most terrifying and terrible secret is the one she cannot speak[,] . . . her own awareness of her love of and for women. (1995, 62)

The first two stories have been incorporated in Gaspar de Alba's 1999 novel, *Sor Juana's Second Dream*, as chapters 3 and 14, respectively. "Cimarrona" is not a part of *Sor Juana's Second Dream*, although certain events depicted in the story are mentioned in the course of the novel.

"Juana Inés" focuses on a known event, the examination of seventeen-year-old Juana by the most renowned scholars of New Spain. Although this incident figures prominently in the legend of Sor Juana, no details of the examination itself are known. The Marqués de Mancera, Sor Juana's patron at the time, described the incident many years later:

> They numbered some forty, of varied professions, such as theologians, scripturists, philosophers, mathematicians, historians, poets, humanists. . . . On the appointed day they gathered for this curious and remarkable competition, and the honorable Marquis testifies that the human mind cannot conceive what he witnessed, for he says that "in the manner that of a royal galleon"—here I transcribe His Excellency's words—"might fend off the attacks of a few canoes, so did Juana extricate herself from the questions, arguments, and objections these many men, each in his specialty, directed to her." (Calleja, quoted in Paz 1988, 98)

In Gaspar de Alba's version, young Juana is preoccupied that morning, not with the examination itself, but with her unspeakable love for her patron, Vicereina Leonor Carreto. It is her desire to atone for that love that drives her to the convent. That lesbian, rather than heterosexual, desire is the cause for Juana's monastic seclusion is in direct contradiction to Portillo's explanation, yet it is historically more viable, in that there is no historical evidence that Juana Inés had a male lover but significant evidence that she had a passionate attachment to Carreto, to whom she wrote love poems.

If Gaspar de Alba's representation of Sor Juana as a lesbian is anachronistic, it is perhaps in the way Sor Juana's desire is represented as "the love that dare not speak its name." The story opens with Juana's internal monologue, in the form of a written confession she lacks the courage to give to her confessor:

> Bless me, Padre, for I have sinned; my last confession was on All Soul's Day. Forgive me for not going to the confessional, but I couldn't speak this sin out loud, Padre, and I may not, may never be able to speak it in

writing. Punish me, Padre, as you would punish the vilest sinner, but don't make me say this to you. (70)[18]

Gaspar de Alba provides an account of the scholarly examination, in which Juana Inés is asked to describe "the five conditions of the solitary bird, according to San Juan de la Cruz" (78), to define the art of poetry (79), "to construct a syllogism" (79), to demonstrate "any scholastic, or even scientific evidence . . . for this quaint conjecture . . . that women can aspire to the same mental and spiritual dimensions as man" (79), to recite a monologue from *Don Quixote* (80), "to define mathematics . . . and explain Euclid's contribution to the field as well as the Archimedean principle" (80), to discuss Copernicus's theory, and to reflect on the influence of the zodiac (81) and the significance of the letter *O* to the Mayan people (82). Like the historical Sor Juana, Gaspar de Alba's character identifies strongly with Saint Catherine of Alexandria, an apocryphal saint who is said to have debated theology with pagan philosophers.

Gaspar de Alba's Sor Juana is well versed in sacred as well as secular literature, the orthodox, the profane, and the pagan. As Rebolledo (1995, 62) argues, "Juana demonstrates her brilliance in European knowledge as well as Nahuatl and Mayan knowledge." Sor Juana demonstrates cultural mestizaje, which Father Núñez de Miranda perceives as dangerous to her immortal soul, for women are not equipped to deal with such dangerous knowledge. Interspersed between each question and each answer, Juana Inés continues her imaginary confession, telling of the unnamable desire for the vicereina. While the topic of the examination worries Father Antonio, he does not realize that her lesbian narrative is much more "dangerous." At the end of the examination, Father Antonio not only steps in to take responsibility for Juana but also convinces her to join the harsh Carmelite order (to cleanse her of her sins), since she is so obviously unsuitable for marriage. Young Juana accepts this as the penance for the confession in her heart.

Gaspar de Alba's "Excerpts from the Sapphic Diaries of Sor Juana Inés de la Cruz" takes place seven years after the death of the marquesa, which Juana depicts in the romantic trappings of the Aztec Legend of the Volcanoes: the death of the Aztec Princess. Sor Juana imagines herself as Popocatépetl, mourning her dead love. Sor Juana's choice of symbolism demonstrates that she is one with the land, not passively but actively, embodying an active volcano linked to sexuality.

The story begins with a long entry in Sor Juana's fictional "Sapphic" diary. This first entry is written as a letter to "Laura" Leonor Carreto, Marquesa de Mancera and Vicereina of New Spain from 1664 to 1673. At the end of the viceroy's term, Carreto and her husband began the overland journey from Mexico City to the port of Vera Cruz, from which they would sail to Spain. Carreto died suddenly before reaching Vera Cruz. Sor Juana's journal entry is written long after Leonor's death.

> You know what that temptation is my lady, and you know, also, how long I have mourned you. For seven years I have stood at my window and gazed out at the volcanoes, imagining that you are still alive out there on that road to Vera Cruz. For seven years I have seen myself as Popocatépetl, smoldering, silent, capped with ice and snow, speaking to you Ixtacihuátl, my Sleeping Lady, in that language of dark smoke. (1992a, 172)

Gaspar de Alba makes use of the historic evidence that Sor Juana grew up in the valley of Anahuac, in the shadow of the volcanoes Ixtacihuátl and Popocatépetl, and that after she entered the convent of San Jerónimo, the window of her cell provided a view of these snowy mountains. I would argue that the radical revision is not Gaspar de Alba's figuration of Sor Juana as a sympathetic lesbian character but rather her use of the mid-twentieth-century Helguera image *Leyenda de los volcanes*. Sor Juana casts herself as Popo and Leonor as Ixta, drawing parallels to the legend:

> When I received your husband's letter explaining to me how you had died, so suddenly, the strange pestilence consuming your body so quickly, as if your heart had just stopped pumping out of sadness at leaving this country you had come to love so much, I felt responsible for your death, in a terrible way, a proud way, believing that you were heartbroken at leaving me. And I swore always to love you; I *married* you in my mourning, Laura. *That* has been the vow I have lived for these seven years, not obedience, not poverty, not enclosure, and certainly not chastity. (1992a, 172; original emphasis)

Like Ixtacihuátl, Laura refuses to live without her beloved. Like Popo, Sor Juana mourns the death of her lover and feels culpability for her death. But Sor Juana is unable to claim Carreto's body and to carry it to the mountains in public mourning. Although the story is set in the seventeenth century, Gaspar de Alba, a twentieth-century Chicana author, appears to draw from Helguera's representations of the Legend of the Volcanoes: just as Helguera depicts a fire smoldering next to the body of Ixta—an offering of incense perhaps to evoke the occasional smoke from the volcanoes—Sor Juana declares, "[I am] speaking to you . . . my Sleeping Lady, in that language of dark smoke." By casting Juana as Popo, she changes the terms of the painting, emphasizing Ixta's death and Popo's grief and reworking the sexualization from the representation of Ixta.

Ironically, this retelling of Ixta and Popo unwrites itself in several ways. This profession of love to the memory of Carreto is upstaged by the news that Juana has to relate: she has fallen in love once more, with the new vicereina, María Luisa Manrique de Lara y Gonzaga, Condesa de Paredes.[19] Thus, Juana explains, she is now setting aside the marriage vow she made at Laura's death. After a page of declaring her love for Carreto, Juana spends three pages singing the praise of the Condesa. This diary entry, then, is hardly a testament to a love as enduring as the volcanoes.

Gaspar de Alba carries the metaphor of the "language of dark smoke" further at the end of this entry:

> I have asked Concepción[20] to bring me the brazier from the bath. She is stoking it now, glancing this way, wondering why I want to burn what I have written. She frowns when I tell her that I am writing to *you*, that I am speaking to you the way Popocatépetl speaks to Ixtaci-huátl, in the language of smoke. . . . Receive the dark smoke of my love, Laura, and remember: Your spirit sleeps at my side.
>
> Your devoted Juana Inés (179)

Thus the reader—who has accepted that she is reading "excerpts from the Sapphic diary of Sor Juana Inés de la Cruz," however unlikely it is that such a document exists—now encounters a paradox: the text itself denies the existence of such a diary. This is no journal entry but a letter that was burned on its completion. Like lesbian desire, it leaves no trace in history.

Sor Juana's servants feature prominently in "Excerpts from the Sapphic Diaries." The slave Juana is called by the English name "Jane."

While in her play *Sor Juana,* Portillo Trambley emphasized both the similarities and differences between Sor Juana and Slave Juana, Gaspar de Alba chooses the English "Jane" over the Spanish "Juana" precisely to distinguish between the two women and to avoid such comparisons. Whereas in *Yo, la peór de todas,* Bemberg removed all reference to the slave woman's African heritage, Gaspar de Alba here depicts Jane as a *mulata,* with a complex *casta* background. Jane marks the hidden "fourth term" in the Mexican national construction of identity as "Spaniard + Aztec = Mexican." Jane is an African, enslaved to build European culture in the Americas.

One of the obstacles to twenty-first-century Chicana and Latina readers' identification with Sor Juana — on a basis other than language or generic "Hispanic" identity — is Sor Juana's position in the racial hierarchy of New Spain. While critical of the structure for her placement in a position inferior to men, *peninsulares,* and highborn *criollos,* Sor Juana seems quite complacent with the system that places her in a superior position to the Indians, Africans, and other *castas.* In "Excerpts from the Sapphic Diaries" in particular, we see examples of women from the different strata of New Spain: the peninsular vicereina; the *criolla* Sor Juana; the *mestiza* Concepción; and the *mulata* Jane. All four of these women experience different social and material realities: the vicereina, though formally excluded by the patriarchal government, is nevertheless a very powerful patron; Sor Juana, though living under a vow of poverty, not only has all of her material needs met but also has the luxury of a spacious cell, fine books, and scientific instruments as gifts of her friends and admirers as well as both a servant and a slave. Concepción, the *mestiza,* has worked as a servant and a skilled seamstress; although illiterate, she is regarded as "teachable" by Sor Juana and is thus being trained as a secretary. Jane, the *mulata,* is "unteachable," that is, illiterate, and perceived as having neither the potential nor the need for literacy.[21] As a slave and the personal property of Sor Juana, she lacks even Concepción's limited social mobility. Her area of expertise is in cooking and housekeeping.

Beyond the Shadow of History

In "Cimarrona" (1994a) the focus shifts from Sor Juana, who views the world through the dichotomy male/female, to Concepción, Sor Juana's *mestiza* servant. For the first time, the reader hears the voices of women who are not of the *criolla* class. In fact, "Cimarrona" is the story of Concepción, the *mestiza* novice who served as Sor Juana's secretary in "Excerpts from the Sapphic Diaries of Sor Juana Inés de la Cruz." To a lesser extent, it is also the story of Aléndula, a woman of African descent who is wrongfully imprisoned after the uprising of 1680. "Cimarrona" brings to the surface tensions about the intersections of gender, race, and class position that are masked by Sor Juana's narrative of all women as subaltern.

I argue that in "Cimarrona," Sor Juana's articulation of gender as the primary factor that affects all women (equally) is undermined by the very different experiences of women in distinct racial/class positions: the *criolla* Sor Juana, protégée of the royals; Aléndula, a *mulata* born of a free mother, who is nevertheless imprisoned as an escaped slave by virtue of her race; Jane, an Indian slave inherited by Sor Juana; and Concepción, the mestiza granddaughter of the abbess of the convent, who engineers Aléndula's escape and flees with her to find a new place in the world. Through the 1683 sacking of Veracruz by pirates, Gaspar de Alba demonstrates just how materially different such women's lives can be.[22]

In the reprint of "Cimarrona," in the anthology *In Other Words: Literature by Latinas of the United States*, Roberta Fernández explains that the term "cimarrona" refers to "a runaway slave." In fact, this feminine form of the noun *cimarrón* is rare. *Cimarrón*, or "maroon," refers to members of autonomous societies of escaped slaves. The *cimarrona* of the title is Aléndula, whose father was a *cimarrón* of the San Lorenzo colony of escaped slaves. Aléndula wants to live up to her *cimarrona* heritage, and to do so she must escape. Concepción and Aléndula become friends, perhaps because they are both outsiders in the convent. "You're the only friend I've ever had," Concepción confesses. "My mistress says I shouldn't associate with the [*India*] maids, but the [*criolla*] boarders won't talk to me either" (410). Aléndula explains that Concepción, too, can become a *cimarrona* by helping her to escape. Thus, like "third world woman" or "woman of color," the title "cimarrona" becomes not an essential identity, determined by birth or race, but a chosen identity acquired through action or affinity. In one sense, Gaspar de Alba considers this identity in relation to the characters Sor Juana, Jane, Concepción, and Aléndula. They are all runaway slaves: Sor Juana escapes through her writing, Jane escapes through drinking pulque, Concepción and Aléndula escape first on foot and later through the water. Yet they all escape to very different futures, as if to emphasize again how gender is only one of the factors shaping the lives of these subjects of colonial New Spain.

"Cimarrona" illustrates how Aléndula's presence (and the contradiction of her imprisonment) motivates Concepción to rethink her own location:

> It had never occurred to Concepción to leave the convent forever or to run away from the place of her birth. But Aléndula had told her stories of the village of San Lorenzo where free Negroes ruled like kings. She spoke of ceremonies that startled Concepción. Of moon mothers and river goddesses and altars piled with coconuts, oranges, and bones. Of old women who smoked cinnamon bark to see the future and sacrificed rooster to talk to the dead. (409–410)

After talking with Madre, the unnamed nun whom we recognize as Sor Juana, Concepción decides not merely to help Aléndula escape, but to leave with her. The two women disguise themselves as flower vendors and quickly disappear into Mexico City. San Lorenzo remains their goal, but as they near Vera Cruz, they see ships entering the port. Believing that these are Spanish galleons, the two women enter the port city to see for themselves the spectacle of Spanish *peninsulares* seasick and helpless as they arrive at New Spain.

What the young women discover instead is a pirate attack, complete with the murder of men and the rape of women.[23] Slaves and freed men and women of African descent are taken as booty by the pirates, who can sell them to the Puritan settlers of New England. Spaniards and *criollos* are ransomed by the viceroy, while the status of the Indians and mestizos/as is unclear, for they are neither commodified in the slave trade nor ransomable by the crown. What we learn, however, is that Concepción defines her own status when she refuses to be separated from Aléndula and makes the pirate captain an offer he cannot refuse:

> It wasn't common buccaneer practice to take Indians or halfbreeds for slaves, but the girl was attached to one of the Negro girls in his share of the plunder . . . and had pleaded with him to take her along, had actually knelt at his feet and kissed his groin, promising to do whatever he wanted in exchange for coming [onboard]. Captain de Graaf had a weakness for brave women. Besides, he had never bedded a wench

that had eyes of different colors: one dark as Jamaican rum, the other green as French chartreuse. (406)

In this, the innocent Concepción makes use of the worldly advice pressed on her by Jane, Sor Juana's slave at the convent. Coming home drunk from the *pulquería,* Jane tells Concepción bluntly what Sor Juana, who knows nothing of men, cannot tell her: "Men are everywhere out there, and they can smell you when you're green and ignorant, the way you are. Just remember this: men got one weakness, and it's always hanging in the same place" (412).

When not "warming the captain's bed," Concepción is sodomized by the cook. She sees her friend beaten violently and for the first time experiences hate, a hate so pure it is like a blessing. Aléndula, who had always sworn that a *cimarrón* "must live free or die," now chooses a different path from the life of slavery laid out before her. She sickens, and prays to Eleggua, and prays for a different kind of release. Concepción later realizes that Aléndula made herself appear sicker than she was to attain her end. One morning, Concepción awakens to find that Aléndula was thrown overboard with the sick slaves during the night. In this way, Aléndula has become free from the slavery that awaited her.

Aléndula's death leads to a mental and spiritual break for Concepción. Her frustration at her helplessness turns to rage:

Suddenly she hated Aléndula—her cowardice, her stupid beliefs. Hated her so much she would black out from hoping with all her strength that Aléndula would be torn apart by every creature in the deep. It was Aléndula's fault that she was here, alone, sodomized and violated by pirates, trapped in a floating prison heading God knows where on the rocking nightmare of the open sea. She had lost everything, and for that she cursed Aléndula to eternal bleeding at the bottom of the ocean.

May the ocean turn red with your blood. May you never stop bleeding. May your blood feed all the fishes and all the monsters and all the spirits of the sea. (415; original emphasis)

This curse seems to rebound onto Concepción: "She remembered nothing except Aléndula, her ghost twitching from the rigging of the ship" (415). Concepción loses any memory of her own identity, name, language. Instead, her head is filled with fragments of Latin songs from the convent, "Sancta Maria mater dei, salve mater misericordia, mea culpa, mea culpa, Ave Maria, Alleluia, mea culpa" (415).

At the same time, Concepción is haunted by the image of a woman in black. Earlier, she had remembered this woman only as Madre, "though her own mother had been a Zapotec [Indian] woman and had died at Concepción's birth" (409). Her paternal grandmother, the Spanish or *criolla* mother superior of the convent, took Concepción in out of a sense of duty and resented the girl's "tainted blood." But the woman in black taught Concepción: "Madre had been her mistress, her teacher. Madre had trained her to take dictation, to read Latin and play chess, to copy manuscripts in the calligraphy of Benedictine monks" (409). In her lucid days before Aléndula's death, Concepción remembers a voice in the shadows warning, "We are all slaves to our destinies, Concepción. Destiny is the cage each woman is born with" (409).

As the ship nears land, Concepción glimpses a whale in the water, leaping into the air and rubbing against the ship. This creature "showed her the dark and massive weight of her own solitude" (416), and a name comes to her, "Jerónima," a code name given to her by Sor Juana, so that she would be able to write to Juana at the convent of San Jerónimo without the abbess suspecting her true identity. Running to the captain's cabin, she looks for paper to write down this name before she forgets it again. She finds the captain's log and discards the written pages, writing "Jerónima" over and over on the blank pages. This writing brings back memories of other writing she has done, copying from "a stack of pages scribbled in an almost illegible hand" (416).

In her mind's eye, she sees those pages again and begins writing out a poem, "Hombres necios que acusáis/a la mujer sin razón, sin ver que sois la ocasión/de lo mismo que culpáis."[24] This poem functions as a motif, so that even readers unfamiliar with Gaspar de Alba's earlier short stories will recognize Sor Juana as the "Madre" of Concepción's recollection. This act of writing brings back all of Concepción's memories; significantly, however, Concepción is not the author but the copyist. Although she uses Sor Juana's words to speak, she cannot speak or write for herself.

Ironically, Jerónima/Concepción's writing separates her even more from the African and mulatto slaves. With proof of her literacy, the captain realizes that he can gain a fixed price for Concepción instead of taking his chances on the auction block, and he sells her to a widowed Puritan minister for fifty pounds. On the bill of sale, Captain de Graaf erroneously records Concepción's name as Jerónima. Her new owner promptly changes her name to "Thankful Breed," thus delineating her newly racialized position in New England.

"Cimarrona" ends with Concepción jumping off the ship into the dark waters. Like Aléndula, she begins by refusing to accept the future laid out for her. However, at the last moment her head breaks the water and she breathes in, a moment that suggests she will take her chances in this "new world."

Although Concepción continually writes out or repeats to herself Sor Juana's views that all women are enslaved, Concepción's story itself deconstructs Sor Juana's argument. Aléndula is truly enslaved, as is Concepción, ultimately. Their options are not to write or submit but to submit or die. Aléndula's actions argue that resistance is more important than life itself. For Concepción, however, the impulse to survive seems stronger than her own will.

Shakespeare's Sisters

Through "Cimarrona," Gaspar de Alba enacts a complex reading of Sor Juana and colonial New Spain, one that goes beyond the social conscience of Portillo Trambley's *Sor Juana*. Concepción and Aléndula constitute a significant intervention into Sor Juana lore: rather than serve merely as props or mirrors for Sor Juana, the two women set out on their own adventures. While Virginia Woolf (1984, 46) imagines "what would have happened had Shakespeare had a wonderfully gifted sister, called Judith, let us say," to depict the social obstacles that women confront because of their sex — obstacles that kept them from becoming world-famous writers, or even leaving traces in history — Gaspar de Alba explores the question, what would have happened had Sor Juana had a *mestiza* assistant, an African slave? Concepción and Aléndula are caught and interpellated as nonhuman subjects because of their race and sex. Commodities in the trade routes of sugar, rum, and slaves, they can be bought and sold in New England and New Spain. Both women attempt to wrest control of their futures once more, and both find their freedom in the water. For Aléndula, water provides the freedom of death, the freedom to die as a *cimarrona*. For Concepción, the future is less clear. Ultimately, the power of "Cimarrona" is its representation of myriad women's lives. Sor Juana is remembered by history because of her reputation but more because of the writings she left behind. Around her were other women who left no documents and who are generally regarded as background figures, symbols, if not subjects, of Mexican and Chicano/a history.

Conclusion

In these works by Portillo and Gaspar de Alba, the ambivalences about the reclamation and representation of Sor Juana come to light. Portillo's Sor Juana is always motivated by her desire for unattainable men, one of whom proffers a political consciousness about race and class oppression in colonial New Spain. Juana's political awakening makes her an acceptable "Chicana" character. Gaspar de Alba's Sor Juana, a lesbian character, articulates a political consciousness about the oppression of women and is likewise made a "Chicana" character through her identification with the Aztec warrior Popocatépetl, the volcano that bears his name, a knowledge of Mayan cosmology, and an appreciation for Mexican cooking.[25] In "Cimarrona," Gaspar de Alba provides a more complex representation of Sor Juana not merely in relation to the vicereinas of New Spain but in relation to the other women of Mexico whose names are not remembered by history.

Ultimately, I argue, it is the author herself and her Chicana reader, more than Sor Juana the character or Sor Juana the historical figure, who best perform the role of the New Mestiza. She demonstrates "a tolerance for contradictions, a tolerance for ambiguity," as she negotiates the complex positions and interrelationships of Jane, Aléndula, Concepción, and Sor Juana Inés de la Cruz.

CHAPTER 5

Memories of Girlhood: Chicana Lesbian Fictions

To link families with four sisters who would be friends longer than their lifetimes, through children who would bond them at baptismal rites. Comadres. We would become intimate friends, sharing coffee, gossip, and heartaches. We would endure the female life-cycle — adolescence, marriage, menopause, death, and even divorce, before or after menopause, before or after death.

I had not come for that. I had come for her kiss.

—EMMA PÉREZ, *GULF DREAMS*

In my research on Chicana literature, I found a series of stories in which girlhood provides a space, however restrictive, for lesbian desire. In the socially sanctioned system of *comadrazgo,* young Chicanas are encouraged to form lifelong female friendships, and it is the intimacy of these relationships that often provides the context for lesbian desire. Specifically, I consider the representation of girlhood friendships in four novel-length works: Sandra Cisneros's *The House on Mango Street* (1991), Denise Chávez's *The Last of the Menu Girls* (1987), Terri de la Peña's *Margins* (1992), and Emma Pérez's *Gulf Dreams* (1996). Of these, only the lesbian-authored texts — those by de la Peña and Pérez — are generally perceived as "lesbian" fiction. By including *Mango Street* and *Menu Girls,* I argue that they, too, are Chicana lesbian texts, not because the characters (or their authors) self-consciously claim a lesbian identity, but because the texts, in their literary construction of such intense girlhood friendships, inscribe a desire between girls that I name "lesbian."

In this, I participate in lesbian textual criticism, which has discussed at length the question, What is a lesbian text? Bertha Harris (1976, n.p.) has defined lesbian texts thus: "If in a woman writer's work a sentence refuses to do what it is supposed to do, if there are strong images of women and if there is a refusal to be linear, the result is innately lesbian literature." This definition seems to use "lesbian" as a metaphor for "feminist" or "woman-identified." Barbara Smith implicitly demonstrates the exceedingly broad scope of Harris's definition when she applies it to black women's writing. Indeed, Smith (1982, 164) argues that according to Harris's definition, the majority of black women's literature is lesbian, "not because the women are 'lovers,' but because they are its central figures, are positively portrayed and have pivotal relations with one another." While I concur that such a definition likewise encompasses most contemporary Chicana literature, so defining all Chicana literature as lesbian would hardly enhance an understanding of either Chicana literature in general or Chicana lesbian literature in particular.

In her well-known reading of Toni Morrison's *Sula*, Smith (1982, 165) gestures toward a more nuanced description of lesbian fiction: "[*Sula*] works as a lesbian novel not only because of the passionate friendship between Sula and Nel, but because of [its] consistently critical stance toward the heterosexual institutions of male/female relationships, marriage, and the family. Consciously or not, Morrison's work poses both lesbian and feminist questions about Black women's autonomy and their impact upon each other's lives." Seemingly, Smith's use of the term "lesbian" to describe a critique of heterosexual institutions is both metaphoric and utopic.[1] Because she seems to use "lesbian" and "lesbian feminist" interchangeably, both the passionate friendship and the critique of institutionalized heterosexuality are necessary to her definition of *lesbian*. However, if one applies Smith's description "both lesbian and feminist" *respectively* to the "passionate friendship" and the critique of heterosexual institutions, one comes closer to a usage of *lesbian* that is neither metaphoric nor interchangeable with *feminist*. Thus the critique of heterosexual institutions makes *Sula* feminist (in a non-heterocentric sense), while the "passionate friendship" invites a lesbian reading.

It is important, I think, to differentiate *lesbian* from other homosocial relations between women and from female desire in general, lest the latter two erase the former, as has been the case in many applications of Adrienne Rich's "Lesbian Continuum" (1983). In *The Practice of Love* (1994), Teresa de Lauretis unravels *lesbian* from its metaphoric and political applications to define it in quite specific terms:

> Whatever other affective or social ties may be involved in a lesbian relationship — ties that may also exist in other relations between and among women, from friendship to rivalry, political sisterhood to class or racial antagonism, ambivalence to love, and so on — the term lesbian refers to a sexual relation, for better or for worse, and however broadly one may wish to define sexual. I use this term . . . to include centrally — beyond any performed or fantasized physical sexual act, whatever it may be — the conscious presence of desire in one woman for another. (1994, 284)

De Lauretis argues that *lesbian* is not equivalent to woman-identified or feminist but derives from desire, that is not simply female desire but desire in one woman (or girl) for another. I feel that Smith was invoking just such an understanding of desire between women in her discussion of Sula and Nel's "passionate friendship," which Lorraine Bethel (1976, n.p.) has characterized as expressing "a certain sensuality in their interactions."

Yet extending de Lauretis's definition to girlhood raises other interpretive questions, for what constitutes "the conscious presence of desire" in girlhood stories? As Bonnie Zimmerman (1993a, 136) has noted, "Lesbian writers of retrospective narratives often claim to have felt themselves to *be* lesbian from birth or age two, or certainly from puberty and thus always to have had a lesbian perspective." Thus, as retrospectives, girlhood stories in particular are "products of the very perspective that they purport to explain" (136). By this logic, *lesbian* girlhood stories are those that retroactively construct adult lesbian identity,[2] but this, too, is a subjective definition; "for example, a woman might focus on the fact that she was intimate friends with Sally at age six and fail to note that so were a dozen other girls, none of whom became lesbians" (Zimmerman 1993a, 136). In the interplay between reader and text, it occurs to me that this retroactive construction might work both ways: a story of being "intimate friends with Sally" might appear to some readers to be a simple girlhood story, with no implications about sexuality outside of gender identity, whereas others might view it as a specifically lesbian girlhood story. Thus for many readers, *The*

House on Mango Street and *The Last of the Menu Girls* would constitute lesbian girlhood stories because the readers identify with the protagonist and her feelings of loss for her friend, whereas other readers, approaching these stories from a heteronormative stance, would emphatically refute such a reading for precisely the same reasons.

Zimmerman (1993b, 39) claims that "if a text lends itself to a lesbian reading, then no amount of . . . 'proof' ought to be necessary to establish it as a lesbian text." As I undertake a lesbian reading of *The House on Mango Street, The Last of the Menu Girls, Margins,* and *Gulf Dreams,* I hope that my readers, though they may remain unconvinced, will yet acknowledge that I am not "demanding a plot . . . that the writer has not chosen to create" but am "picking up on hints and possibilities that the author, consciously or not, has strewn in the text" (Zimmerman 1993a, 144). While both Cisneros and Chávez depict the cultural structures of institutionalized heterosexuality, neither fixes a heterosexual ending for her protagonist, who is alone at the end of the text, with many possibilities open to her.

In Chicana/o literature, stories of girlhood and adolescence provide a glimpse into the construction of sexual identity when "the girls come . . . face to face with . . . their prescribed roles" in Chicana/o (hetero)sexual economies (Saldívar 1990, 184). The stories show how and what the young female characters learn about sexuality and the sense they make of it. The girls are frequently perceived as asexual, since they are not sexually active, or more specifically, not (yet) heterosexually active. They are discouraged — by mothers, family, community, and religion — from recognizing or exploring their sexuality. At the same time, the cultural role of *comadres,* which raises lifelong friendships to the status of kinship, is both encouraged and recognized. Here I want to focus on the representation of desire as it develops between girlhood friends and on the ways in which that desire, and any explicitly sexual perception of it, is masked by the presumed sexlessness of adolescent girls.[3]

In all four works that I am discussing here, girlhood friendships have a very specific relationship to institutionalized heterosexuality. These works critique the limited and heterosexual roles open and indeed prescribed to young Chicanas, as well as the ways in which female friendships are less valued than heterosexual relationships. However, I have chosen these texts neither for their critique of heterosexual institutions nor for their depiction of the role of girlhood friendships within their respective Chicano/a communities but because they locate certain erotic elements in girlhood friendships.[4] Chicana/o literary criticism has not yet discussed these texts in terms of lesbian sexuality.[5] While more scholarship on Chicana lesbian literature is being produced, most of it focuses on the two best-known Chicana lesbian writers, Cherríe Moraga and Gloria Anzaldúa. As the coeditors of the 1981 anthology, *This Bridge Called My Back,* Moraga and Anzaldúa were instrumental in the circulation of writings by lesbians of color. Many of their subsequent individual works have been widely anthologized, often several times over. Both have taken pains to develop and promote the work of other writers — through editing, teaching, and workshops — but they are often taken as representative of Chicana lesbians in general and thus are published in lieu of other Chicana lesbian writers. Because of the prominence of these two authors, criticism on Chicana lesbian writers has focused mainly on the genres of drama and nonfiction prose. In looking at girlhood friendships, I hope to broaden the scope of Chicana lesbian literary criticism, both by bringing attention to less well known writings and authors and by reevaluating Cisneros's and Chávez's works in light of the explicit representation of lesbian desire in girlhood in the novels of de la Peña and Pérez, and thus to expand Chicana lesbian literature beyond the writings of lesbian-identified authors. In my readings, I dwell on the "passionate friendships" between girls that other scholars have been at pains to ignore, rationalize, or misrepresent.

The House on Mango Street

Sandra Cisneros's *The House on Mango Street* was first published in 1984 by Arte Público, a small press under the aegis of the University of Houston that features the works of Latino writers in English and Spanish. In 1991 the third edition was published by Vintage and has been an international best-seller. It is frequently referred to as a novel-in-stories; it is, in fact, a series of forty-four vignettes that feature the same narrative voice and cast of characters. Alvina Quintana takes exception to the tendency to classify *Mango Street* as a novel, which she sees as a means of incorporating Cisneros's work into traditional forms:

> Cisneros defined a distinctive Chicana literary space — oh so gently she flung down the gauntlet, challenging, at the least, accepted literary form, gender inequities, and the cultural and economic subordination

of minorities. Theoretically speaking, this little text subverts traditional form and content in a way that demonstrates how conventional applications of literary genre and the social construction of gender undermine a "feminist aesthetic." (1996, 55)

Ironically, in spite of its classification as a novel, critical discussions of *Mango Street* (Herrera-Sobek 1987; Saldívar 1990) often approach it as a collection of separate stories, with little effort to appreciate the complex relationships among the characters as they develop throughout the work. As a departure, then, I examine one relationship as it is developed in five of the vignettes, "Sally," "What Sally Said," "The Monkey Garden," "Red Clowns," and "Linoleum Roses." These stories focus on the developing relationships between Esperanza, the narrator, and Sally, with whom she shares a particular friendship.

All the stories (or vignettes) in *Mango Street* are told by the adolescent Esperanza in first person. She discusses the other inhabitants of Mango Street, sometimes giving her own views on people, sometimes repeating what she has been told. Most of the secondary characters are also girls: Nenny, her younger sister; Lucy and Rachel, her friends across the street; Marin, Alicia, and Sally, the older girls in the neighborhood. In this community, an adult woman is one who has a house, and women are classified according to whether they have husbands or whether their husbands have died or have left them. Women are viewed primarily in relation to men, in heterosexual terms. The narrator begins describing herself by explaining her name, Esperanza, which means both "hope" and "waiting." She does not want to wait for a man to change her life; she wants to write her own changes. Esperanza seeks an alternative to the options presented to her, options proscribed by sexism and institutionalized heterosexuality. One of Esperanza's dilemmas is how to reconcile her desires with her opportunities. She looks forward to having her own house, without a husband to lock her in or leave her lonely. Such a thing is unheard of on Mango Street, where women are confined to the home, where a woman is alone not by her choice but by necessity or a man's choice. Thus Esperanza, who looks for something more, must look beyond Mango Street.

Ramón Saldívar (1990) discusses *Mango Street* at length in his chapter, "Gender and Difference in Ríos, Cisneros and Moraga." Like many other critics, including Julián Olivares (1987), Alvina Quintana (1996), and Renato Rosaldo (1991), he focuses on the space of Mango Street, the houses, the gender roles, and the confinement of women. Ironically, while addressing the limited roles made available by the patriarchal structure, he is caught up in its discourse, defining women in relation to men and thus missing the significant relationships between girls that occur in the novel. Saldívar places the intense friendship Esperanza feels for her friend Sally solely in the realm of emulation or shared experience and does not differentiate it from Esperanza's other friendships, such as those with Rachel and Lucy, who are nearer her own age, or the significant but less charged older girl/younger girl friendships she enjoys with Marin and Alicia.

For Esperanza and for her world, adulthood — that is, womanhood — is defined by men. In "The Family of Little Feet," Esperanza, Lucy, and Rachel are given three pairs of fancy high-heeled shoes by a neighbor lady.[6] They practice walking and running up and down the street with them. Then:

Down to the corner where the men can't take their eyes off us . . .
Mr. Benny at the corner grocery puts down his important cigar: Your mother know you got shoes like that? Who give you those?
Nobody.
Them are dangerous, he says. You girls too young to be wearing shoes like that. Take them shoes off before I call the cops, but we just ran. (40–41)

The shoes enact one transformation on the girls and the men another. On the one hand, the shoes make the girls into desirable objects; they see their legs becoming long and shapely because of the high heels: "the truth is it is scary to look down at your foot that is no longer yours and see attached a long long leg" (40). On the other hand, the men, through their desiring gaze, make the girls into women: here, clearly, to be a woman is to be an object of desire to heterosexual men. The male attention places the girls in the adult world; they are solicited by the men and finally run away home to hide the shoes for another day because they "are tired of being beautiful." But that other day never comes, and they leave the shoes hidden, to be thrown away later by a cleaning mother.

"The Family of Little Feet" is a good example of the ways in which Esperanza keeps coming up against adulthood, womanhood, which means adult heterosexuality, and her resistance to that change. At the same time, Esperanza distinguishes herself from her younger sister, Nenny, who is firmly in the realm of childhood. In "Hips," Esperanza, Lucy, and Rachel are discussing their desire to grow hips, what hips mean, and what they are for. As they jump rope, each girl makes up a rhyme about hips. Nenny does not understand the conversation: "Everybody is getting into it now except Nenny who is still humming *not a girl, not a boy, just a little baby*. She's like that" (51).[7] Instead of making up her own song about hips, Nenny uses standard jumping rhymes, like "Engine, engine number nine" and "My mother and your mother were washing clothes," even when the other girls tell her she's not playing right. In contrast to Nenny, who is a child, and Esperanza, Lucy, and Rachel, who are adolescents, the teenage girls in the stories are constantly circulating in the male sexual realm. Whether under the control of their fathers, meeting boys at dances, fulfilling the roles of absent mothers, or marrying and being confined to the house, Marin, Sally, and Alicia are clearly situated within adult heterosexuality. While Esperanza is friends with most of these older girls, one in particular — Sally — has a transformative effect on her. Esperanza admires Sally, and desires her, although that desire is not explicitly sexual. Through Sally, Esperanza comes to understand the value system in which female friendships are relegated to childhood and adulthood is reserved for heterosexuality.

"Sally," the first of the stories to depict Sally and Esperanza's relationship, introduces "the girl with eyes like Egypt and nylons the color of smoke" (81). Esperanza describes Sally first as Sally's father perceives her — "to be this beautiful is trouble" — and then as Esperanza's mother sees her — "to wear black so young is dangerous" — both parents implying that Sally's sexual desirability will bring her grief. Indeed, this is already the case, as she has no best friend, "not since [Cheryl] called you that name" (82), that is, presumably, since Cheryl labeled her as sexually dirty. Though it attracts males, Sally's sensuality creates a barrier between herself and other girls. She is judged fast or dirty or ill-fated and is thus left alone. Furthermore, Sally seems afraid to go home and attempts to "clean herself up" before entering her house: "You pull your skirt straight, you rub the blue paint off your eyelids. You don't laugh, Sally. You look at your feet and walk fast to the house you can't come out from" (82). Both Saldívar and Quintana look at "Sally" as being primarily about the danger of sexuality. Yet they do not contextualize this story with the other Sally stories but see it as one of a series of introductions, not as part of a larger narrative about this one character. Cisneros introduces Sally between "Rafaela Who Drinks Coconut & Papaya Juice on Tuesdays," a view of a young married woman locked up in her house, and "Minerva Writes Poems," the story of a friend "only a little bit older than me but already she has two kids and a husband who left" (84). The Sally stories are unique in *Mango Street* because they are not isolated vignettes but chart the development of the character Sally and her relationship with Esperanza. The stories dealing with Lucy and Rachel, for example, could be read in any order, whereas the Sally stories chronicle the growing intimacy between Esperanza and Sally, the ending of that intimacy, and the subsequent distance from which Esperanza perceives Sally.

Saldívar (1990, 185) argues that "Esperanza wishes to be like Sally, wishes to learn to flick her hair when she laughs, to 'paint [her] eyes like Cleopatra,' and to wear black suede shoes and matching nylons as Sally does." Yet Esperanza's desire to be taught how to paint her eyes "like Egypt" is less about being *like* Sally than it is about being *with* Sally.[8] It is intertwined with the desire to lean against the fence with Sally and share her hairbrush, to hear Sally's dreams. Esperanza then goes on to articulate a world for Sally—like Esperanza's own dreams for a "real" house, far away from the barrio and the limits of Mango Street—a world where Sally keeps walking to a quiet, middle-class neighborhood, where she can dream her dreams, where her desire for desire is innocent and not damning, and where her desire for love is not "crazy" but the most normal thing in the world.

Quintana (1996, 69) is most interested in the way the depiction of Sally and her desires "illuminates the contradictions in an ideology whose primary objective is masculine gratification." The negative opinions of Sally, such as those voiced by Esperanza's mother and Sally's father, and "the stories the boys tell in the cloakroom" are clear evidence of the contradiction that women face: they must reproduce themselves for a desiring male gaze, but in doing so, they incur censure. Although she labels this ideology "heterosexist," Quintana does not herself go beyond a heterosexual framework, and in my view she fails to fully appreciate Sally the character and her significance for Esperanza. Esperanza's descriptions of Sally are poetic and appreciative, although when she describes Sally as pretty she does so in reference to male approval: "The boys at school think she's beautiful because her hair is shiny black like raven feathers and when she laughs, she flicks her hair back like a satin shawl over her shoulders and laughs" (81). In her own mind she poses questions to Sally, in a bantering, flirtatious tone quite unlike Esperanza's usual form of address: "Sally, who taught you to paint your eyes like Cleopatra? And if I roll the little brush with my tongue . . . will you teach me?" Here she goes on to articulate a desire to be like Sally, to have shoes and nylons like hers, but again her means of express- ing this point out how much it is Sally she desires. Precisely because they do read "Sally" in conjunction with the other four Sally stories, Quintana and Saldívar miss the development of Esperanza and Sally's relationship throughout the book. Perhaps they see no reason to privi- lege female friendships or to consider lesbian desire in their critique of the gender limitations in *Mango Street*. Instead, they see "Sally" as merely one of a sequence of character introductions, between Rafaela and Minerva.

Of all the characters, however, it is Sally whom Esperanza desires, and it is Sally who betrays her. In "The Monkey Garden," Esperanza is torn between running with the children and talking to the boys with Sally. "Play with the kids if you want to," Sally says, from the circle of a boy's arms, "I'm staying here" (96). In their sexual banter, the boys take Sally's keys and refuse to return them unless she gives each of them a kiss, and the group enters the garden to accomplish this:

> One of the boys invented the rules. One of Tito's friends said you can't get the keys back unless you kiss us and Sally pretended to be mad at first but she said yes . . .
> I don't know why, but something inside me wanted to throw a stick. Something wanted to say no when I watched Sally going into the gar- den with Tito's buddies all grinning. It was just a kiss, that's all. A kiss for each one. So what, she said.
> Only how come I felt angry inside. Like something wasn't right. (97)

Esperanza is incensed at this manipulation of her friend. Confused by Sally's compliance, she interprets it as passivity and attempts to inter- fere with the male coercion. She first complains to the mother of one of the boys, who tells her, in effect, that boys will be boys. Frustrated, Esperanza decides she has the responsibility to rescue Sally.

> I . . . ran back down the three flights to the garden where Sally needed to be saved. I took three big sticks and a brick and figured this was enough.
> But when I got there Sally said go home. Those boys said leave us alone. I felt stupid with my brick. They all looked at me as if I was the one that was crazy and made me feel ashamed. (97)

Esperanza is shown that her assistance is neither required nor desired. In fact, her aggression, if you will, her refusal to accept this male sexual barter as "justo y necesario,"[9] is precisely what marks Esperanza as "childish" rather than "womanly." Furthermore, Sally not only demonstrates that she thinks Esperanza is childish for resisting, but she is quite clear in expressing her preference for Tito's company over Esperanza's. Sally, articulating her adult (hetero)sexuality, mocks Esperanza and signifies her as infantile both because of her active role (attempting to rescue the seemingly passive Sally) and because of her perception of male sexuality and heterosexuality as dangerous. It is this rejection by Sally that affects Esperanza so strongly that she feels sick and angry and "wrong." She hides herself in the monkey garden, weeping and praying for death: "I wanted to will my blood to stop, my heart to quit its pumping. I wanted to be dead, to turn into the rain, my eyes to melt into the ground like two black snails. I wished and wished. I closed my eyes and willed it, but when I got up my dress was green and I had a headache" (97–98). The violence of her reaction demonstrates the depth of her feeling for Sally and the pain of betrayal. Yet her feelings, her love, are clearly of little value in comparison to male attention. Although Esperanza frequently expresses feelings of rebellion and resistance toward the limited gender roles available to girls, in this instance, she resents heteronormativity as well as sexism, because it limits not merely what she can do but also who she can love and how. Sexuality—heterosexuality—however it is naturalized, defined, and promoted, remains outside the realm of Esperanza's understanding. "They were laughing. She was too. It was a joke I didn't get" (96). For Sally and Tito and the other boys, the joke is heterosexuality: it's fun, it's funny, it's a game they all know. And yet, like Nenny singing her childish rhyme, oblivious to the advantages of hips, Esperanza lives in a world that does not accommodate such things. Heterosexuality is, throughout the novel, a brutal intrusion into the world of girls.

In Chicana contexts, girlhood is a space and time before the imposition of normative heterosexuality and, as such, provides a site for texts to stage lesbian desires, such as those of Esperanza, whose feelings for Sally go beyond simple friendship. According to the institutions of heterosexuality, Esperanza's reluctance to enter into (hetero)sexuality is both validated by and a symptom of her sexual immaturity. Because she is a child, she is repulsed by the mature reality of heterosexuality. When she is older, she will get the joke. Yet throughout *The House on Mango Street* Esperanza resists this forced heterosexualization. In "Red Clowns," she is violently initiated into heterosexuality by a boy who says, "I love you, Spanish girl" (100). She and Sally are at a carnival, and it is while she is waiting for Sally, who has gone off with another boy, that she is forced into sex. She cries out against the act, which is not like the stories of her girlfriends, or the songs, or the movies, but is painful and unpleasant and a manifestation of male desire that has little to do with her as a person. Esperanza's resistance constitutes what Smith (1982, 165) would describe as the text's "critical stance toward the heterosexual institutions of male/female relationships, marriage and the family." And yet, what moves *Mango Street* into the realm of lesbian text is Esperanza crying out to Sally: "Sally Sally a hundred times" (100). As in "The Monkey Garden," Sally chooses male company over Esperanza, leaving the latter confused and vulnerable. Esperanza very clearly voices her desire for Sally and the ways in which she perceives it to differ from male desire: "And anyway I don't like carnivals. I went to be with you because you laugh on the tilt-a-whirl, you throw your head back and laugh. I hold your change, wave, count how many times you go by. Those boys that look at you because you're pretty. I like to be with you, Sally" (99). Esperanza is attempting to articulate a desire for Sally that she differentiates from the mere physical attraction of "those boys that look at you because you're pretty." She is unable, however, to find words to express that differentiation and thus falls back on the acceptable description of female intimacy: "You're my friend." Saldívar (1990, 186) misses the nuances of this story, stating only, "Waiting to meet Sally at an amusement park, Esperanza is assaulted by three white boys."[10] Esperanza's love for Sally and Sally's preference for a boy are precisely what has placed Esperanza in this vulnerable position; Sally's action represents not merely "complicity in embroidering a fairy-tale-like mist around sex" (Herrera-Sobek 1987, 178) but the further betrayal of Esperanza's love for her.

What stands out about both "Red Clowns" and "The Monkey Garden" are the ways in which Esperanza relates to heterosexuality, not through boys, but through Sally. Sally desires male attention; Esperanza desires Sally's attention. She wants to be Sally's friend and confidante, to stand by her when others do not. Instead she is rejected and left waiting while Sally chooses to kiss the boys. It is Esperanza's desire for Sally, both in the way that it differs from her friendships with Lucy and Rachel and in the way that it pushes Esperanza into heterosexuality, that makes this a lesbian girlhood story. I do not mean that Esperanza chooses heterosexuality but merely that she is violently initiated into it because of her desire to be with Sally, who does not prefer to be with her. "Linoleum Roses," which follows "Red Clowns," effectively brings Sally's narrative, and Esperanza's involvement in her life, to a close. Sally is married and locked away in a man's house. Although he is prone to violence, Sally says her new husband is "okay. Except he won't let her talk on the telephone. And he doesn't let her look out the window. And he doesn't like her friends" (101–102). Thus Sally is lost to Esperanza, who is not allowed "to visit her unless he is working." Not even able to gaze at roses outside the window, Sally can only view those printed on her linoleum floor.

The Sally stories, "The Monkey Garden" and "Red Clowns" in particular, have a transformative effect on both the narrator and the text. They are situated near the end of the collection[11] and suggest "a change in Esperanza's attitude" (Quintana 1996, 65). In these stories Esperanza passes out of adolescence, not in the patriarchal sense of "being made a woman" through intercourse with a man, but because she is passed over in favor of a male and then subsequently used for male pleasure. These traumatic events are marked off, as is Esperanza's perception of her self: "I looked at my feet in their white socks and their ugly round shoes. They seemed far away. They didn't seem to be my feet anymore. And the garden that had been such a good place to play didn't seem mine either" (98). Esperanza's world, her self, and the way she views everything have dramatically shifted as a result of the loss of Sally's friendship. However, while the world in which Esperanza moves is exclusively heterosexual, she is not recuperated by heterosexuality at the end of the book. The ending, in fact, raises more questions about Esperanza's future than it answers:

Friends and neighbors will say, What happened to that Esperanza? Where did she go with all those books and paper? Why did she march so far away?
They will not know I have gone away to come back. For the ones I left behind. For the ones who cannot [come] out. (110)[12]

Perhaps Esperanza will come back one day for Sally, the one "who cannot come out."

The Last of the Menu Girls

Denise Chávez's 1987 work, *The Last of the Menu Girls*, has enjoyed a good deal of success, especially for a small press book. Like *The House on Mango Street*, *Menu Girls* is a series of interrelated stories about an adolescent female character negotiating her womanhood. Also like Cisneros's work, *Menu Girls* resists easy classification. Though the seven stories are distinct, their depiction of Rocío Esquibel, the primary narrator, demonstrates the depth and movement of her character. Several of the stories were originally published individually, yet as a collection the stories achieve a certain unity that informs the minor aspects of the individual stories.[13] However, Rocío's world is very different from Esperanza's: women are not defined by men or dependent on them for identity or support. Rocío herself comes from a household of women, although traces of her mother's two husbands can be found in dusty corners.

The stories are set in the area of Las Cruces, New Mexico, just north of El Paso, Texas, which in turn borders Ciudad Juárez, Mexico. They are generally told from the perspective of Rocío, who lives with her younger sister, Mercy, and their mother, Nieves, a schoolteacher. Her father, Salvador, has deserted the family and is working up north, and Ronelia, her elder sister, has left home to marry. Although she is looking back on her adolescence and captures the bluntness of that period, Rocío clearly speaks as an adult through most of the stories. In *Menu Girls*, I am primarily interested in Chávez's portrayals of the relationships among girls and between girls and women and in the way that Rocío's eroticism and desire focus on women. Chávez is quite frank in depicting the sensual dynamics of these relationships, and in fact it is the sensual dimension that causes Rocío to question herself continually. Rocío is a challenging narrator, for unlike Esperanza of *Mango Street*, who holds little back, Rocío is often coy and evasive, providing only hints of her true feelings.

The book begins with the title story, which describes Rocío's first job, delivering menus to patients at the local hospital. Being in the presence of the "sick and dying" reminds her of caring for her dying great-aunt Eutilia four years earlier. Following a multitude of visceral images of Eutilia's illness, Rocío recalls dancing "around her bed in my dreams, naked, smiling, jubilant. It was an exultant adolescent dance for my dying aunt. It was necessary, compulsive. It was a primitive dance, a full moon offering that led me slithering into her room with breasts naked and oily at thirteen" (14). This "full moon offering," charged with imagery of female sexuality, is not solely self-expression. In her mind, Rocío performs not merely in the presence of Eutilia but for Eutilia:

> Down the steps I leaped into Eutilia's faded and foggy consciousness where I whirled and danced and sang. . . . Eutilia stared at me.
> I turned away.
>   I danced around Eutilia's bed. I hugged the screen door, my breasts indented in the meshed wire. In the darkness Eutilia moaned, my body wet, her body dry. Steamy we were, and full of prayers. (15)

While one could perhaps read this scene as solely a fantastic healing ritual, it seems clear that Rocío sees it as distinctly sexual. Renato Rosaldo (1991) describes this dance in terms of "sexuality and danger" and acknowledges a "bodily sexual connection" between Rocío and Eutilia, but he does so, perversely, without considering the implications of that "sexual" connection being between women. Instead he reads it exclusively as an aspect of her familial ties to generations of women (1991, 89–90).[14] However, Rocío's fantasy of offering her own oiled breasts, pressing them against the screen door that separates her from Eutilia, the contrast of "my body wet, her body dry," Eutilia's stare — which simultaneously draws Rocío and drives her away — and Eutilia's moans mark this not merely as female sexuality but as sexuality between women.

Throughout the stories Rocío's sexuality is expressed most profoundly in relation to other women. Although Rocío does not identify as a lesbian — and she does know lesbians — she repeatedly expresses complex desires for other female characters. For example, Rocío describes a significant week:

> When Arlene took a short vacation to the Luray Caverns, I became the official menu girl. That week was the happiest of my entire summer.
>   That week I fell in love.

ELIZABETH RAINEY (26)

The name Elizabeth Rainey marks a section break in the story. The previous sentence, "That week I fell in love," sets up an expectation that Rocío will tell of her first boyfriend, perhaps of an awkward court-ship or a romantic one. Instead she describes Elizabeth Rainey, an ele-gant young Anglo patient at the hospital, who impresses Rocío with her beauty and sorrow.

> I ran out, frightened by her pain, yet excited somehow. She was so beautiful and so alone. I wanted in my little girl's way to hold her, hold her tight and in my woman's way never to feel her pain, ever, whatever it was. . . .
>
> It was this woman in her solitary anguish who touched me the most deeply. How could I, at age seventeen, not knowing love, how could I presume to reach out to this young woman in her sorrow, touch her and say, "I know, I understand." (27)

Elizabeth Rainey has an aura of sexuality, for she "was in for a D and C." "I didn't know what [that] was," Rocío says, "but I knew it was mysterious, and to me, of course, this meant it had to do with sex" (26). This is another example of the difference from *Mango Street*, where, although girls may marry before high school or leave home be-cause of pregnancy, they do not get abortions.[15]

Elizabeth Rainey is indeed marked by sexuality but not treated kindly by it: "She looked fragile, and yet her face betrayed a harsh indelicate bitterness" (26). Although her hospital room is full of flow-ers, there is no tender lover to greet her, to inquire anxiously about how she is feeling. Instead there is only a seventeen-year-old menu girl fascinated and yearning but unable to act: "As long as I live I will carry Elizabeth Rainey's image with me: in a creme-colored gown she is propped up, her hair fanning pillows in a room full of deep sweet acrid and overspent flowers. Oh, I may have been that summer girl, but yes, I knew. I understood. I would have danced for her . . . had I but dared" (28). Yet in spite of foreshadowing the week of Elizabeth Rainey as "the week I fell in love," Rocío avoids actually saying that she has fallen in love with Elizabeth. Rather, she articulates those qualities that attract her to Elizabeth—her beauty, her pain—and then her own inability to reach out, to give the comfort or understanding expected of the Florence Nightingales of the hospital. Although she expresses her desire in terms of nurturing, she also dwells on her desire to dance na-ked for Elizabeth as she dreamed of doing for Eutilia. Yet, whereas she was able to fantasize quite explicitly about that dance for Eutilia, something—perhaps the fact that Elizabeth is marked by sexuality—keeps her from actively fantasizing that dance for her. Instead she regrets her lack of daring.

Here and elsewhere in *Menu Girls,* Rocío attempts to explain away her desire in terms of identification. "I shrank back into myself and trembled behind the door. I never went back in her room. How could I? It was too terrible a vision, *for in her I saw myself,* all life, all suffering. What I saw both chilled and burned me. I stood long in that darkened doorway, confused in the presence of human pain. I wanted to reach out . . . I wanted to . . . But *how?*" (27; ellipses in original, first italics mine). However, "it is important to consider that identification and desire can coexist, and that their formulation in terms of mutually exclusive oppositions serves a heterosexual matrix" (Butler 1991, 26). One need not choose either to identify with a person or to desire that person (see Butler 1993, 99). Such an argument seems to refute the distinction de Lauretis (1996, 120) makes between (lesbian) desire for a woman and "'intrafeminine' self-directed, narcissistic 'fascinations,'" which she sees as "quintessentially heterosexual." However, in the cultural contexts of both *Mango Street* and *Menu Girls,* the narrators are unable to articulate desire for females except through socially acceptable identification.

Unlike *Mango Street,* which does not include the possibility for women loving women, Rocío's world is inhabited by lesbians. Quite a few lesbians, in fact, such as "the Nurses González and González—Esperanza, male, and Bertha, female" (28).[16] "Esperanza the dyke" is the head nurse of the surgical floor (32). She is bossy, prejudiced against immigrant Mexicans, and wholly unsympathetic, in stark contrast to the feminine women to whom Rocío is attracted. Far from identifying with this lesbian character, Rocío seems quite repulsed by this "Esperanza of no esperanzas" (32), who is "without hope" both because of her own aggressive belligerence and because, looking back from the future, Rocío knows of her early death in a car accident: "Later when Esperanza was killed my aunt said, 'How nice. In the paper they call her lover her sister. How nice!'" (32). This incident marks both the visibility and the invisibility of lesbian relationships. Everyone knows that Esperanza and Bertha are lovers. The author of the newspaper obituary recognizes the significance of that relationship by claiming Bertha as "sister," that is, as the closest legitimate female kin. Yet that same claim simultaneously erases their lesbianism by conflating it with nonsexual blood ties. Anyone not personally acquainted with González and González will merely see that a woman has died in a car accident and was survived by her sister. Meanwhile, the ending of the story links Rocío back to Esperanza the dyke because her summer also ends with a car accident, although not a fatal one. Like Elizabeth Rainey, she is installed in a hospital room full of flowers, and she curses her own stupidity, which has brought her to such a pass.

While Chávez thus creates a chain of signification from Esperanza to Rocío and back to Elizabeth Rainey, Rocío is at pains to distance herself from Esperanza and thus from lesbianism. The sections of the story are named for the characters who are most prominent in them (Mr. Smith, Arlene Rutshman, Elizabeth Rainey, and Dolores Casaus): this section should logically be named "Esperanza González." Instead it is named for a rather minor character, Juan María—an undocumented Mexican worker disfigured in a barroom brawl—as if Rocío is afraid to put too much emphasis on "Esperanza the dyke." In the stories dealing with Rocío's desires for women, Chávez repeatedly invokes lesbian figures, who stand simultaneously for lesbian potential and the denial of that potential. The lesbian serves as a marker, as if to say, "Something queer is going on here," and yet, because of her unsympathetic portrayal, that queerness is never claimed for Rocío. Instead the narrator chooses to rearticulate that desire for women as an identification.

"Shooting Stars," the third story of the collection, deals at length with Rocío's relationship to other girls, specifically her friend Eloisa, who is sixteen and "already a woman" in comparison to the still-girlish Rocío. During her annual summer visit with relatives in Texas, Rocío discovers that Eloisa is a cousin of sorts: "Her aunt wore men's shirts and pants and bound her breasts with rags. One day I found that Eloisa's mother and aunt (half men to me) were relatives! This made Eloisa, too, part of my mother's family. Most of them were a queer, unbalanced lot" (55). Eloisa's nameless "aunt" is clearly a butch lesbian. The earlier euphemistic representation of González and González as sisters provides a certain ambiguity as to whether Eloisa's mother is the "aunt's" lover rather than her sister. That Eloisa's mother is included in the designation "half men to me" seems to support the possibility that the two women are lovers. These queer women serve to introduce Rocío's relationship with Eloisa, whose "womanliness" or maturity makes her desirable to Rocío and at the same time contains the rejection of that desire. "How I admired Eloisa! How grateful I was for allowing me into her magical woman's world. Eloisa and I were bright girls, mature girls. . . . Later, after the nightly watermelon, I would fall asleep under the stars thinking about Eloisa. She was Venus, I myself was a shooting star. The two of us were really one. We were beautiful girls, bright beautiful girls spitting out watermelon seeds. We were coyotes calling out to the moon" (56). Representing Eloisa as Venus, the bright planet and also the goddess of love, Rocío again emphasizes identification with her: "The two of us were really one." Yet the title, "Shooting Stars," emphasizes the ephemeral quality of their relationship.

Rocío's love for Eloisa, like Esperanza's for Sally in *Mango Street*, eventually comes up against socially sanctioned heterosexual relationships. Rocío's reverential love is destroyed when she sees Eloisa at a movie theater, smoking lasciviously and allowing some faceless man to paw her. Eloisa, then, implicitly rejects Rocío's love through her desire for a man, and Rocío retaliates by withdrawing entirely and curtailing their rambling walks together. This new image of Eloisa as fast, as wanton and decidedly heterosexual, produces a physical revulsion in Rocío: "[I felt] sick with nicotine, faint with its smell . . . sick to my heart . . . faint with disappointment" (56), just as Esperanza was sick in the Monkey Garden. Even after her return to New Mexico, Texas and Eloisa continue to haunt Rocío, taunting her to make sense of her feelings and her memories:

> To me, Texas signified queer days, querulous wanderings, bloody fairy tales, hot moon-filled nights . . . Texas was women to me: my fading grandmother, my aunt dying of cancer, my mother's hunchbacked aunt and Eloisa. All laughing, laughing. . . . When I lay in the solemn shade of my father's study, I thought of myself, of Eloisa, of all women. The thoughts swirled around like the rusty blades of our swamp cooler. . . . Perhaps someday when I grow older, I thought, maybe then I can recollect and recount the real significance of things in a past as elusive as clouds passing. (57)

Rocío specifically expresses her desire for women, always placing it in the context of exploring womanliness. Thus as she conjures up images of women she has loved from the patterns in the stucco walls, she wonders, "What did it mean to be a woman? To be beautiful, complete? Was beauty a physical or a spiritual thing, was it strength of emotion, resolve, a willingness to love? What was it then that made women lovely?" (53).

Rocío's next "crush" is on Diana, an occasional domestic worker in the Esquibel household. She cleans and acts as older sister to Rocío, whose sister Ronelia left home to marry. Diana is a beautiful innocent, "unlike her Texas counterpart." And for Rocío she was "first and foremost: a friend who could never betray, no never. Nor could she see the possibility of betrayal. In this assumption of hers and mine lies all the tragedy of young womankind" (58). Diana's loyalty clearly constitutes one part of Rocío's attraction: she is still smarting from Eloisa's betrayal. She attempts to articulate what it was about Diana that attracted her, whether it was her beauty, her body, her laughter, which "crossed the fields and fogged all consciousness" (58). She then swiftly side steps any suggestion of lesbianism by asserting, "[I]n observing Diana, I observed myself" (58). This is in spite of the fact that Diana and Rocío are not otherwise represented as similar. Diana is not a fully formed character, nor yet a fully formed person. Her speech, always formal and polite, always yielding gracefully, nevertheless takes the form of "monosyllabic utterings of someone dependent upon the repetitious motions of work, the body and its order." When she speaks she is "naive, a little girl" (58). Her "weakness of spirit" separates her from Rocío, as she marries, has children, and is neglected by her straying husband. She thus ultimately accomplishes another kind of betrayal—a betrayal of Rocío's image of her, Rocío's hopes for her. When she becomes a good wife to a bad husband, Diana's youth, beauty, and laughter fade to a yellowed shell. Rocío cannot even recognize "Diana the huntress" in the wrinkled, whiskered woman with sad eyes whom her mother points out at church. She feels a deep sense of loss for the beautiful Diana.

The perceived betrayals by Eloisa and Diana and Rocío's subsequent rejection of them are ultimately refigured as their unsuitability as "role models." In actuality, of course, within the cultural constraints of institutionalized heterosexuality, they are unsuitable objects of desire. Thus Rocío tells herself to "let them go." She thinks about "*loving* women. Their beauty and their doubts, their sure sweet clarity. Their unfathomable depths, their flesh and souls aligned in mystery" (63). However, given the apparent fact that women are destined for heterosexual relations, Rocío sternly puts this thought from her mind, supplanting it with the image of her sister Ronelia, a more suitable (heterosexual) role model. Yet, inevitably, the thought of them comes back to her: "Women. Women with firm, sure flesh of that age in time. In dreams. Let them go . . . They were clouds, soft bright hopes. Just as quickly as they were formed, they dissolved into vast pillows. Their vague outlines touched the earth and then moved on" (65). This passage from the end of "Shooting Stars" articulates very carefully that one should not love women precisely because of an inherent flaw, their propensity for betrayal. This awareness is charged with regret and nostalgia for Rocío, as if to say: Who can help loving women, even if there is no future to it?

The final story, "Compadre," demonstrates the different ways in which Rocío expresses desire toward women and toward men. Her repulsion for the large daughters of Regino Suárez (her mother's *compadre*) clearly does not extend to all members of the family: "The car was being driven by Eleiterio, Regino's only son. Handsome, handsome young man, with Regino's dark skin and bright eyes, he was the embodiment of whatever passion there was in the union between Braulia and Regino" (150). Later, Rocío thinks she has seen Eleiterio cruising Main Street, pachuco-like, but convinces herself that she has not: "I imagined things. Almost always imagined things, and only once or twice with Eleiterio. *Su apá era adventista*"[17] (159). Rocío is conscious of a desire for Eleiterio but speaks of him very briefly. His younger sister, Zianna, however, draws Rocío's sustained attention during an unplanned visit to the Suárez family. Unlike her sisters, Zianna is slender and attractive.

> Zianna, the darkest, loveliest flower in the Suárez garden. A hose in hand, fingers laced over the hose head, Zianna watered the roses that grew near the street side of the house. She stood between the tame and the untamed worlds, that of her father's constant laborings and that of her mother's rampant, uncontrollable life.
>
> Zianna's face, lovely as a dark brown, dusky rose, was lit with natural highlights. Her neck was long, her small proud head balanced by a full, fleshed mouth. Her luminescent eyes shielded themselves against the elements and luxuriated in the absence of explanations.
>
> Full, lush and firm, her breasts were carefully rounded swells of female flesh, flowerets full of awakening fragrance. Zianna stood straight, her face in the direction of her thirsty charges. Her feet were planted firmly on the grateful grass. (154)

Rocío dwells on the "lush" curves of Zianna's body as the girl stands in the garden watering flowers. After the scene in which Rocío thought she had seen Eleiterio cruising, she fantasizes about Zianna:

> Ssssmmosh. MMMMmmmmm. Patter, patter, patter, patter. Black bird, blackbird, *what are you thinking*? Zianna stood nearby, a part of the landscape. She was too wild for the garden's cultivation, yet too re-

fined for the wildness of the Suárez home. She was a small, silent black bird on the nearest branch.

Ssssmooosh. Mmmmmmm. Patter, patter, patter . . .

I imagined Zianna standing in the grass, watering wearing [my] squash dress. That dress will be hers. Dark girl in the sunshine, seeking shade. (159; emphasis and ellipses in original)

The language used to describe Zianna, in direct contrast to that used for Eleiterio, is wholly unrestrained and exults in Zianna's physical beauty, her flesh, and the eroticism she inspires in Rocío. Rocío imagines Zianna in her own dress (the Esquibels generally give their old clothes to Zianna's family) and dwells on how well it will suit her and on the visual pleasure of Zianna: "Zianna would get her dress wet; she never wore pants like the other girls. She stood on the grass barefooted, with no shoes on and in a wet dress and never caught cold" (158).

While critics such as Rosaldo are quite vocal about the sexual energy of *Menu Girls*, and even direct attention to many of the same examples I draw from the text, they completely avoid the possibility that Rocío actually desires these women. Rosaldo (1991) recognizes the "bodily, sexual connection" with other women but considers only the context of female desire without respect to its object. Quintana (1996) does not examine the intimate relationships between Rocío and the different women: she sees them (as she did in *Mango Street*) as merely "a catalogue of female characters[,] . . . a variety of female options for solving the riddle of female self-fashioning" (104). Such themes are certainly present, and even Rocío herself offers them as explanations for her interest in women, but they are not the whole story. Although Rocío is attracted occasionally to men, her most passionate, sexual desire is directed toward a series of feminine women. It is that desire I name "lesbian."

Margins

Terri de la Peña's 1992 novel, *Margins*, is sometimes incorrectly identified as "the first Chicana lesbian novel." If this means a Chicana lesbian–authored text with Chicana lesbian characters, then that honor more properly belongs to Sheila Ortiz Taylor's *Faultline* (1982). Nonetheless, Ortiz Taylor, de la Peña, and Pérez all prepared their manuscripts for publication conscious of the scarcity of fiction focusing on Chicana lesbians. De la Peña initially published a series of short stories imagining a community of Chicana lesbians from the West Los Angeles area while at the same time creating an audience for the novel to come.[18] Like *Margins* itself, the majority of these stories were published in mainstream lesbian anthologies and journals and are concerned with the positive representation of Chicana lesbians in relationships with one another.[19] *Margins* is primarily a coming-out novel, emphasizing lesbian identity, coming out to family, and adult relationships with lesbian-identified women.[20] I want to concentrate on how this novel deals with the subject of lesbian girlhood, as it recalls the first lesbian love relationship of the main character, Veronica Melendez.

The novel opens as Veronica is recovering from an automobile accident that killed her "best friend," Joanna Nuñez. Veronica and Joanna had been best friends since girlhood, and their relationship had become sexual during adolescence. They lived together as "roommates" throughout their college years and lived a closeted life, without participating in a lesbian community or referring to themselves as lesbians outside of their relationship. And yet throughout their girlhood, adolescence, high school, and college years, both their families accepted their "particular friendship" without perceiving the possibility of sexuality or homosexuality. That Veronica and Joanna could carry on a sexual relationship for over ten years without anyone else noticing demonstrates both the cultural validation of same-sex friendships for girls and the heterosexual structure within which those relationships are presumed to exist. When Isabel, Joanna's mother, explains her obliviousness to the sexual aspect of the relationship, she dwells on the perceived sexlessness of girlhood friendship:

"Roni, I'm not sure I understand. I had favorite girlfriends too. We just never—"

"Joanna and I were so close that loving each other came easily, too."

"I remember how you girls could practically read each other's minds . . . I thought that was friendship, nothing else . . . I never thought of you two—that way. I knew Joanna and you were always together, and had been for years, but I thought she was close to you because she didn't have a sister . . . All the time you girls were growing up, I was always glad Joanna had you for a friend. You're such a good student, a nice quiet girl—never in trouble."

> "You have to watch those quiet ones," Veronica quipped.
>
> Isabel ignored that modest attempt at levity. "I thought you were a good influence on her." (111–113)

Although she comes to accept the truth, Isabel initially insists on the "innocence" of the girls' friendship, echoing the literary criticism of *Mango Street* and *Menu Girls*. She later tries to reestablish this narrative of innocence when Steve, a teenage boy, begins showing pornographic pictures of lesbian sex and telling both Isabel's younger sons and Veronica's nephew, Phil, that Veronica and Joanna used to "do that." Isabel exclaims, "Oh, Roni. It isn't your fault. You and Joanna loved each other in an innocent way. It wasn't like — in that magazine" (180). This narrative is further developed by other family members, including Veronica's older sister, Lucy, a Carmelite nun: "You're the baby of the family. I think Mama wanted to keep you inocente as long as she could. . . . You loved Joanna from the day you met her in kindergarten. Everyone knew that. We just never looked beyond the friendship" (248). Veronica's relatives rely on the idea that there is an innocence, a sexlessness, to young Chicanas that by definition precludes the possibility of homosexuality. This is clearly marked in the novel when rumors of the sexual aspect of Veronica and Joanna's relationship begin to spread. When Phil is asked to explain to his grandparents his argument with the boy who showed him the magazine, he does not reveal the discussion of lesbianism. Instead the topic of conversation becomes his own (hetero)sexuality:

> "And what were you y Steve arguing about?"
>
> "Some girl," Phil murmured.
>
> "Ay, que muchachos! You're too young for that, Philly."
>
> "Sara, he's old enough to shave." Joe offered his grandson a conspiratorial smile. "Just be careful next time, Phil." (146)

This "boys will be boys" discussion makes it clear that while the fourteen-year-old boy is perceived as a sexual being, his twenty-four-year-old aunt is not. The issue of female sexuality is further complicated because there are no women in the family, other than Veronica, who claim an active sexuality. Her mother, Sara, clearly thinks of sex as dirty, and her sister Lucy has taken a vow of celibacy.[21]

Whereas Veronica blames her parents for the family's silence about sexuality, Lucy argues, "Es la cultura" (248). This is a very different world from Cisneros's *Mango Street* and Chávez's *Menu Girls*, in which female heterosexuality is an explicit force to be reckoned with. It is precisely because of this erasure of all female sexuality that Joanna's family attempts to produce Veronica as the "living lesbian" who seduced their innocent Joanna. Threatened by the attack on Joanna's "honor," they react first by denying that the two women had a lesbian relationship; then, when Veronica begins living openly as a lesbian, they refigure her as their daughter's seducer.

Veronica attempts to displace this narrative of "innocent girlhood," arguing for an active *lesbian* girlhood. For Veronica, same-sex play is a natural (physical) extension of the emotional intimacy of girlhood bonds, one that does not change the nature of that relationship but extends it.

"Joanna and I were so close that loving each other came easily, too."

". . . Joanna wasn't interested in a men in a sexual way. How could anything compete with what we had?"

". . . At first, we thought we were going through a phase, experimenting with each other before getting involved with men. We both tried dating, but we realized right away we were much more comfortable with each other." (111)

She argues against being cast as the "lesbian seducer" by stressing the mutuality of their relationship and again by attempting to show that for both of them there was a natural progression from friendship to sexual intimacy:

"Well, no one stays innocent for long. Joanna and I started playing around when we were in grammar school. I still can't believe no one caught on." (248)

"Joanna and I used to spy on you [and your boyfriend]. Afterwards we'd go to her house and practice kissing." (264)

Both of these examples are from a conversation Veronica has with Lucy. She emphasizes the sexual precocity of her relationship with Joanna — how early they started "playing around." When she reveals that she and Joanna used to spy on Lucy, she is talking about a time before Lucy entered the convent, which took place when Veronica was thirteen. Veronica is articulating a specific model of lesbian identity, the "born lesbian" who never has voluntary sex with men. Although Lucy does not respond directly, she accepts Veronica's explanation, perhaps because she believes that homosexuality is innate and therefore not a "choice."[22] While she can accept Veronica's homosexual feelings, she cautions Veronica against claiming a lesbian identity without Joanna. To some extent, then, the ground conceded in the natural extension of particular friendship is taken back by arguing that with the end of that girlhood friendship, lesbianism need not be embraced.[23] Implied is the idea that this lesbian adolescence must come to an end, must be replaced by adult heterosexuality.

Because of Joanna's early death, de la Peña avoids the question of betrayal of a "passionate friendship" in the sense that we have seen, albeit in less explicit form, between Esperanza and Sally and between Rocío and Eloisa in the two earlier books. Veronica is, to some extent, betrayed in adulthood when her affair with her initially heterosexual neighbor Siena ends abruptly and Siena begins sleeping with a man. The characterization of Siena is caught up in the question of coming out. Siena is explicitly criticized by the other lesbian characters in the novel for not being "out" as a lesbian, a bisexual, or a woman-loving woman. This is in marked contrast to their acceptance of Veronica, who is not criticized for being closeted in her ten-year relationship with Joanna, although Siena has had a sexual relationship with a woman for less than a week. This double standard is tied to the representation of the Chicano/a community: to be close to their families, to be within the culture, Veronica and Joanna needed to be closeted. However, the same argument is not held valid for Siena, an Italian American from a Catholic background no less conservative than Veronica's. Like Elizabeth Rainey in *Menu Girls*, Siena is recovering from the after-effects of an abortion. Thus she, too, is "marked" by sexuality, but, in the new context of lesbian identity, she is also marked as untrustworthy. Her sexual desire for Veronica is invalidated by her inability to claim a lesbian identity and trivialized by the other lesbian characters. The novel privileges the "born lesbian" and views women who have been heterosexually active with suspicion.

Ironically, Veronica herself sets aside her relationships with Joanna, just as Esperanza's and Rocío's "passionate friendships" are expected to be set aside. In this case, however, the relationship is not superseded by institutions of heterosexuality but is replaced by Veronica's new lesbian identity and lesbian relation. Joanna is relegated to the past and to the "innocence" of girlhood as the novel turns toward Veronica's mature, adult relationship with a Chicana lesbian, René Talamantes. The novel ends with Veronica giving a public reading from her short story collection, a "fictional recreation of Joanna" (328). As she reads, Veronica looks to René for encouragement and to the multiethnic audience at Sisterhood bookstore for affirmation. Because of its emphasis on lesbian identity, in particular because it privileges identity over desire, *Margins* reinforces the division between (innocent) girlhood friendships and adult sexual relationships portrayed in both *The House on Mango Street* and *The Last of the Menu Girls,* with the significant difference that in this case adult relationships are not exclusively heterosexual.

Gulf Dreams

Emma Pérez's 1996 novel, *Gulf Dreams,* first appeared in short story form in the anthology *Chicana Lesbians: The Girls Our Mothers Warned Us About* (Trujillo 1991). The novel is ambitious in both range and style as it addresses socialization and sexuality in the fictional Texas Gulf town of El Pueblo. The novel has a loose chronological structure that is abruptly contested by a competing narrative of memory, which is violent, fragmented, and often cinematic in the ways in which it evokes images. The narrator meets and falls in love with a young woman, the sister of her sister's best friend. Their relationship is extremely passionate, although, at least initially, the actual sexual activity is limited to that between the young woman and her first boyfriend, which she describes to the narrator in detail. Eventually, the two women enroll in a nearby junior college, where the young woman begins dating Pelón, a male pre-law student from the university. The two women become more intimate while their relationship is entangled with that between the young woman and Pelón and with physical and emotional violence. Although we are not told the details of the young woman's childhood history, Pérez makes it clear that she has been emotionally scarred by violence from those she loves. According to the narrator, the young woman thus seeks out violence along with love, first going from Pelón, who abuses her, to the narrator, who comforts her, and later verbally abusing the narrator until she too marks the young woman with bruises.

The narrator then leaves Texas for California; the novel reveals little about her life there, except that she hides in anonymous sex and perhaps makes a living as a sex worker. After her departure, the young woman marries Pelón.

The narrator returns to El Pueblo some years later, after she reads a newspaper account of a gang rape in the town: Ermila, a young Chicana, is picked up and raped by five Chicanos. Pelón is the defense attorney for the offenders; he builds his case on the negative representation of Chicanos by the Anglo media — completely erasing Ermila as a Chicana, as well as the violence done to her — and on the premise that, as the type of woman "who says yes," Ermila did not have the option of saying no. The narrator stays for the trial and verdict, seeing the young woman again and resuming their relationship, from which she has never truly been free. Four of the five rapists are acquitted. The fifth, the ringleader, is convicted and receives a thirty-year sentence. The narrator leaves before the appeal and returns to Los Angeles.[24]

Having given a very basic sketch of the novel, I now want to focus specifically on the relationship between the narrator and the young woman. The two girls are brought together when the narrator is fifteen by their sisters who are best friends, *comadres*. In the passage that I have taken as my epigraph, Pérez introduces their relationship, contextualizing the expectations for close female friendships in this Chicano/a community:

> To link families with four sisters who would be friends longer than their lifetimes, through children who would bond them at baptismal rites. Comadres. We would become intimate friends, sharing coffee, gossip, and heartaches. We would endure the female life-cycle — adolescence, marriage, menopause, death, and even divorce, before or after menopause, before or after death.
>   I had not come for that. I had come for her kiss. (13)

Pérez is referring here to the cultural system of *comadrazgo*. The masculine term, *compadrazgo*, refers to the relationship between the father and godfather, or the parents and godparents, of a child. The baptismal ceremony unites these people, raising their friendship to the level of kinship in recognition and mutual commitment. Thus their relationship is extended beyond the present through the lives of their children. The terms *compadre* and *comadre* are also used more informally to refer to friendships that are as close as family ties and to specify the relationship between the parents of married children. *Compadrear,* the verb formed from the masculine noun *compadre,* means to be on familiar terms with another person. Pérez is talking specifically about the relationship between women, *comadrazgo.* The verb *comadrear,* however, has a slightly different meaning—"to gossip"—which she acknowledges with the phrase "sharing coffee, gossip, and heartaches" and by stressing the verbal aspect of the relationship—the telling, the sharing, the speaking. Notice that men are not essential to *comadrazgo* and that this relationship extends beyond that of the heterosexual marriage through which it is evoked. Withstanding "even divorce, before or after menopause, before or after death," *comadrazgo* emphasizes the permanence of women's relationships, over the temporality of men. *Comadrazgo* itself, then, is constructed paradoxically: women are simultaneously central and marginal in each other's lives. They are central because their friendship, their intimacy, will outlast the passion, the trauma, the infidelity, or the demise of heterosexual relationships. And yet they are marginal because these friendships function as a constant prop to the heterosexual structure—maintaining and always yielding precedence to heterosexuality or, in effect, to the male.

Pérez ruptures these narratives—both of the "female life cycle," which is, by definition, heterosexually proscribed, and that of the "platonic intimacy" achieved by *comadrazgo*—by foregrounding the sexual desire of the narrator for the young woman: "I had not come for that. I had come for her kiss." She does not want a platonic intimacy with other heterosexual women but rather a sexual union of the flesh. Precisely because of its built-in deference to the male and to heterosexuality, the narrator attempts to avoid the pattern of *comadrazgo*: "The promise of female rituals enraged me" (15). Here it may be enlightening to think back on Esperanza's relationship to Sally, particularly in "Red Clowns," where Sally, who is forbidden to associate with boys, is allowed to go to the carnival with Esperanza. Their friendship provides the opportunity for her heterosexual rendezvous, ultimately at Esperanza's expense.

The narrator's desire is created and inspired by the young woman. Although she says "I met her in the summer of restless dreams" (11), it becomes clear that the restless dreams are brought on by their first meeting, when, with a glance, the young woman "caressed a part of me I never knew existed." For weeks after their brief meeting, the narrator is haunted by dreams of the young woman's erotic touch: "I dreamt of her fingers brushing my skin, lightly smoothing over breasts, neck, back, all that ached for her. A fifteen-year-old body ached from loneliness and desire, so unsure of the certainties her body felt" (12). The early part of the novel focuses on this lesbian desire, awakened by the young woman, and on the frustration of that desire both by the heterosexual limits of female friendship within the community and by the young woman's flirtatious rejection of the narrator. The desire between the two girls is tangible and even articulated but only as mediated by the young woman's relationships with men: "That day under the shaded tree, she had spoken about a young boy. She craved his delicious, expert mouth, she said. She told me he had sucked her nipples. He was careful not to hurt her or impregnate her. Instead he licked her moistness. . . . I revered the lips that relived desire for him" (14). The young woman seduces the narrator emotionally, by verbalizing her sexual experiences. By describing her erotic activities, she gives form to what the narrator, with her more limited sexual experience, has not yet imagined that she would like to do with the young woman. Because the young woman's desire is described through her sexual behavior with the boy, the narrator's fantasies in relation to the young woman become heterosexually marked. No longer visited in her dreams by the young woman alone, instead she sees at night the scenes described under the shaded tree, sees him pleasuring the young woman in the ways she has described.

The young woman is clearly aware of the narrator's susceptibility: "She longed for someone to arouse her. Each time she dared to look directly into my eyes, she quickly averted hers. She alerted the passion, repressed it immediately" (14–15). The very structure of girlhood friendship allows the young woman to solicit the narrator's desire. Because the two girls do become "intimate friends, sharing coffee, gossip, and heartaches," the young woman can tell the narrator of her sexual activities, continuously drawing her in closer, so that she becomes both voyeur and participant in the young woman's sexual relationships: "She confessed details, delightfully. She told me how she shook with pleasure from the strokes of a ravenous tongue. I listened, opening to her seductive words, wanting more particulars to bond us intimately" (52). The narrator attempts to resist the "promise of female rituals," albeit unsuccessfully. The *comadrazgo* she sought to escape is precisely what creates and aggravates lesbian desire in this situation. Desire exists — is created — in the telling. Although she resents its inevitable frustration, the narrator cannot resist the telling: "Intimacies of the flesh achieved through words. That was our affair. Years later, I rediscovered my compulsion to consummate intimacy through dialogue — to make love with a tongue that spewed desire, that pleaded for more words, acid droplets on my skin. With her, I learned to make love to women without a touch. I craved intimate, erotic dialogue. I was addicted to words and she had spawned the addiction" (52). Ironically, then, the young woman, who is not identified as lesbian, instructs the lesbian narrator, teaching her how to make love to a woman with her tongue, literally and figuratively, by narrating eroticism. She speaks of the pleasure she receives and in doing so gains pleasure and inspires it in the narrator.

The narrator attempts to resist this sexually heightened *comadrazgo* but is unable to do so precisely because of the level of eroticism it contains: "She half-expected me. Took my hand, led me to her bedroom, shoved me playfully on her twin bed next to her. She spoke reasonably. She had missed me. Why had I stopped coming? Why had I stayed away? She relied on my friendship, a passionate friendship, she called it. Mute, I looked away, paralyzed, embarrassed, hurt. She played at my emotions under the guise of friendship" (17). The narrator's words bring to mind both Smith's (1982, 165) discussion of *Sula* —which works as a lesbian novel in part "because of the passionate friendship between Sula and Nel" — and Esperanza's inability to fully articulate her desire for Sally — "those boys that look at you because you're pretty. I like to be with you, Sally. You're my friend" (99). Yet for the narrator, the young woman's words are harsh, an insult, a blatant denial of her own active participation in this sexual game. However, the young woman uses the "guise of friendship" not only to incite the narrator's desire but also to supplement her own heterosexual relations: "We became enraptured, entrapped, addicted to each other's eroticism. A kiss on the cheek inflamed me for hours. I witnessed her greed. Teasing reached new heights. . . . The desire to desire her — my weakness. . . . Her boyfriend grew more threatened each time I appeared. . . . She and I, trapped in social circumstances. Propriety kept us apart" (28). The boyfriend's antagonism is one of the early signs that the narrator's participation in the young woman's relationships with men is not limited to voyeurism: "After rushing to him, he would oblige her by hurting her, then she would come to me. I rescued her, then resented my duty to her. And so we played this deceitful game, angry because we didn't know how to quit" (29). In a sense, then, the narrator is the conventional *comadre*, in that she provides support for the young woman in the latter's heterosexual relationship; in addition, she acts as a sort of lesbian supplement to heterosexuality, providing a love and a level of eroticism that balances the inadequacies (for the young woman) of the heterosexual relationship and helps to maintain it.

Gulf Dreams contrasts with de la Peña's *Margins* in the way it represents female friendships within the community. Because neither Joanna nor Veronica dates or is sexual with men, both are, in the eyes of the community, sexually infantilized, which provides a screen behind which they explore their sexuality together. They are, in effect, good girls, and as Veronica wryly explains to Joanna's mother, "You have to watch those quiet ones." Ironically, their hidden lesbianism is what earns them the classification "good girls." In the world of *Gulf Dreams*, the luxury of being a "good girl" is rather limited. Both the narrator and the young woman are introduced to sex before they are old enough to make such choices for themselves. The young woman seeks out strong men to protect her from the caresses of her stepfather, and the narrator chooses a quiet boy from Alabama whose demands are easy to fend off. But because the young woman is actively and visibly sexual, her relationship with the narrator is also more visibly marked as "queer": her first boyfriend, who has evidence enough of her heterosexuality, complains of her relationship with the narrator and finally uses it as an excuse to break up with her, saying he wants only her and "not some lezzy and a pet dog" (53). Like so many other aspects of sexuality in the novel, the young woman's heterosexual activity simultaneously masks and promotes her own "lesbianism."

Sexism and heterosexism are pernicious in the Pérez novel to a degree unseen even in *Mango Street*. In El Pueblo, the potential for male sexual violence is omnipresent. As a two- or three-year-old child, the narrator is molested by a group of adolescent and preadolescent boys. As a nine-year-old, she is sexually harassed publicly by a thirteen-year-old, to the extent that she no longer feels safe, and yet she is told to accept it, while the boy is never disciplined or even discouraged. Packs of boys roam the railroad tracks and, catching up with the narrator and her younger brother, force kisses on her, leaving her smeared with saliva. In the schoolyard, a group of boys will chase a younger girl and pull down her underwear. All of these images build up to the gang rape in El Pueblo, which becomes notable because the woman in question,

Ermila, refuses to accept predatory male sexual violence and refuses to see herself as merely a tool for male sexual use. This is an atmosphere in which male sexual violence is normalized and female sexual assertion is punished with more sexual violence. Lesbian desire, while clearly present, is not only circumscribed but often violently policed. In fact, at one point, the young woman claims that her husband's domestic abuse was not a result of his personality or behavior but of her relationship with the narrator. The narrator is justifiably suspicious of such an argument, which displaces the responsibility for the husband's violent behavior onto her, but the possibility that lesbian relationships would be policed in an even more violent fashion is real enough. The possibilities for a public lesbian identity under such circumstances are severely limited. *Gulf Dreams* foregrounds the restrictions imposed by normative heterosexuality, as the young woman is confined to her house after her marriage, staring at the linoleum, just as Sally does after her marriage in *Mango Street*: "She stood in the middle of her kitchen, gaping at her floor, absorbed in the linoleum's stain, a muddy brown stain in the same corner of the kitchen. For years she had tried chemicals of every brand. . . . But the floor covering only looked thinner and paler and the dirty film reminded her that her world was imperfect" (47).

Unlike Veronica in *Margins*, the narrator of *Gulf Dreams* does not write herself a happy ending. Instead she writes herself out, writes the young woman out, writes everything out of her narrative. She writes the young woman out of the story by obfuscating how much she exists independently and how much she is merely the narrator's creation:

> With phrases I create you. I create you here in text. You don't exist.
> I never wanted you to exist. I only wanted to invent you like this, in
> fragments through text where the memory of you inhabits those who
> read this. You have no name. To name you would limit you, fetter you
> from all you embody. I give you your identities. I switch them when it's
> convenient. I make you who I want you to be. And in all my invention,
> no matter how much I try, you don't have the skill to love, to love me
> as I am. (138–139)

For the narrator, there is no ultimate resolution, no utopia to be gained in lesbian identity. The girlhood friendship, so casually glossed over in the criticism on *Mango Street* and *Menu Girls*, so easily recuperated in the narrative of an adult lesbian relationship in *Margins*, is here revealed as the most important relationship of the narrator's life, the one for which all others are pale substitutes.

Conclusion

The House on Mango Street, The Last of the Menu Girls, Margins, and *Gulf Dreams* construct images of intense emotional attachment and erotic attractions between girls and women. They contribute to the representation of Chicana lesbianism by providing images of intimacy and intensity beyond that considered appropriate for proper heterosexual girls. While such friendships are initially encouraged, especially over heterosexual relations that might result in premature sexual activity and pregnancy, the girls are expected to relinquish the primacy of these friendships as they become part of the grown-up heterosexual world. Within these fictional Chicano/a communities in Chicago, New Mexico, southern California, and Texas, the female protagonists are confronted by limited options for women. Both Esperanza and Rocío leave or will leave their communities of origin so that they can make different lives for themselves. The narrator of *Gulf Dreams* also leaves her community but finds no solace in the outside world. Certainly within the Chicano/a communities depicted in these four works, there are no women actively claiming a Chicana lesbian identity, in spite of forming love relationships with other women. The exception here is René Talamantes of *Margins*, who lives as a lesbian with her mother in the barrio and whose relationship with Veronica Melendez gives the latter a sense of deep connection to her cultural heritage. Veronica makes this move to cultural identification, although it is fraught with tension with regard to her family, but prefers not to live in Chicano/a neighborhoods. In addition, the Los Angeles of *Margins* is both more "multicultural" than the rural or barrio worlds in which the characters of the other three books live — thus escaping a rigid Anglo/Chicano or Anglo/Latino dichotomy — and more permeable, so that Veronica can move to a different part of the city. She clearly has more options than the other women.

The representation of Chicano/a families is significant in all four of these works but especially in *Mango Street* and *Gulf Dreams*, which deal with domestic violence and sexual abuse. While all of the protagonists come from families free of abuse, they are constantly confronted by the reality that the same does not hold true for many of their friends; Esperanza and the narrator of *Gulf Dreams* are also aware that even their families cannot protect them from harm. These families, too, provide mixed messages about sexuality: daughters are protected but restricted; daughters are kept ignorant of sex to preserve their innocence; daughters are expected to fulfill the roles of mother and wife.

Throughout these stories, intimate girlhood friendships are predetermined to end in loss. Esperanza loses Sally, who prefers male sexual play to Esperanza's childishness. Rocío, while not rejected by Eloisa, is nevertheless disillusioned when she sees her friend enjoying lascivious male attention. Veronica loses Joanna to an automobile accident, but Joanna's death begins to take on the aspect of a natural progression, necessary in order for Veronica to live openly as a lesbian and to enjoy an "adult" relationship with René. Pérez's narrator alone does not "lose" her young woman, but she does not "keep" her either, nor can she successfully negotiate adult relationships because of the scars she carries both from childhood sexual abuse and from the emotional dynamics of her obsessive relationship with the young woman.

Mango Street, Menu Girls, and *Gulf Dreams* all show that these girls' behaviors, identities, and desires are mediated by the heteronormativity of the worlds in which they live. Love and desire are constituted in relation to heterosexuality: Esperanza knows that the way she likes Sally is different from the way boys look at Sally, even as it is different from her platonic girlhood friendships. Although Eloisa does not explicitly choose a boy over Rocío, Rocío sees Eloisa's heterosexual behavior as contaminating the "brightness" of their relationship. Her perception of the inevitability of heterosexuality leads her to perceive of the "brightness" of the desire between girls as that of a shooting star, intense and fleeting.

The ways in which female friendships are socially perceived and encouraged provide a space, however restrictive, for lesbian desire in these texts. The intimacy itself provides the context for lesbian desire. Because they are intimate friends, the young woman in *Gulf Dreams* will tell the narrator of her sexual pleasures, knowingly exciting the narrator and deriving pleasure from that knowledge. On a less overtly sexual level, Esperanza can be close to Sally, hold her hairbrush, and wave to her on the tilt-a-whirl, because they are close friends. That intimacy provides a space for Esperanza's feelings of love to grow, feelings that are distinct from the male desire based on Sally's appearance.

Esperanza's desire is based on Sally's self, the way she laughs, her pleasure in a carnival ride, her own desire to be loved. In *Margins* this space
for lesbian desire is much more literal: their very intimacy provides Joanna and Veronica with a "good girl" image, which in turn gives them
the freedom to develop a lesbian relationship. This freedom is quite
material: both Veronica's and Joanna's parents are paying the rent on
an apartment for their two "good girls" while they are in college.

In *Gulf Dreams* female friendship is articulated in terms of *comadrazgo*,
a friendship and commitment that is perceived as being stronger than
the heterosexual marriage around which it is constituted. At the same
time, the women's relationship is a supplemental component of the heterosexual marriage, providing constancy and support alongside the
fluctuations of heterosexuality. Because they require deference to heterosexuality, such female friendships are undesirable to the narrator;
because they provide intimacy, they are also irresistible. While Rocío
consciously makes a decision to "let them go," Pérez's narrator cannot
do so and instead strikes back at one of the forces that has imposed heterosexuality on her world, with a violence that equals the violence done
to her.

All of these fictions represent same-sex love and desire at approx-
imately that moment at which girls are expected to set aside female
friendships in favor of heterosexual relations. Within these texts is a
recognition that however privileged heterosexual desire may be, it is in
no way more natural or innate than homosexual desire. Indeed, I would
argue that, with one exception, these works depict a fluid and dynamic
notion of female sexuality. Only in *Margins* is sexuality explicitly tied
to claiming a lesbian identity. Pérez, while perhaps privileging her lesbian narrator (who has had both positive and negative relationships
with men), complicates binary heterosexual/homosexual models of female sexuality through her portrayal of the young woman. Ostensibly
a "heterosexual" teenager, she teaches her "lesbian" best friend about
teasing, eroticism, and making love through words alone, as well as the
mechanics and pleasures of oral sex. The stories that *Gulf Dream*'s narrator weaves for the young woman, of an idyllic future where she has
a good husband, children, and secret male and female lovers, combine
what the young woman needs socially (a good husband as equivalent to
a stable family) with what she desires (children, passion, variety, and
secrets).

Finally, although the lesbian content of *Mango Street* and *Menu Girls* has been ignored by literary critics, I have tried to show how that very erasure constitutes part of the representation of lesbianism. That is to say, like the social perceptions of female friendships in the four books, this very silence about the possibility of lesbianism has nevertheless provided a space for a lesbian reading.

CHAPTER 6

Shameless Histories:
Talking Race/Talking Sex

How will we choose to describe our past, now, at this moment, as an enunciation in the present?
—EMMA PÉREZ, *THE DECOLONIAL IMAGINARY*

Chicana lesbian fictions demonstrate a pressing concern with history.[1] Many of the stories I am discussing in this work create historical narratives that situate characters within a long line of women who were proud of their sexuality and their Mexican heritage.[2]

To understand this literary engagement with queer Chicana history, I have found it extremely valuable to examine the research of Chicana feminist historians. For example, Deena González, in her study of Spanish-Mexican women in Santa Fe, New Mexico, from 1848 to 1898, articulates how feminism informs her work:

> Widows are frequently described as wives without husbands. I instead view them as unmarried women, women unpartnered with men; and I place them in the context of generally being unmarried, which was a far more important condition in frontier New Mexico than we have been led to believe. Most adult women spent their lives in a state of unmarriedness. . . . If we focus on their relationship primarily to [men] . . . we miss some crucial elements of their existence. Women were indeed bound in marriage. . . . Women also managed to disavow marriages, to obtain annulments, and, in many cases, to outlive husbands and never remarry. (2000, 7)

González argues that the historical means of evaluating women — that is, in relation to men — obscures "crucial elements of their existence," including their work, their class status, and their relationships to other women. By showing that many women "managed to disavow marriages[,] . . . obtain annulments[, and] . . . outlive husbands," she seems to be saying that the women themselves refused to be defined solely by their marital status.

Like González, the authors of Chicana lesbian fictions create Chicanas of the past who live their lives independent of men. In so doing, they are both claiming and creating a history of Chicana lesbianism. Their work confronts the erasure of Chicanas/os from the history of the American West, of Chicanas from Chicano history, and of Chicana lesbians from gay and lesbian histories.

In this chapter I focus on three short stories published during the 1980s: Jo Carrillo's "María Littlebear" (1982), Gloria Anzaldúa's "La historia de una marimacho" (1989), and Rocky Gámez's "A Baby for Adela" (1988). I do not claim that these authors are representative of Chicana lesbians writing in the 1980s — indeed, only Anzaldúa and Gámez identify as lesbians — but argue that the stories reveal a search for and creation of legitimating histories of lesbians in Chicana communities. As the other chapters in this book show, these are not the only stories in which this theme can be found, nor is history the only theme in Chicana lesbian fiction. My goal is to introduce a particular group of texts to demonstrate how they take up and remake history for Chicana lesbians. Their stories, whether passed on, reprinted, or lost in the archives, tell "histories" through short fiction.

These three stories employ three different popular forms: Carrillo's "María Littlebear" creates fiction in the form of an oral history; Anzaldúa's "La historia de una marimacho," employs the Mexican *corrido;* and Rocky Gámez's "A Baby for Adela" plays with pulp fiction. Carrillo's story tells a first-person narrative as if it were oral history, a form that has emerged as the optimal methodology for documenting the lived history of working-class people. Progressive programs such as women's studies and Chicano/a studies employ oral history in their pedagogy: undergraduate students become researchers, taking down the histories of parents and grandparents, community elders, migrants and immigrants.

In "La historia de una marimacho," Anzaldúa creates her own version of the *corrido* — the Mexican border ballad, a narrative produced

by the border cultures of South Texas. The *corrido* has been an oppositional form of history since the eighteenth century. Widely recognized
as a forerunner of Chicano/a literature and Chicano/a history, it praised
male heroes such as Gregorio Cortez, who stood up against the racial
violence of the Texas Rangers.

In contrast to these "organic" narrative forms that emerge from
the community, engaged by Carrillo and Anzaldúa, Gámez references
pulp fiction, mass-produced paperback books of the 1950s and 1960s.
Though lurid, sensationalist, and sexy, these books were available at
any corner drugstore and told stories of "wayward girls and wicked
women," shameless lesbians and their deviant lifestyle. Catering to
male readers and often written by men using feminine pseudonyms,
this genre of fiction nevertheless made public the image (or specter)
of the lesbian, in a way that affected the sexually identity of hundreds
of women. All of these popular forms represent groups often left out of
official histories. As such, they offer authors a productive ground for
producing a fictional account of queer Chicana histories — histories that
are no less "real" for being fictional.

"My History, Not Yours":
The Fictional Autobiography of María Littlebear

In 1993 the historian Genaro Padilla published his research on autobiographies of Californios, Tejanos, and *nuevomejicanos* during the period
immediately following the U.S. annexation of northern Mexico under
the title *My History, Not Yours*. Padilla argues that through their narratives, Mexican Americans "gave utterance to the threat of social erasure
[,] . . . opened a terrain of discursive necessity in which fear and resent-
ment found language[,] . . . [and] made *los americanos* the subject of
ironic humor, linguistic derogation, and social villainy" (4). Padilla is
involved in the archaeological project to "recover the nineteenth-century formations of Chicano autobiography [by] . . . digging through the
archives — layer by textual layer — gleaning those personal narratives
with which we may construct an autobiographical tradition" (5).

Padilla takes his title from a statement by Mariano Guadalupe
Vallejo, who in 1875 sold his library and allowed his own history to
be transcribed for the collection of H. H. Bancroft. Vallejo articulates

a resistance to being archived, recorded, and confined by the Anglo ethnographer:

> I am willing to relate all I can remember, but I wish it clearly under-
> stood that it must be in my own way, and at my own time. I will not be
> hurried or dictated to. It is my history and not yours I propose to tell.
> (Quoted in Padilla 1993, 3)

Vallejo clearly differentiates "my history"—a Mexican American history—from "yours"—that of Anglo-Americans.

Feminist historians and literary critics participating in the "Recovering the U.S. Hispanic Literary Heritage" project, including Rosaura
Sánchez, Tey Diana Rebolledo, Antonia Castañeda, Clara Lomas, and
Amelia Montes,[3] have focused their research on fiction, nonfiction, and
autobiographical writings by the women of northern Mexico after annexation. To date, no Chicana lesbian autobiographies have been re-
covered.[4] For representation of their lives, Chicana lesbians must look
to fiction it seems, for it is only in fictional writings by contemporary
authors that Chicana lesbians become subjects of history. At the time
of this writing, Chicana scholars have drawn on historical research to
fictionalize queer Chicana histories: Graciela Limón, Alicia Gaspar de
Alba, Amelia Montes, Yxta Maya Murray, and Emma Pérez have written or are completing historical novels about queer Chicanas.[5]

In short stories, however, Chicana lesbian history was created much
earlier. In 1981 the Chicana feminist Jo Carrillo published "María
Littlebear" in *Lesbian Fiction,* an anthology edited by Elly Bulkin. The
book was published by Persephone Press, a "white women's press of
Watertown, Massachusetts," that "ceased production in the spring
of 1983" (Moraga and Anzaldúa 1983, publishing note).[6] Carrillo's
short story thus had very limited circulation. During the early eight-
ies, Carrillo was active in women of color publishing circles and is well
known for her poem in *This Bridge Called My Back,* which issues a challenge to white women who would exoticize women of color: "And when
you leave, take your pictures with you" (Carrillo 1981b).

"Maria Littlebear" takes place in the mid-twentieth century in
rural northern New Mexico. It describes New Mexico several generations after annexation. Anglo-Americans control the state apparatus,
but Chicana and Chicano characters like María Littlebear also "give

utterance against a threat of social erasure," to resist the dominant discourse, to mark their families' long histories in the area before "the West was won," and making *los americanos* "the subject of ironic humor, linguistic derogation, and social villainy" (Padilla 1993, 4). Carrillo skillfully weaves this first-person narrative into a tale of Chicana lesbian history.

"María Littlebear" is the fictional story of love between two women. The eponymous narrator describes her relationship with her lover, Elisa Alvarado, by situating their lives in the racial context of that period. Carrillo begins her story with María describing the apparition of God on the chapel wall in Holman, New Mexico, in either 1939 or 1940. *Nuevomejicanos* came from all over the state to view this miraculous sight and to learn their fate, "to know if you were damned or saved."

> Everyone who saw God or the Virgin was safe, if you saw a saint you
> still had a chance, but if you saw the Devil you were damned. . . . The
> gringos thought we were all nuts. They wrote an article about us in the
> Journal. Something like "there were Mexicans standing around just
> looking at the Holman wall.[7] They claimed to see God but they say
> that this is only possible when the moon is full." It was in the back
> by the obituaries. Can you *believe* they put God by the dead people?
> (Carrillo 1981, 17; original emphasis)

María adds that the Anglos attempted to stop the Mexican pilgrimages by painting over the chapel wall. Thus the opening of this story sets up an oppositional relationship between *nuevomejicano* popular history — the apparition of God in Holman — and official Anglo history — the *Albuquerque Journal*'s report about superstitious Mexicans. Furthermore, that the story is hidden "back by the obituaries" and that the Anglos whitewash the chapel wall indicates an erasure of *nuevomejicano* history literalized by whitewash.

This is an example of the way Carrillo's narrator, María Littlebear, contextualizes her place, not merely as a Chicana lesbian, but also as a *nuevomejicana* living in a racialized state. María is using this instance of popular history to establish the year Elisa Alvarado was born. I like to imagine this story as an oral history, in which an interviewer asks María, "What was it like for lesbians during that time?" María responds with stories describing the racial context of New Mexico, because for her there is no way to separate being a *lesbiana* from being a *nuevomejicana*.

María admits that she fell in love with Elisa immediately. Yet she downplays the romantic aspect to illustrate that Elisa, a waitress at a truck stop and a Mexican woman, was perceived by Anglo truckers as being "for sale."

> The day I first ate there, this one guy was yelling at Elisa, calling her "senorida" and saying things like he'd give her ten big ones if she'd go with him. . . . [H]e slapped her real hard, right on the ass. . . . Elisa was just standing there, her face was all twisted and she looked like she was going to start crying any minute. (19–20)

Implicit throughout María's telling is a critique of racialized power in New Mexico, the Anglo truckers who "thought they owned the place and everything in it," including the women. Not only does this trucker attempt to buy Elisa, he hits her hard enough so that everyone in the place knows she has been hit. It's a sexual gauntlet thrown down, daring anyone to tell him he can't take her and inviting others to appreciate his mastery over her.

The response he elicits surely could not have been anticipated. María Littlebear admits, "[I] just couldn't take it . . . because I hate to see a woman treated like meat" (20). The way she tells it, María had not yet spoken a word to Elisa, yet she feels compelled to rise to her defense and to this racialized sexual challenge.

> Me being who I am, I got up, stuck my thumbs in my pockets and walked over there real cool like. I was shaking, but I would never have let him know it. And I told that guy in Spanish that he was a cabrón, who didn't even know how to shit let alone how to treat a woman. He died! Mostly because Elisa was standing behind me sort of laughing and he didn't know what I was saying. When he left, there was a fifty-cent piece — that was a big tip back then — still, he should have left the ten big ones he was bragging about. (20)

Rather than, say, punch him in the nose (something she admits she would be more inclined to do "nowadays, since I'm a lot stronger"), María changes the terms of the exchange by cursing him and criticizing him in a language he doesn't understand, a language of New Mexico. María thus destabilizes the trucker's ability to control the terms of the exchange, both verbal and sexual.

Elisa and María together mean something different from what they mean separately, in part because, at least in this instance, they are coded as femme and butch. When Elisa is alone, the truck driver reads her as heterosexually available to his desire. Situated in alliance with María and laughing at her "reading" of him, Elisa's position is quite different: she becomes a Mexican woman who is neither single (unprotected) nor necessarily heterosexual and thus doubly unavailable. While the story itself makes it clear that Elisa is "already" a lesbian, that she has loved women since she was five years old, in this scene Elisa "becomes" lesbian symbolically and physically in relation to the butch María.

María is performing both for the truck driver and for Elisa: for the former, she answers a challenge; for the latter, she issues an invitation. In a sense María's action is the beginning of the two women's lifelong relationship. In her representation of that moment, however, Carrillo shows how inextricably love between the two women was intertwined with their gender, racial, and class positions.

"María Littlebear" also depicts Chicana lesbian characters living not in isolation but as members of families and of communities.[8] María remembers:

> Her grandma could have died the day she found out about Elisa's . . . feelings, you know, about women and all? . . . The day she found out about Elisa and me, she cried and cried. . . . After at least a week of crying and a month of penance she calmed down. Like nothing ever happened. Ay! She just came into our kitchen—we were living together then—plopped down a bag of flour and started to make tortillas. All she ever said about our being together from then until the morning she died was "you think you're so great? You're not the first two people to fall in love." (19)

The grandmother's initial reaction—shame, mourning, penance—gives way to defiant acceptance, a challenge to her *two* granddaughters not to think themselves so special. That the grandmother starts making tortillas signifies her acceptance of their relationship; but it is also likely that Carrillo is punning: the grandmother is making tortillas in the house of *las tortilleras*.[9]

At the same time that Carrillo emphasizes the significance of one's family of origin, she also shows how lesbian couples, while silently acknowledged, may be erased. María tries to avoid discussing the way that she, as a lesbian and thus Elisa's illegitimate partner, was erased from the discourse of family following Elisa's death. "At her funeral, everyone was crying except me. They brought lots of food and flowers, the kind she hated, the kind she always said looked too sad — like little kids who can't even run around without getting in trouble." Almost as an afterthought, María adds, "Oh, and I didn't get to ride in the limo with the 'immediate family' either — that's what Gonzalez, the funeral man called her brothers and her papa. Didn't bother me none. I was the one who loved her and I was proud of it" (22). In a sense María is refusing to accept the official discourse: Elisa Alvarado, *soltera*, was survived by her father and brothers.[10] As María's narrative so eloquently demonstrates, the official discourse tells as much about Elisa Alvarado's life as the *Albuquerque Journal* tells of the apparition of God.

This fictional story consistently marks out Chicana lesbian history, both in relation to the erasure of Mexican history by Anglo-American political and social structures and in relation to the erasure of lesbians through the Mexican discourse of "legitimate" family. Carrillo emphasizes the raced and gendered position of her lesbian characters, thus pointing out how the two discourses that assign them subordinate positions have combined to erase Chicana lesbians from history.

La marimacho alzó su machete/ The *Marimacha* Raised Her Machete

"La historia de una marimacho,"[11] by Gloria Anzaldúa, was first published in a special issue of the journal *Third Woman*. Edited by Norma Alarcón, Ana Castillo, and Cherríe Moraga, this special issue was initially intended to focus on Chicana lesbians but was later broadened to discuss the sexualities of all Latinas. *Third Woman*, published from 1981 to 1989, promoted critical and creative writing by Chicanas, Latinas, and other women of color. In 1989 the journal announced its transition to a book series before ceasing production entirely.[12] In 1993 the special volume was reissued as an anthology titled *The Sexuality of Latinas*. Of the more than one hundred short stories, plays, and novels by or about Chicana lesbians that I have studied, "The Marimacha's Tale" is one of only two texts written entirely in Spanish — in Anzaldúa's case, the regional Spanish of South Texas.[13]

Marimacha is a slang term for "lesbian," roughly equivalent to "bulldagger." As Angela García (1994) suggests, the term unites two words that are intended to be mutually exclusive: María (woman) and macho (masculine).[14]

In spite of the use of the singular in the title, this is a story of two women, because, as Teresa de Lauretis (1994, 235n) argues, "it takes two women, not one, to make a lesbian." Neither of the two female protagonists is given a name: they are "I" and "she," the butch and the femme, *la marimacha* and *la chaparrita*, the subject and the object of desire. *La marimacha* pursues *la chaparrita* through the streets and woos her earnestly. They are subject to the gossip of the neighbors. When an old woman spies them kissing in the dark, she runs off crying, "Ave María Purísima," as if she had seen the devil himself.

In the course of the story, *la chaparrita*'s father learns that she has been seen with *la marimacha*, and he confines her to the house. The two women run off to the north, with *la marimacha* passing as a man. Although they make several stops, they are always driven farther when the townspeople begin to look at them strangely. At long last they find a place they can call their own. One day, *la marimacha* arrives at home and finds her father in the kitchen. He has struck *la chaparrita* in the face, and she is on the floor, tears and blood streaming down her cheeks. His daughter tells him he must accept their relationship. With her machete, *la marimacha* cuts off the fingers of the hand that struck *la chaparrita* and the ear that would not listen to her cries. The father repents and comes to live with the two women. The story ends with what appears to be the final verses of a *corrido*, telling of the valor of the *marimacha* and the lesson she has taught the local machos:

> La mujermacho alzó su machete
> Allá en San Juan Puñacuato.
> Los dedos de don Rafo saltaron
> Y se le escurrió su coraje.
> De la gente se oye decir
> Que ya un hombre no vale nada
> y hasta los huevos le estorban
> a los machos de San Juan Puñacuato. (68)[15]

When the father ultimately joins the two women in their life, there is no sense that he has left his country behind. *La chaparrita*, expressing her initial fears about running away with *la marimacha*, asks,

"¿Qué vamos hacer dos mujeres, sin dinero, sin amigos, sin tierra?" (65).[16] Yet Anzaldúa is not implying that lesbians are "women without a country."[17]

I read Anzaldúa as deliberately refuting the notion that lesbians share a "more profound nationality of their lesbianism" (Harris 1973). Bertha Harris, in her article on lesbian society on the Left Bank in the 1920s, develops this notion, drawing from Virginia Woolf's (1938, 197) statement, "As a woman I have no country." Harris recalls her twenty-one-year-old self following Djuna Barnes through the streets of New York, cherishing the fantasy that Barnes "would stop and take [her] hand . . . and then tell [her] how it was to be a dyke in Paris, in the Twenties," a world into which the young Harris believed she ought to have been born (Harris 1973, 77). She reads Colette and Gertrude Stein as "the books of [her] ancestors" even as she recognizes the disparities between her life and theirs:

> But I was poor and grubby; naive, emotional, sweaty with lower-class need. I was short and peasantmade — and my ancestors, I learned, as I read my censored history, were rich or nearly rich; sophisticated, cool; longlimbed; and our family bloodline, the common identity among us, would always be nothing more, nothing less, than our common need for the world of consequence: will always be my acknowledgment of these women, despite all material difference between us, as my first ancestors, the women my father stole me from. (1973, 78–79)

For Harris, the disjuncture between her self as lesbian and her self as "poor and grubby[,] . . . lower-class[,] . . . peasantmade" are competing identities between the name of the lesbian (Djuna Barnes) and the name of the father. The choice between is quite clear. "They were," writes Harris, "American and English and French but mostly American but with the father's nationality in effect wiped out by the more profound nationality of their lesbianism" (79). Their lesbianism was like their aristocracy and their expatriate circle: all three represented beauty and distance from the mundane world.

I believe that Anzaldúa is writing a very different kind of lesbian history, one that challenges the idea that "to be lesbian was at its finest to be also upperclass" (Harris 1973, 79). "La historia de una marimacho" is in fact a "peasantmade" history, with sweat and manual labor. Anzaldúa creates a tradition in which lesbianism is not separate from race, class, and location, a tradition in which the young Harris might have found both her working-class self and her lesbian self represented.

For Anzaldúa, land itself does not represent merely *la tierra patria*, the father's land and the father's name, but the actual means by which to earn a living. At the same time, the emphasis "sin tierra" resonates with Chicana/o history of not possessing the "lost land" (see Chavez 1984). To paraphrase the poet Jimmy Santiago Baca (1990), Chicanas and Chicanos are "immigrants in our own land." As Chicana/o historians (and indeed the Chicano/a movement) have consistently argued, we didn't cross the border, the border crossed us.

"La historia de una marimacho" is a border story in the sense that it is situated in "the greater border region": a geographic region both to the north and south of what is now the Mexico-U.S. border. But it might more accurately be considered a story of the Mexican frontier—alluding to a historical past, before Mexicans felt the northern encroachment of Anglo settlers. When *la chaparrita* and *la marimacha* are met with "malas caras" (dirty looks) from the people they encounter, they simply continue to head farther north—not to the United States but to an area less settled. In fact, there is the sense that the two woman can continue north through unsettled lands until they find some place they can call their own.[18]

Thus Anzaldúa establishes a popular history of queer Tejanas. It is precisely for that reason that the story ends with a *corrido*: the *corrido* is a popular form of history that contests the official Anglo account of Texas. Anzaldúa deliberately links lesbian history to a butch/femme economy of desire. In spite of the *marimacha's* assumption of masculine power in the tale, the *chaparrita* is imbued with her own subjectivity. Whereas the narrator suggests that the father repents either because of her chastisement or because he does not want to lose his daughter, I would argue that it is actually the *chaparrita* character who persuades him to accept their relationship. She declares: "No cambiaré por oro o plata ni un segundo de mi vida con ella" (67).[19] Her final argument is, "Nuestro cariño es tan fuerte, papi, como el tuyo pa' mamá. Ningún amor es corriente, ni el de una mujer pa' otra" (67).[20] This is the appeal that the father is unable to refuse.

Indeed, the text highlights the subject position of *la chaparrita*, the femme, showing her fears and her courage. Initially, she is afraid to leave home: she says to her lover, "Pa' ti la vida es tu lucha . . . Pero . . .

yo soy miedosa" (65).[21] When her partner asks if she wishes to return home, because "[n]uestra vida no va ser fácil" (66),[22] *la chaparrita* is offended and responds, "[L]a vida amenaza a todos, rico o pobre, hombre o mujer" (66).[23] When *la marimacha* persists, "[P]ero amenaza más a la mujer, y más todavía a las mujeres como nosotras,"[24] the *chaparrita* ends the conversation and continues the journey upriver.

The time period of "La historia de una marimacho," is unclear. The *corrido* was popular from roughly 1830 to 1920, especially during and after the Mexican Revolution. That the women do not cross a border indicates that the story takes place before 1920; the absence of references to Anglo settlers in the region suggest a much earlier time. The story could take place in 1820, 1720, or 1620 — in any of a variety of periods of the history of what is now northern Mexico and/or the U.S. Southwest.

Rebolledo (1995, 201) describes the story as "Anzaldúa's creation of a lesbian Chicana mythos." It seems that Rebolledo is arguing that the story has become part of the mythology of Chicana lesbians, who we are, where we come from. I would argue further that the story creates a history. Indeed, I believe that Anzaldúa writes this story in Spanish precisely so that it may serve as a "historical" text, as an artifact of Chicana lesbians who have gone before us. "The Marimacha's Tale" functions like Paredes's study to produce a history of Chicanas/os — or in this case, Chicana lesbians — in the greater border region. We can imagine that this is a long-lost document, recently discovered, precisely because Spanish was the language of the Mexican frontier. By writing in Spanish, Anzaldúa creates new "ancestors" for contemporary Chicana lesbians, a new "tradition" in this story and *corrido* that can be claimed as Chicana lesbian heritage.

Odd Girls of the Rio Grande Valley

Since 1981 Rocky Gámez has written three short stories detailing the adventures of Gloria, a working-class Tejana butch from the greater border region: "From *The Gloria Stories*" ([1981] 1983b), "A Baby for Adela" (1988), and "A Matter of Fact" (1990). The first story in the series has been reprinted no fewer than four times since its original publication in the now-defunct journal *Conditions*.[25] Its popularity and success is due to Gámez's humorous characterization of Gloria as a

Chicana butch from the lower Rio Grande Valley of Texas and of her narrator, Rocky, who represents Gloria without being seduced by her. Like "María Littlebear," the Gloria stories depict the lives of working-class Chicanas in Chicano/a communities claiming a queer Chicana heritage.

Although I want to focus on the second of the tales, "A Baby for Adela," it is helpful first to put it in context by giving a brief description of the first story, titled simply "From *The Gloria Stories*":

It is set in fall 1969, and our narrator, Rocky, has gone away to college. Through letters, she receives news from home, including the scandalous behavior of her friend Gloria, who has been going around dressed as a man and accompanied by loose women. While Rocky is recovering from an automobile accident, she receives a letter from Gloria herself, announcing that she has finally met a nice girl, Rosita, and they have shared wedding vows in a church (albeit silently, during a heterosexual wedding ceremony). When Rocky returns home to the valley, she is greeted by a strutting Gloria, who announces that she has successfully impregnated her girlfriend, because "every time I do you-know-what, I come just like a man" (Gámez 1983b, 139–140). With the aid of her college biology text, Rocky explains to Gloria that this just isn't possible, and Gloria makes the obvious connection that Rosita has been unfaithful. Gloria, who has attempted to be a good husband and father, has instead ended up the *cabrón*, the cuckold. The story ends abruptly with a devastated Gloria leaving Rocky on the curb as she drives home to settle things with Rosa.

This is the background for "A Baby for Adela," set in December 1970, which is the tale of Gloria's second attempt at marriage and fatherhood. Gloria has once again found herself a "real nice" woman, Adela, and they are making a home together. Visiting the happy couple in Gloria's little house, Rocky notes:

> There were bookshelves lining the walls, with real books on them . . . my entire collection of lesbian literature that I had not wanted my family to know I read: *Odd Girl Out*,[26] *Shadow of a Woman*,[27] *Beebo Brinker*,[28] *Journey to a Woman*,[29] *The Price of Salt*,[30] *The Well of Loneliness, Carol in a Thousand Cities*,[31] *We, Too, Must Love*,[32] all of them! (1988, 102)

This is the first time in any of the stories that Rocky is marked as queer. Her cache of books are mainly lesbian pulp fiction of the late 1950s and early 1960s.

The message of the lesbian books is somewhat deflected by the new book on the shelves, *How to Bring Up Your Baby*. Once again, it seems, Gloria is looking forward to "the pattering of tiny feet on the brand new rug" (102). "I'm going to get Adela pregnant. . . . This time, I'm really going to get her pregnant. I have the ammunition all ready to go" (102). She has contracted with a local gay Chicano to pay him for his sperm, which she plans to introduce into Adela's ready womb. Rocky constantly challenges Gloria on what she sees as Gloria's sick obsession with getting her women pregnant. Gloria replies that she is merely expressing the natural human urge to procreate. She knows it is possible because one of the lesbian novels depicts artificial insemination, and, of course, Rocky's father has artificially inseminated his cows. Rocky argues that the process is bound to be much more difficult than Gloria has assumed. And so it proves, though for reasons neither woman can foresee.

Gloria drives to a nearby town to introduce Rocky to her selected sperm donor, Moctezuma, who is a waiter at his aunt's restaurant. The aunt caters to gays and lesbians as long as they are not too overt, so Gloria dons purple lipstick before entering the establishment. Indeed, her style has changed noticeably in the past six months:

> She even looked a little more feminine than her usual butchy self. She was wearing a brown wool cardigan sweater, women's chino pants, and penny loafers. Her hair was a little longer over the ears. Did I like her new look?
>
> "Oh yes, Gloria," I replied. "But you don't look like Sal Mineo anymore. You look like Toña la Negra."
>
> "Helps me sell more brooms though," she chuckled. "At least the housewives won't bolt their doors on me when they see me stomping up their driveway with my load of brooms." (101)[33]

On the previously arranged evening — Christmas Eve — Rocky and Gloria go driving in Gloria's old truck on the bumpy back roads of South Texas. Moctezuma does not meet them at the appointed time. After a great deal of pressure, his aunt tells them how to get to his house in El Granjeno. Rocky and Gloria arrive to find a repentant Moctezuma regretting his bargain, trying to reconcile his sexuality and his religion, and tapping out a suicide note on his typewriter. Gloria has neither time nor patience for Moctezuma's crisis. While Rocky waits outside, Gloria threatens the young man with physical violence. When Gloria emerges from the house, it is with a spoon full of semen, which, she mutters to Rocky, was all she could scrape off the sheets.

Their delivery to Adela is destined never to arrive. Gloria drives too fast on the pothole-ridden roads, attempting to get Rocky home in time to take her mother to midnight mass. They're signaled by a police car to slow down, and when Gloria attempts to outrun it, she drives the truck off the road. Rocky loses her grip on the spoon, and the ammunition drips from the dash to the floorboard. A very glum Gloria drops Rocky at the church door and goes home to her Adela.

Gámez raises many issues in this story. What interests me is the relationship among history, identity, and literature. Rocky's reference to "real books on the shelves" is significant, first because it suggests that Gloria is no great reader of books: her usual reading material consists of magazines such as *True Confessions* and perhaps *fotonovelas*. All the books that Rocky is describing are lesbian pulp fiction. Radclyffe Hall's *The Well of Loneliness* and Claire Morgan's *The Price of Salt* were both published earlier as literature but were reissued in pulp editions during the heyday of pulp fiction.[34] Aldrich's books *Carol in a Thousand Cities* and *We, Too, Must Love* were sensational nonfiction, journalistic pulps,[35] an insider's look at the lurid lives of lesbians. The majority of the other titles focus on white women in New York City.

In "Pulp Passions" (1997), Yvonne Keller discusses the significance of lesbian pulps in terms of representations of lesbians for a mainstream audience, but more important, in the ways that lesbian readers were hungry for their own lives in literature.[36] She describes the books listed above as the most "lesbian-positive" of the genre, written mainly by women and lesbians, rather than — as was more often the case — written by men using feminine pseudonyms. If we examine Gámez's Gloria stories as a response to this pulp fiction, we see the disparity between Greenwich Village and the Rio Grande Valley.[37] In the former, as depicted in *Women in the Shadows*, the lesbian Laura is inseminated by her wealthy gay male friend, Jack, while in the latter, where farmers routinely inseminate cattle, Gloria's attempts to inseminate Adela are foiled by church and state.

Gámez also parodies the powerful and benevolent white gay male of Bannon's novels in the character of Moctezuma, a gay Chicano albino who performs Ravel's "Bolero" on the clarinet at his aunt's restaurant, the Magic Cocina. Moctezuma is clearly not a player in the patriarchy but a pawn. His "male privilege" is negligible. A drunk patron derides him—"¡Maricón! ¡Pinche joto!"—and his priest convinces him that suicide would be less sinful than a homosexual life.

Keller argues that pulp fiction was expected to depict a racist and homophobic viewpoint. In a variety of complicated ways, lesbians read these books against the grain to find positive representations of lesbians. Gámez is very clearly marking the racism and exclusion practiced both in the representation of the lesbian pulps and in the public spaces of queer life. Duffy's in McAllen, Texas, is "a redneck bar but catered to jotos if they weren't too overtly nelly. A few old gringa dykes that passed as rodeo cowgirls went in to play pool regularly, but they were too prejudiced to talk to Mexicans, so it was best to ignore them" (Gámez, 102).

Furthermore, Gloria, who has left her job at the slaughterhouse for a new profession selling brooms door-to-door, is herself constructing community. There are no bars or support groups specifically for Chicana/o queers, but Gloria is meeting *jotos* and *tortilleras* "from Rio Grande City to Brownsville" (101), in Falfurriás, San Juan, and El Granjeno, and is able to "represent" those people to Rocky: "There were thousands like [Moctezuma] all over the Valley, but they were all closeted because of the shitty attitude of the people of the area. Anglos and Mexicans were alike in their intolerance of gays. But she had met zillions of them on her broom-selling route" (105). This is an awakening for Rocky, because "[i]n the Valley, overt homosexuals were as rare as wings on donkeys" (105), and she had never known any other queers besides Gloria.[38]

Rocky is able to find her queerness reflected in the lesbian pulps, but they are clearly inadequate to represent the lives of queer Chicanas in the valley. The character Rocky is not able to find either herself or Gloria in these books, but the author Gámez succeeds in writing Chicana lesbian history, in true pulp fiction style.

Together the stories discussed above speak to a variety of popular traditions in creating Chicana lesbian history. Through a fictional character, Jo Carrillo contrasts Nuevomejicano memory with official history as represented by the *Albuquerque Journal* and then similarly contrasts the "official" (patriarchal) family with lesbian *familia*. Gloria Anzaldúa uses regional Spanish, high drama, humor, and the *corrido* to tell "la historia de una marimacha." Rocky Gámez, in her picaresque adventures of la Gloria, uses pulp fiction as signifier of lesbianism while critiquing the racial exclusivity of the books and of lesbian communities. At the same time, Gloria, as the traveling salesman, herself makes a community, discovering the other queers all over the southern Rio Grande Valley and representing them to Rocky while the author represents them to her readers.

Through their portrayal of Chicana lesbians, these authors provide a revisionary reading of Ramón Saldívar's argument:

> In Chicano narrative, . . . history . . . is the subtext which must be recovered from the oblivion to which American social and literary history have consigned it. Our literary texts will show how aesthetic and cultural productions often turn out to be the ideological rewriting of that banished history. (1990, 19)

The banished history that is being rewritten is not merely that of the Mexican in the American West but also that of the Chicana lesbian in Chicano/a communities.

In the 1980s Chicana feminist writers used fiction to write histories of the unnameable: lesbians in Chicano/a communities. Just as many other Chicana/o writers have used their fiction to show the ways in which the history of Mexicans in the United States has been systematically erased from the history of the American West, these Chicana writers used the *corrido*, oral history, and pulp fiction to represent Chicano/a history *as* queer and to attempt to show Chicana lesbians in their sexed/raced positions in the U.S. Southwest. These tales, which on the surface appear quite simple, are actually playing on the notion of *lo popular* to create popular histories, histories of the people, to argue that *marimachas, maricones,* and *tortilleras* are part of Chicana culture and history.

CHAPTER 7

Queer for the Revolution:
The Representation of Politics
and the Politics of Representation

*What was right about Chicano nationalism was its commitment to pre-
serving the integrity of the Chicano people. A generation ago, there were
cultural, economic, and political programs to develop Chicano consciousness, autonomy, and self-determination. What was wrong about Chicano
nationalism was its institutionalized heterosexism, its inbred machismo.*
— CHERRÍE MORAGA, *THE LAST GENERATION*

*It is not very difficult to be a "nationalist feminist." What is difficult is to
be a feminist without nationalism.*
—NORMA ALARCÓN, "RE: THE NEED FOR NEW WAYS OF THINKING"

This chapter focuses on the representation of Chicana/o politics in
queer Chicana writings, specifically in two plays by Cherríe Moraga,
Heroes and Saints (1991) and *Watsonville: Some Place Not Here* (1996). I am
interested in the different ways these plays represent Chicana/o politics
as well as their intervention in Chicana/o representation. I argue that
they tie the figure of the Chicana lesbian to an activist politics; they
draw from history, from legal cases, from oral history and ethnography;
they render the political sphere so that it does not separate sexuality
from "larger" political questions; and they draw connections between
environmental racism, dangerous working and living conditions, and
global issues such as U.S. interventionist policies in Latin America.
These works create bridges between political discourse, Chicano/a
teatro, and passion plays. They employ and emplot Chicano/a religions
onto the drama of Chicano/a lived realities. Their apocalyptic endings
can be read as cynical, as prophetic, or as hopeful.

Nationalism and Chicano/a Literature

At times Chicano/a literature has been judged against the nationalism of the Chicano/a movement, which argued for a unified, masculinized community voice in its calls for justice.[1] Chicano nationalism coalesced in the production and dissemination of two pivotal texts — *El Plan Espiritual de Aztlán* (1969), a manifesto, and *Yo soy Joaquín* (1967), an epic poem — and in the plays and performances of the theater collective El Teatro Campesino (ETC).

Rafael Pérez-Torres (1995) discusses the significance of *El Plan Espiritual de Aztlán* and *Yo soy Joaquín*. He argues that *El Plan* — a collectively authored manifesto for the Chicano/a movement produced at the Denver Youth Conference in 1969 — echoes such calls for revolution as the 1810 "Grito de Dolores"[2] in which the Mexican subjects of Spain rose up in opposition to the crown.[3] *El Plan* builds its claim to land on both the historic presence of Native Americans and mestizos in what is now the southwestern United States and the preponderance of Mexican Americans in agricultural labor in the same region. Rudolfo "Corky" González, an important member of the group that produced *El Plan* created an Everyman hero for the Chicano/a movement in his poem, *Yo soy Joaquín*. Through the character of Joaquín, the poem traces Mexican history as five hundred years of resistance and shows "the" Mexican and "the" Chicano as colonizer and colonized, tyrant and slave. Not so, however, for both men and women, for the narrative voice embraces male historical figures in the first person — "I am Cuahtémoc . . . / I was part in both blood and spirit of that courageous village priest Hidalgo . . . I fought and died for Don Benito Juárez . . . / I rode with Pancho Villa" — but shifts back and forth between the first and third persons when it attempts the feminine voice:

> I am in the eyes of woman,
> sheltered beneath
> her shawl of black,
> deep and sorrowful eyes
> that bear the pain of sons long buried or dying,
> dead on the battlefield or on the barbed wire of social strife.
> Her rosary she prays and fingers endlessly
> like the family working down a row of beets
> to turn around and work and work.

There is no end.
Her eyes a mirror of all the warmth
and all the love for me,
and I am her
and she is me. (González 1967, in Foster 1997, 219–220)

"The" Mexican woman is defined through her love for the male hero, Joaquín: her eyes mirror him and mirror her warmth and love for him. Thus she exists only through the heterosexual family romance.

El Teatro Campesino (1965–1980) was a theater troupe devoted to raising consciousness and support for the unionization of farmworkers. Yolanda Broyles-Gonzalez (1994) argues in her feminist study of the troupe that although it operated as a collective, it has been signified primarily through the person of its founder, Luis Valdez. The troupe drew from standard commedia dell'arte characters and employed them in the political themes of the farmworker movement. The troupe included both men and women, and the women played both male and female characters. In the surviving scripts of ETC, published by Valdez, the roles for female characters were—like *Joaquín*'s black-shawled women—defined through heteronormative relations to men: mother, daughter, wife, whore. Broyles-Gonzalez maintains that the women in the troupe continued to resist the stereotyping but were frustrated because it excluded mature actresses from pivotal roles:

[Actor] Socorro Valdez's appropriation of male roles provided an opportunity for her to stretch her own self-image, to grow: "[The female roles] are very limiting. There is the mother type, then there is the 'mutha': the whore type, sleazy, cheap. There is always the mother, the sister, the girlfriend, or the grandmother. That's very limiting, and that's one of the reasons I dove so deep [into playing male roles]. I needed exploration in my work." (1994, 150)

As Broyles-Gonzalez argues, drawing from the oral histories she conducted with the women of ETC, both the collective nature of the group and the subversive potential of the women's performances are erased through the exclusive focus on the plays as single-author texts. She emphasizes that the women were active participants in the theatrical process while acknowledging that a text-based theater history will by definition silence subversive voices.

Queer Women of Color beyond the Nation

Both during and since the Chicano/a movement, Chicanas have articulated feminist challenges to male-centered, homophobic nationalism. Early on, feminist, gay, and lesbian voices were often silenced through sexist and homophobic discourse. In the four decades since *el movimiento*, both straight and queer Chicanas "reinvented" nationalist mythologies to better portray the participation of women and of gays and lesbians, in spite of obstacles.[4] For example, Cherríe Moraga articulates a nostalgia for Chicano nationalism, not as it was, but as it could have been. She envisions a new, queer Chicano nationalism:

> One that decolonizes the brown and female body as it decolonizes the brown and female earth. It is new nationalism in which la Chicana Indígena stands at the center, and heterosexism and homophobia are no longer the cultural order of the day. I cling to the word "nation" because without the specific naming of the nation, the nation will be lost. (1993, 150)

While recognizing the dangers of nationalism, Moraga clings to it as hope for the future, based on the notion that a Chicana/Chicano movement can only be built on a foundation of cultural nationalism.

I have found that Chicana lesbian representation has a complex relationship to Chicano nationalism. In some instances, this representation poses a strong challenge to nationalist ideology. In other instances, it attempts to reconfigure the nation, and often it is itself created in and through nationalist desire and longing.

However, nationalism is not the only resistance strategy open to Chicana lesbians. Chicana lesbian politics has been informed by the coalitional and inorganic politics of women of color organizations of the 1980s. Chela Sandoval (1991, 1992) argues that one problematic of "third world feminists" is that this is not an organic essential identity. One is not born a third-world woman of color. There are clearly larger structures that interpellate us in a variety of ways, but we can also choose to come together to make common cause.

Lesbians of color, such as Pat Parker, Hilda Hidalgo, and Audre Lorde, moved into the construction of postnationalist images in their critique of nationalist rhetoric that continues to be used against women, against gays and lesbians, and in the service of male privilege.[5] The

Puertorriqueña Hilda Hidalgo tells a coming-out story, "El ser yo no es un lujo" (Being Myself Is Not a Luxury) (1987),[6] which rejects the unified identity usually implied in such stories and also constitutes a new type of Latina lesbian identity. I discuss Hidalgo's oral history in relation to a fictionalization of the same story that was published earlier (by Nicholasa Mohr, 1983). Although both stories describe one pivotal racial incident, Hidalgo ties the incident to sexual identity in a way that Mohr does not.

Mohr first tells Hidalgo's story in "An Awakening . . . Summer 1956," a short story published in 1983 in a special issue of *Revista Chicano-Riqueña* devoted to Latina writing. Mohr dedicates her short story to Hidalgo. Four years later, Hidalgo herself retells the story in her oral history, "El ser yo no es un lujo," in the collection *Compañeras: Latina Lesbians* (1987). Both stories illustrate a young woman's traumatic confrontation with North American racism and the way it forces her to reconceptualize her position racially. Hidalgo's oral history — one of a series of Latina lesbian coming-out stories and *testimonios* — is clearly marked as "lesbian." Mohr's story evades the topic of sexuality through its exclusive focus on racism.

In both versions, the protagonist is visiting a friend in Texas in the late 1950s. Mohr's version is figured as a short story, with the confrontation itself as the central issue:

"A Pepsi-Cola, cold if you please . . .

"Don't have no Pepsi-Colas," he responded loudly . . .

The man gestured at the wall directly behind her. "Can't you read English."

Turning, she saw the sign he had directed her to. In large black letters and posted right next to the door she read:

NO COLOREDS
NO MEXICANS
NO DOGS
WILL BE SERVED ON THESE PREMISES

All the blood in her body seemed to rush to her head. She felt her tongue thicken and her fingers turn as cold as ice cubes. Another white man's face appeared from the kitchen entrance and behind him stood a very black woman peering nervously over his shoulder.

The silence surrounding her stunned her as she realized at the moment all she was — a woman of dark olive complexion, with jet black hair; she spoke differently from these people. *Therefore,* she was all those things on that sign. She was also a woman alone before these white men. (Mohr 1983, 110; emphasis added)

Mohr distinguishes her protagonist from "these white men" and "a very black woman." She marks her visible difference from the others as "a woman of dark olive complexion, with jet black hair" and her linguistic difference from the group: "she spoke differently from these people." At the same time the text privileges the protagonist, giving her agency. Unlike the "very black woman," who can only watch nervously, the protagonist is able to act against the sign.[7] Furthermore, the black woman's gender is erased when the protagonist becomes "a woman alone before these white men."

The sign in the café functions on two levels. First, it enacts an exclusion: No Coloreds, No Mexicans, will be served. Second, it argues an equation:

Coloreds = Mexicans = Dogs

The protagonist recognizes that though she is neither African American nor Mexican American, she is nevertheless implicated in its system of categorization. Her differences from the white majority, "dark olive skin" and the fact that she "spoke differently," place her among those who are excluded. In the resolution of Mohr's short story, the protagonist spends the rest of the summer in Texas working against racism before finally taking a bus to the East Coast and reflecting back on the incident.

A Series of Political Awakenings

Hidalgo's own version of the story is presented in the first person as an oral history, one in a sequence of important events in Hidalgo's construction of who she is.

Me puse a caminar y después de un rato entré a un sitio a tomarme un refresco. Cuando pedí una Pepsi-Cola, el hombre que trabajaba allí me enseñó un letrero que tenía en la parte de atrás y decía: "No Niggers,

No Mexicans, No dogs," o sea, no se permitían negros, mejicanos, or perros. La primera impresión mía fue que yo no era ninguna de esas cosas. Pero esa impresión duró sólo una fracción de segundo y entonces me di cuenta de que sí, *yo era todas esas cosas y más*. Sentí una furia tremenda y pensé: "Ud. me va a servir." Yo creo que el señor leyó la expresión en mi cara porque me servió la Pepsi-Cola. Yo cogí el refresco, y de la furia que tenía, rompí la botella llena contra el mostrador y le dejé medio peso. (1987, 73)[8]

In reaction to the sign and its systems of exclusion and equation, "Hidalgo" catches herself trying to make meaning out of racist discourse and falling into the trap of differentiating herself from those who are named. Her reaction is not merely because the sign equates [Hilda Hidalgo], "negros" and "mejicanos" with "perros," nor is it simply the practice of discrimination. In effect, her motivation comes from her realization of the danger of constructing privilege in racist discourse. Significantly, "Hidalgo" does not claim a nationalist identity by asserting, for example, I am not black or Mexican: I am Puerto Rican. Instead, and in contrast to Mohr's protagonist who sees that to these people "she was all those things on that sign [and] also a woman alone," Hidalgo first recognizes that she fits none of those labels and then that she is all of those things and more.

In addition, Hidalgo's oral history frames sexuality as an integral aspect of this story as a political awakening. "El ser yo no es un lujo" articulates a specific Latina lesbian coming-out story: rather than focus on the "moment" at which one realizes one is, was, and always will be a lesbian, she constructs her Latina lesbian identity through a series of stories that detail her continuing political development.[9] In so situating her coming-out stories, Hidalgo makes her sexuality an integral part of herself without divorcing it from her political and educational work. By articulating the complexities and the contradictions of her multiple subjectivity — she is all that and more — Hidalgo narrates a lesbian identity that moves beyond a nationalist construct.

While Chicano/a activist literature of the 1960s and 1970s assumed a unified Chicano subject, the infusion of Latina feminism, Xicanísma, and lesbian of color representational strategies have put forth significantly different models in turn-of-the-millennium activist literature. Moraga's plays *Heroes and Saints* (1992) and *Watsonville: Some Place Not*

Here (1996) deal with social and political issues that affect Chicano/a communities and are informed by Mexican-Chicano/a theatrical traditions, including religious plays and the work of El Teatro Campesino, as well as by women of color feminisms. Although the plays have specific characters in common, they are quite distinct and have very different implications for Chicana lesbian identity, politics, and context. These dramatic fictions publicize environmental racism and challenge such universal notions as the significance of religion in Chicano/a activism and the centrality of "the" Chicano/a family. The plays employ magical realism, telenovelization, and history, all the while featuring lesbian and gay characters.

Heroes and Saints is set in McLaughlin, a central California farmworker community, a "cancer cluster" contaminated by pesticides and toxic waste. Children are born with deformities, and one of the main characters has no body: no limbs, no torso. Moraga is explicitly making connections with the works of El Teatro Campesino, specifically, *The Shrunken Head of Pancho Villa* (1967), a dystopic satire of underclass Chicanas/os and the wages of assimilation. Like *Heroes and Saints, The Shrunken Head of Pancho Villa* focuses on one Chicano/a family as emblematic for Chicanas/os in general. The family members include Pedro "the jefito, an old Villista con huevos, Cruz, the madre, long-suffering but loving, Joaquin, the young son, a vato loco and a Chicano, Lupe, the daughter, Mingo the son, a Mexican American, Belarmino, the oldest son . . ." (153). Belarmino, like Moraga's Cerezita, has no body, only a head, but rather than being the family's salvation, he is their damnation: his insatiable hunger adds to the family's poverty. (He never becomes full because he has no stomach.) Valdez also uses character names to signify religiosity (Cruz and Lupe, two generations of sorrowful mothers), Joaquín — obviously a reference to *Yo soy Joaquín* — and Mingo, who changes his name from "Domingo" to "Mr. Sunday" as he assimilates into gringo society. Mr. Sunday forgets that he is even related to the other characters, and his only interaction with them is as their welfare caseworker. Joaquín is imprisoned for playing at being a nationalist Robin Hood, and when he returns from jail he, too, is fully assimilated and returns a silent body with no head.

While Moraga focuses on the politicization of the Chicano/a community in *Heroes and Saints,* she does so in a metacritical way — visible to the characters and to the audience. Historically, the story derives from environmental racism in an actual Central Valley town in California.[10] The essential unit of the Chicano/a community is *la familia*, in this case, the Valle family, which is represented as primarily women: a mother, Dolores; her gay son, Mario; her daughters, Yolanda and Cerezita; her infant granddaughter, Evalina; her *comadre*, Amparo, a political activist; and her *compadre*, Don Gilberto. Moraga uses familiar "types" for her characters—the politically conservative, religious and sorrowful mother; the *activista;* the middle-class assimilationist—as well as new types—the butch queen Mario and the second-generation mixed-race Chicano Juan Cunningham. Moraga also uses religious iconography and *teatro* antiromance techniques that culminate in the "transcendence" of Cerezita as La Virgen de Guadalupe.

Watsonville: Some Place Not Here combines an account of the cannery women's strikes on California's Central Coast with the apparition of La Virgen de Guadalupe in the "holy tree" and anti-immigrant legislation passed in California in the 1990s. The play is a sequel to *Heroes and Saints* that depicts the lives of Dolores del Valle, Amparo, and Juan Cunningham after the events in McLaughlin. Moraga follows the same working-class family, the Valles, to emphasize that they represent all working-class Chicanas/os and that their struggles represent working-class struggles generally, much like Harold Biberman's *Salt of the Earth*. *Watsonville* moves beyond the clear "us/them," "privileged/ disenfranchised" dichotomies of *Heroes and Saints* to illustrate that there are different layers of privilege and different ways of claiming an identity. Dolores del Valle, the poor Chicana mother who represents the disenfranchised farmworker family in *Heroes in Saints,* in *Watsonville* is able to recognize how even she has a more secure position than Lucha Lerma, who, without papers, is doubly vulnerable.

Heroes and Saints and *Watsonville* engage in discussions concerning nationalism, neonationalism, and postnationalism. Whereas *Heroes and Saints* seeks to modify Chicano nationalism to make spaces for women and queers, *Watsonville* challenges such a reappropriation by demonstrating the deep sexism and homophobia ingrained in nationalist institutions and ideology and the dangers of succumbing to a logic that renders Chicano/a workers—especially undocumented workers—subhuman. *Watsonville's* critique shows how easily sexism and homophobia are employed by both politicians and unions to divide communities, to privilege "us" over "them," and to lose sight of the individual struggles in the bigger picture.

Martyrdom of the Bodiless Subject

The plot of *Heroes and Saints* begins with reports that the bodies of children are appearing on crosses. The children have died from cancer, and unknown activists have been taking them out of their coffins to draw attention to the extremely high incidence of cancer in McLaughlin. Dolores wants to keep to herself, even though her daughter, now eighteen, was one of the first to be born with birth defects, in her case, no body. Amparo, who works with Dolores in the produce packing house, begins to take an active role in protesting the pesticides and demanding that the government investigate. The growers respond with increasing violence against the protestors. The police brutally beat Amparo during a rally. Juan realizes that Cerezita and the children are responsible for the crucifixions. He pledges to help them for the next action but flees, guilt-ridden, after a sexual encounter with Cerezita. In a final act, Cerezita (with the children's help) dons the robe of rose and blue and embodies an apparition of La Virgen de Guadalupe. She goes out into the fields — joined at last by Juan — and is shot down by patrolling helicopters. In anger and dismay, the community sets fire to the fields.

The play focuses on the Valle family. Unlike the traditional representation of "the" Chicano/a family, the Valles are a female-headed household: the mother, Dolores; her children, Yolanda, Mario, and Cerezita; and her grandchild, Evalina.[11] Included in the extended family are Dolores's *compadres* — Mario's baptismal godparents, the friends who are as close as kin, Amparo and Don Gilberto. That this play has an allegorical quality is evident from the names: Valle = Valley.[12] The Valle family thus represents first- and second-generation Chicano/a families working in the fields and in the canneries, producing the food that feeds the nation. The mother, Dolores, is the Mater Dolorosa, the mournful mother of the crucified Christ.

Dolores achieves a *marianismo* ideal, in which a true mother emulates the Mater Dolorosa, by sacrificing everything for her children. In effect, suffering is her only outlet, for she cannot curse; she cannot fight; she can only weep. Dolores del Valle works to support her three adult children: her son, Mario, chooses a single, homosexual lifestyle; her daughter Yolanda struggles to care for her own infant; and her third child, Cerezita, is a perpetual child — not because she lacks an adult mind but because she lacks an adult (or any) body. Dolores is a *dejada*, an abandoned woman, left by her husband to support her children on her own. Asking charity of no one, she implores only God and does not look for comfort from fellow sufferers. She has her cross to bear; it cannot be lightened by sharing it. Dolores's long suffering masks anger and fear. She has no sorrow to spare for anyone else: she sees only what she has endured, that she has endured it, and that she must go on. Thus she sees Amparo's activism as rabble-rousing and *metiche* troublemaking.

Cherríe Moraga's heroine Cerezita (little cherry) is a sixteen-year-old head with no body. Like Sor Juana, she is fully living the life of the mind, able to read philosophy, theology, poetry, and tragedy. At the same time, she is the hybrid Chicana, combining Old World with New. Alongside the Western canon, she reads Mexicans, queers, Aztecas: Rosario Castellanos, García Lorca, the Popol Vuh. She reads in English, in Spanish, in Latin, in Nahuatl. Far from being satisfied with her mind that is free of corporeality, Cerezita rails against her situation, not by feeling sorry for herself—though she does try to get others to see the world from her position—but by fighting back against the growers, government, and agribusiness. Cerezita feels keenly the loss of her female body, and while she feels sexual desire, it is her own body she wants.[13]

Mario, the firstborn, the son, is his mother's hope. He is also his people's hope, for his goal is to go to medical school, become a doctor, and return to heal his ailing community. Ironically, the gay Chicano Mario is the *marimacha* figure in the play.[14] This Macho-María enjoys male privilege—the limited male privilege of poor Chicano men—most evidently in the freedom allotted him. And while he and Cerezita take great delight in reliving his seduction by his Mexican cousin Freddie, most of his male sexual partners are older, wealthier Anglo men.[15] At the end of the first act, Mario leaves his family and goes to San Francisco, not to medical school, but to the gay Latino community for the freedom to live openly, to live "one life, not two." Yet Mario does not escape his family's doom. Just as everyone in McLaughlin is poisoned by the "environment," the gay *raza* in San Francisco are also poisoned: HIV, homophobia, governmental disinterest, and lack of health care. With the optimism of youth, Mario first believes he can heal the pain of racism and homophobia in his Latino lovers with love. He ultimately contracts HIV. Like the rest of the people in the valley, he realizes how little his life is worth to the government, to the drug companies, and to mainstream America.

With his freedom to come and go, Mario contrasts sharply with Cerezita, who lacks the limbs for perambulation. He fashions for her an electric cart that she can operate with a chin control. Dolores places limits on Cerezita, however; she forbids her to take the cart outdoors (or even near windows where she can be seen) and eventually disengages the chin control to prevent her from moving herself at all.

Juan Cunningham is the new priest assigned to McLaughlin. A mixed-race Chicano from an agricultural background, Juan had specifically requested to be assigned to a farmworker community. Inspired by César Chávez's 1988 fast,[16] Juan returns "to the valley that gave birth to [him]." His goal is to serve the working-class, *los pobres*, and to participate in their struggle against oppression. He is active in the protests against the use of pesticides and tries to get Dolores to permit Cerezita to attend. He identifies strongly with Cerezita and enjoys discussing politics and poetry with her. He realizes that she has been the one behind the "crucifixions" of the dead children while other children of the valley have served as her arms and legs. He fears that he lacks the courage of his convictions, and indeed when he has the chance to join the children in the fields he fails to show up. In spite of his theology of liberation, Juan suppresses his own desires beneath the priests robe, "battling . . . internal doubts, Inquisition style" (115). He romanticizes martyrdom, though Cerezita wryly tries to show him that the world has enough victims already. Dolores observes that though Juan has been a priest for ten years, he "still has the eyes of a man" (100).

Yolanda, Dolores's elder daughter, is a single mother who works as a hairdresser. Throughout the first act of the play, she tends her infant daughter's ailments: a diaper rash that never heals, skin burned raw from the polluted water, red lesions. At the beginning of the second act, the baby Evalina refuses the breast and is hospitalized and diagnosed with a malignant tumor. Following Evalina's death, Yolanda wants to strike back against the faceless corporations that are responsible. Her mother's pain is embodied by her milk-swollen breasts, which ache for her child.

While Mario is the explicitly queer Chicano, in the play's reality, heteronormativity does not necessarily hold sway. For example, Juan Cunningham is clearly attracted to Mario. Cerezita shares in Mario's description of gay male eroticism, and the sexual encounter between Juan and Cere is far from normative.[17] The scene ironizes safe sex in the age of AIDS, ironizes Juan's self-absorption, which makes him forget that Cerezita is a participant, and calls into question Cerezita's own sexuality, as she confesses that it was not Juan's masculine body that she yearned for but her own lost female body.

> All I wanted was for you to make me feel like I had a body, because the fact is I don't. . . . But for a few minutes, a few minutes before you started thinking [i.e., intellectualizing, doubting], I felt myself full of fine flesh filled to the bones in my toes. . . . I miss myself. Is that so hard to understand? (144)

In addition to challenging heteronormativity, Moraga takes the Chicano/a family away from the androcentric narrative and tries to imagine a different story for the daughters, the mothers, the sisters. When Yolanda's daughter, Evalina, dies from cancer, it appears as if Yolanda will inherit Dolores's role of the sorrowful mother. However, she chooses political action over private sorrow; Yolanda does not retreat into herself and her house but directs her sorrow into community action, permitting the activists to display Evalina's corpse as a symbol of the endangerment of the community.

Doña Amparo, *la comadre*, is a prop to Dolores, but she is also in a sense another Dolores, with many of the same histories and problems but who works for her community, for change. Amparo, who is inspired by Dolores Huerta and Emma Tenayuca, is an uneducated woman whose politics are leftist. She knows a worker's struggle and refuses to accept it as an individual one (as Dolores does). For her, the personal is political, and the community must find common cause.

Moraga does not imagine Chicana and Mexican women in labor organizing simply to posit a female counterpart to male leaders such as César Chávez. Rather, she looks back into the history of Chicano/a labor struggles to reveal and acknowledge the female participants. From the Mexican American women active in United Cannery, Agricultural, Packing, and Allied Workers of America (UCAPAWA)[18] to Emma Tenayuca's leadership of the pecan shellers' strike in Texas, Chicanas have been active in the struggle for justice, not merely hand in hand alongside their men, but in the cotton fields, in the canneries, and on the picket lines. In one sense, the stakes of representation are actually working against an ideology of heroes and an inclusive model of community.

Cerezita is the hybrid character who puts all these different aspects in play. She is the mastermind behind the direct action in which the

dead children's bodies are displayed as crucifixes. She uses this religious symbolism as a way to say to American society at large, "Children
are being sacrificed, and for what?" If the sacrifice of the innocent is
emblematic of Western Christianity, then shouldn't society at least care
about these children's deaths, at least take notice of them, not as statis-
tics, but as they are memorialized in the procession, as individuals, as
little lives lost?

Heroes and Saints is a product of 1980s political movements. During
the 1980s, Chicana/o politicization in the universities was frequently
tied to support for the Sandinista revolution in Nicaragua and protest against U.S. support of El Salvador's death squads.[19] Organizations such as the Committee in Solidarity with the People of El Salvador (CISPES) educated college students about U.S. intervention in
Central America. Not all Chicano/a college students were involved in
CISPES, but the organization played a crucial role in consciousness
raising with regard to international policies.

Moraga acknowledges this significance by the ways in which she
represents the 1989 murders at the University of Central America
(UCA) in San Salvador, El Salvador:

> The radio music is suddenly interrupted by a news break.
> *Radio:* This is KKCF in Fresno. News brief. San Salvador. UPI reports
> that at 6 a.m. this morning, six Jesuit priests, along with their
> housekeeper and her daughter, were found brutally murdered. The
> priests, from the Central American University, were outspoken op-
> ponents to the ruling rightist ARENA party.
> *Dolores:* Cere! Baja la radio! (To the women:) We got enough bad
> news today without hearing about the rest a the world también.
> (1994b, 117)
>
> . . . .
>
> [Crossfade to *Juan*, who is walking to the Valle home, books stuffed
> under one arm. He reads from a newspaper article.]
> *Juan:* They blasted their brains out in their sleep! Just like that!
> [*Don Gilberto* enters . . .]
> *Gilberto:* Read some bad news, Father?
> *Juan:* Yes. (He shows *Don Gilberto* the article)
> *Gilberto:* Did you know the guys?
> *Juan:* No, but they were Jesuits, my order.

Gilberto: You'd think a priest in a Catholic country couldn't get shot up
   in his pajamas.
Juan: But they were intellectuals.
Gilberto: That didn't seem to matter too much to the bullets, Padre.
   (118–119)

Moraga's play images solidarity between Chicanas/os and Central
American peoples to show common cause — we are both subject to an
ongoing conquest — and to more clearly mark the sinister processes of
colonization and institutional repression. The nameless, faceless killers
survive. Moraga does not limit her representation to the Jesuits but
includes the two women among the martyrs of the UCA.

Cerezita: You know when they killed those priests in El Salvador? . . .
   Did you know they killed the housekeeper and her daughter too?
Juan: Yes.
Cerezita: If the Jesuits died as priests, does that make them saints?
Juan: I don't know. They're martyrs, heroes. They spoke out against
   the government.
Cerezita: Did the housekeeper and her daughter?
Juan: What?
Cerezita: Speak out against the government?
Juan: I don't think so.
Cerezita: I don't either. It wasn't their job. I imagine they just changed
   the priests' beds, kept a pot of beans going, hung out the sábanas
   to dry. At least, the housekeeper did and the girl, she helped her
   mother. She did the tasks that young girls do . . . girls still living
   under the roof of their mother. (139)

In this passage Moraga raises questions about the nature of martyrdom
and heroism and the way in which these gendered discourses efface
women's labor and women's communities. Moraga emphasizes that intellectuals were not the only enemies of the terrorist regime. Just as it
"didn't seem to matter to the bullets" that the priests were intellectuals, it didn't matter that the women were not. Moraga recognizes them
as witnesses, martyrs. Similarly, the children whose bodies Cerezita
and her group display on the grapevines — tiny crucifixions, tiny crucifixes — were not actors against environmental racism. The shrines not

only turn the children into witnesses but also demand that the community (local and televisual) bear witness to their deaths.

Moraga takes pains in her depiction of Mario to argue against AIDS campaigns that promote the notion of innocent victims, a discourse that focused attention on (middle-class Anglo-)Americans, often children, who had been infected by the virus medically, through blood transfusions, unlike the "guilty" or deviants who were infected through sex or IV drug use. Mario is no such "innocent" figure, but his illness, tied as it is to the deaths of the children in McLaughlin, argues that *all* these victims are innocent. Moraga pushes her audience to see AIDS, the birth defects, the murders by U.S.-supported death squads in El Salvador, and the grower's murder of Cerezita as part of a whole enterprise that devalues the lives of people of color in favor of a bottom line.

The play ends with Cerezita's transformation into La Virgen de Guadalupe. The truth in the event is revealed when Dolores at last permits her daughter to pass out of her domestic cage and into the public and political realm. No more must Cerezita act behind the scenes. She goes to her martyrdom with her eyes wide open, knowing that she will be killed but knowing that the most important thing she can accomplish is to speak out for her community. Because her martyrdom will be captured on television and witnessed by the whole community, Cerezita believes she can bring an end to the violence it represents.

Throughout the play, the narrative of McLaughlin has been framed by Ana Pérez, a Latina reporter covering "human interest stories" in "Hispanic California." At the beginning of the play, Pérez is situated outside the Chicano/a community. While reporting for her television audience, she frames an interview of Amparo by saying, "Possibly this neighbor can provide us with some sense of the emotional climate prevalent in this small, largely Hispanic farm worker town" (93). Yet the interview and its aftermath show that Pérez has no real understanding of Amparo or of life in the valley:

Ana Perez: Señora, what about the boy?

Amparo: ¿Qué boy?

Ana Perez: The boy on the cross . . . in the field

Amparo: Memo?

Ana Perez: Yes. Memo Delgado.

Amparo: He died a little santito, son angelitos todos . . .

Ana Perez: Why would someone be so cruel, to hang a child up like
that? To steal him from his deathbed?

Amparo: No, He was dead already. Already dead from the poison.

Ana Perez: But ma'am . . .

Amparo: They always dead first. If you put the children in the ground,
the world forgets about them. Who's gointu see them, buried in the
dirt.

Ana Perez: A publicity stunt? But who's —

Amparo: Señorita, I don't know who. But I know they not my enemy.
(Beat.) Con su permiso. (AMPARO walks away.)

Ana Perez: (with false bravado) That concludes our Hispanic hour for
the week, but watch for next week's show where we will take a
five-hour drive north to the heart of San Francisco's Latino Mis-
sion district, for an insider's observation of the Day of the Dead, the
Mexican Halloween. (She holds a television smile for a full three
seconds. To the "cameramen.") Cut! We'll edit her out later.

[. . . group of small *Children* enter wearing calavera masks. They startle
her.]

Children: Trick or treat!

Ana Perez: No. I mean . . . I don't . . . have anything to give you.

[She exits nervously.] (94)

Doña Amparo brings a close to the conversation, politely putting Ana
Perez in her place by showing that she, unlike Amparo, cannot tell the
good guys from the bad and uses terms such as "publicity stunt" to
describe the ritualistic direct action being performed by the silent pro-
testers. Tellingly, she is startled by the trick-or-treating children, whose
calavera masks represent not only Día de los Muertos — which Pérez
grossly oversimplifies by calling it "the Mexican Halloween." The larger
significance of the children in the *calavera* masks is that it is the children
who die first: they are the canaries in the coal mine whose deaths indicate that things are not as safe as they appear. Ana Pérez's response to
the children, "I don't have anything to give you," like her questions to
Amparo, illustrate her inability to connect with the Chicano/a working
class whom she represents (if only to her Anglo audience). She is not
truly providing an insider's view because she is outside this community:
she has sought her fortune far away from her (presumed) farmworker
origins.

By the final scene of the play, Ana Perez has been changed by the events in McLaughlin. She covers Cerezita's apparition of/as La Virgen, at Father Juan's invitation, to bear witness, both personally and televisually, to the impending "crucifixion." Throughout the procession and Cerezita's final speech, Ana Perez "stands on the sidelines, observing."

> [*Cerezita* and *Juan* proceed offstage into the vineyards. Moments later the shadow and sound of a helicopter pass overhead. *El Pueblo* watch the sky. Then there is the sudden sound of machine gun fire. *El Pueblo* lets out a scream and drop to the ground, covering their heads in terror. *Mario* suddenly rises, raises his fist into the air.]
> *Mario:* Burn the fields!
> *El Pueblo:* (rising with him) ¡Enciendan los files!
> (They *All*, including *Ana Perez*, rush out to the vineyards, shouting as they exit.)
> ¡Asesinos! ¡Asesinos! ¡Asesinos!
> [Moments later there is the crackling of fire as a sharp red-orange glow spreads over the vineyard and the Valle home. The lights slowly fade to black.]

In this final moment of the play, Ana Perez has joined the community. She is part of El Pueblo, striking out at last, burning the fields and the town, uniting in communal action. She is no longer the observer, the *vendida*, selling a packaged version of her *raza* to the camera.

Heroes and Saints joins social protest with religious imagery and queer subjectivities. The farmworker community — traditionally represented as the very heart of the Chicano/a movement — is now peopled with strong women, gays, and Marxists. The play offers no resolution, no solution to the problems faced by the characters. At the same time, it seeks to raise the consciousness of the audience, in the manner of the traditional *actos* of El Teatro Campesino.

Watsonville: Some Place Not Here

Watsonville: Some Place Not Here, like *Heroes and Saints*, is based on actual events in a California Chicano/a community, in this case, Watsonville. This play, along with *Heroes and Saints*, *Circle in the Dirt* (2002),[20] and *Who Killed Yolanda Saldívar?* (2000b),[21] marks a significant shift in Moraga's work to a different kind of theater. Combining the updated politics of El Teatro Campesino with the ethnojournalism of Anna Deveare Smith, Moraga works in the realm of ethnomythography. Extensively researching, learning the local "language," and interviewing dozens of people for their perspective on the political events, she weaves characters and the story together with a healthy dose of Mexican religion-cum-mythology and a queer ethos.

Activism

Watsonville is based on the 1985–1987 cannery workers' strike in this Central Coast agricultural community composed largely of Chicana and Mexican immigrant workers. When the workers went on strike for wages and job security, they encountered the racism of the growers *and* their union. This most vulnerable workforce succeeded after an eighteen-month strike, during which workers faced evictions and ever more grinding poverty. In the spirit of the 1966 march from Delano, California, strikers—mostly women—brought civil disobedience and their Mexican folk Catholicism to bear. The Delano marchers had carried a banner of Nuestra Señora de Guadalupe. The Watsonville strikers walked on their knees, praying to La Virgen.[22]

The Chicana anthropologist Patricia Zavella (1987) has discussed the significance of women of color achieving victory over a large national company in the changing economic contexts of the 1980s and 1990s. This victory was later subsumed, for transnational capital closed the Watsonville plant and moved its business to Mexico in order to exploit that country's similarly vulnerable workers. Indeed, the challenge of turn-of-the-century labor activism was to organize transnational movements.

The play is in some ways dedicated to Chicano labor activist and United Farm Workers (UFW) cofounder César Chávez, but it is also a testament to the history of Chicanas' history of labor activism. It suggests such David-and-Goliath success as the San Antonio pecan sheller's strike and, in fact, the successful organizing of Chicana labor groups in which the big unions had no interest and no faith. Mexican American women are generally regarded more as strikebreakers than as successful labor activists, and this short-sightedness on the part of organized labor has been demonstrated again and again in Chicana victories such as Watsonville and the California Sanitary Canning Company (Cal San) strike of 1939 (see Ruiz 1987, 69–86).

Though *Watsonville* is tied to these historical events, Moraga is imposing a particular narrative structure on the different histories of Watsonville, California. She pursues parallels between the events of the women workers' strike in Watsonville and the Silver City zinc miner's strike dramatized in *Salt of the Earth* (Biberman 1953). Moraga draws out these similarities and also carries them forward, beyond the heterocentrist narrative embedded in *Salt of the Earth* to show how a woman's political awakening can be tied to her (homo)sexual awakening, and also to give credit to the many lesbians who have been activists in Chicano/a communities. Whereas Esperanza (Hope) in *Salt of the Earth* is a Chicana living under patriarchy who is instrumental in winning the strike and changing gender regulations, Lucha, whose name means "struggle," is a Mexicana single mother who is becoming politicized and ever more wary, to the extent that she boards a bus of Mexican and Mexican American strikebreakers to tell them how her family and by extension their families are hurt by crossing the picket line. Thus Lucha shows that she will not assume Dolores's role as the sorrowful but helpless mother. At the same time, Lucha becomes aware of Sonora, a second-generation Chicana lesbian activist. Ultimately, this meeting facilitates Lucha's articulation of her own lesbian desire, to show how her political work has changed her life in more ways than one.

Where Will You Be When They Come?

Watsonville is set in 1996, amid the strike, its limited victory, and the economic fallout of agribusiness's move from California's Central Coast to Mexico. Moraga ties these political events to natural and supernatural phenomena: the 1989 Loma Prieto earthquake, whose epicenter was twenty miles outside the hard-hit town of Watsonville; and the apparition of La Virgen de Guadalupe in the bark of an oak tree at Pinto Lake.[23]

The political climate is framed by the melancholia following the AIDS wars and concomitant anti-immigrant sentiment and legislation. From 1992 to 1994 the conservative Save Our State organization mobilized anti-immigrant sentiment in support of Proposition 187, an amendment to the state constitution to systematically exclude undocu-

mented workers and their (U.S.-born) children from the legal, education, and social systems of the state of California.[24] The passage of the
amendment was a shock and a wakeup call to the millions of California
Latinos. I frame my discussion of *Watsonville* with Pat Parker's 1978
poem, "Where Will You Be," which draws attention to the dangers of
accepting civil limitations against a particular group, in Parker's case,
gays and lesbians. Parker, like Moraga, warns that this is not the end of
the repression but only the beginning:

> Citizens, good citizens all
> parade into voting booths
> and in self-righteous sanctity
> X away our right to life (Parker 1978, 74)

Many Latino groups chose to disassociate themselves from the undocumented workers who were targeted in the legislation. That even
Latino communities were split on the issue demonstrates a larger communal amnesia concerning struggles against the Immigration and Nat-
uralization Service's (INS's) detention of anyone who looked Mexican,
actual citizenship notwithstanding. This practice, which today would
be known as racial profiling, makes all Latinos "potential wetbacks"
and thus "potential criminals." The struggle against these policing practices — and against the forced sterilization of Mexican and Mexican
American women — was a defining call for 1970s Chicano/a/Latino political action. Such amnesia ignores (and facilitates) state and federal
governments' disinterest in distinguishing "legal" from "illegal."

> I do not believe as some
> that the vote is an end,
> I fear even more
> It is just a beginning. (Parker 1978, 74)

Watsonville carries the anti-immigrant sentiments behind Proposition 187 forward to their logical conclusions, demonstrating Chicano
nationalist struggles can be suborned by the narrative that *they*, the undocumented, are not like *us*, even if the "difference" is predicated solely
on one generation or a change in circumstance. In the play, Lucha and
Chente are both working in the United States without papers, but

Chente eventually obtains his green card. However, Chente is quick to side against Lucha, especially when she refuses him her sexual favors.

> You have the straight brothers and sisters quoting that now famous line about the women's movement being a white woman's trip filled to the armpits with bulldaggers and castrating bitches and of course no self-respecting 100% Mexican will have jack shit to do with that unless you don't mind being called a vendida, sellout. . . . The only way out is to walk hand in hand with your man and together battle the white devils of oppression. (Morena 1980, 346)

Behind this contemporary struggle, other struggles from the 1970s emerge, homophobia in the Chicano/a movement, for one. The quotation above, from Naomi Littlebear Morena's *Survivors: A Lesbian Rock Opera*, was written close enough in time to *el movimiento*, to the years of dyke-baiting that the bitterness and pain are still sharp. Moraga's play, set some thirty years after those times, has softened the edges of history, naming the homophobia but also striving to remember what struggles took place, what worked.[25] Sonora and Juan demonstrate how sexual identity, or, to use Audre Lorde's terms, the power of the erotic, can be central to our political awareness, activism, and conscientization. Sonora says:

> I came of age in 1970 . . . And it gave me a very skewed view of reality. [Beat] In '68, my brother's dragging me over to Garfield High School to go to barricade the East L.A. streets with our bodies. I went from the [school blow-outs] on a weekday to grape boycotts on the weekend. Standing out there in front of the Safeway passing out UFW leaflets and bumper stickers. (Pause) Then in 1970 I am kissing Teresa Treviño, a verifiable brown Beret, behind the speakers at the Chicano Moratorium. (Morena 1980, 375)

In describing her political coming-of-age, Sonora waxes nostalgic for those days of activism. At the same time, she is arguing that she was queer from the very beginning. Indeed, the final details, "kissing Teresa Treviño, a verifiable brown Beret, behind the speakers at the Chicano Moratorium," first articulates how sexually charged the political environment was. Teresa Treviño embodies the erotic power attached to the militant Chicano/a group, the Brown Berets. Sonora romancing this woman at this moment argues, in fact, that the movement was always already queer, even from its purest, most nationalist origins.

In spite of the potential for change in the power of the erotic, nationalist structures such as the sexist *movimiento* employ sexual identity to separate the good women from the bad. In other words, when cultural nationalism attempts to encompass even sexuality itself—when homosexuality, like feminism, is named as the white man's/white bitches' disease—gays and lesbians are excluded from the political communities they call home.

> *Sonora:* Then in '76, after a decade of marches and boycotts, and
> door-to-door canvassing, and school lunch programs and self-help
> groups, I'm booted out of MEChA for being a dyke and there's a
> whole women's movement (white as it was) to break my fall. (375)

While trading confidences, Juan confesses to Sonora his secret fantasy.

> *Juan:* (After a pause) Okay, I'd love to make love to Che Guevara . . .
> Well, that's my fantasy. The oldest one I've had. You had Teresa
> Treviño and the Chicano Moratorium. Well, I had my revolutionary
> pressed into the smooth sheets of a paperback . . . Always wanted to
> kiss that Jesus Christ mouth, stare dreamingly into those brooding
> never-satisfied eyes. Che, the lover . . .
> *Sonora:* Now I'm really depressed.
> *Juan:* Why?
> *Sonora:* Two queers without a date on a Saturday night.
> *Juan:* Just queer for the revolution, baby. (400–401)

Juan explicitly demonstrates that the erotic can hold a powerful charge for political activism. Indeed, in his case, his sexuality exists only for "the revolution." While both characters tie their sexual identity to icons of the Chicano/a movement, just as in the reality of Sonora's 1976 MEChA experience, Sonora the lesbian or Juan the mixed-race Chicano would have been cast unhesitatingly as the *vendido* in nationalist *teatro*.

> So I must make assessment
> Look to you and ask:
> Where will you be
> when they come? (Parker 1978, 74)

In *Watsonville,* the union organizer Chente is, ironically, the first person to fall in line with the new legal mandate to distinguish the "legal" from the "illegal."[26]

> *Chente:* We got to be realistic here. We've got to find out who's legal, who isn't . . . Really get a sense of the numbers and let the union know. Maybe it's fewer than we think. Maybe the loss of a few workers won't . . .
> *Sonora:* You can't do that.
> *Chente:* I didn't say turn them in, I said just find out cuantos son ilegales. (Moraga 1996c, 377)

Chente alone seems to be able to divide people up in this way. In the second act of the play, he takes what he believes to be justified measures to stop the scabs: he reports them to the INS:

> *Juan:* How could you do that, man? . . . (Pushing [Chente] away in disgust) Give up your own Raza to la migra.
> *Chente:* They were scabs. They were vendidos—
> *Juan:* No they're just people, man, just people trying to make a living.
> *Chente:* That's very nice, Juan, pero not too practical.
> *Juan:* Is it practical to split up families?
> *Chente:* I couldn't think about that . . . I had to show the union we could win. The union bosses were caving in on us . . . All they saw was a strike with no end in sight. They wanted to settle . . . We would have lost everything. Everything we'd done for the last eighteen months would have been for nothing.
> *Juan:* You gonna turn us in, too? You gonna turn the huelguistas in too, Chente?
> *Chente:* I wouldn't do that. (403)

Initially concerned only with the numbers, with being "practical" and looking at the "big picture,"[27] Chente is quick to invoke the nationalist rhetoric of labeling those who are not "with us" as "vendidos."[28] Chente makes his quest much more personal, luring Lucha's son into revealing that Lucha's immigration papers are forged and then using this information to pressure her into sex. When Lucha refuses, Chente is quick to turn against her.

Lucha: Díme in voz alta en frente de toda esta gente, why Lucha
   Lerma won't be getting a thing after eighteen months on the
   picket line.
Chente: Because you're illegal . . .
Lucha: And because I won't open my legs to you . . . Tell him. Tell my
   son to his face how you got him to confide in you, Cabrón, so you
   could turn your back on his mother when she doesn't give you what
   you want. Tell him how you lied about wanting to help me and my
   kids out. That you could fix my papers, if I needed. Pues, I needed
   bad, but not that bad. Mándanos a México si quieres, pero por lo
   menos regreso con mi dignidad. (412)

Like the feminists struggling within the Chicano/a movement, Moraga's narrative turns sexist and homophobic logic back in on itself to
argue that the *machistas* are the real sellouts for privileging patriarchal
rhetoric over their Chicana compañeras.[29]
   The ensemble play calls for a large number of roles, but interestingly, the notes for *Watsonville* indicate that it needs only three male
actors: one to play JoJo (Lucha's son), one to play Juan, and one to
play Chente, Don Arturo, and the Monsignor. This is another instance
of Moraga turning the sexism back on itself, for in Chicano/a *teatro* one
way in which companies could economize was to cast the same actress
for more than one of the female roles (an easy task since most of the
female roles were quite small). Significantly, then, Moraga reverses this
character typing by making all of the "negative male characters" interchangeable: Doña Lola's useless *viejo* Arturo is interchangeable with
Chente, the *real vendido*, and with the Monsignor, who values the hierarchy of the church over the faith of *los pobres*.

Revising History

Although *Watsonville* is a sequel to *Heroes and Saints* and the characters Dolores, Amparo, and Juan appear in both plays, there is significant revision taking place in the time/space between McLaughlin and
Watsonville. First, throughout *Watsonville*, Dolores views the lesbian
character Sonora as Cerezita returned. (Sonora may also represent a
combination of Mario and Cerezita: she is the political physician's assistant ministering to her pueblo, which goals both Mario and Cerezita

articulated in *Heroes and Saints*.) Retroactively, then, the text inscribes Cerezita as lesbian.[30] This is what Dolores recognizes in Sonora.

Second, Dolores remembers the events of McLaughlin and weeps for her children but names only Mario and Cerezita. Her eldest daughter, Yolanda, whose infant daughter died of stomach cancer, is not mentioned and appears never to have existed at all.

Third, in spite of recognizing Cerezita in Sonora, that is, recognizing the lesbian in Cerezita, Dolores also attempts to reinscribe Cerezita in a heteronormative frame, arguing that when Cerezita went to her death robed in white, she was a bride, either the bride of Juan Cunningham or a Bride of Christ.

> *Dolores:* She was a bride, vestida de blanco. She died for God.
> *Juan:* She died for change.
> *Dolores:* Era una santa.
> *Juan:* She was a hero.
> *Dolores:* Is that what they teach you in your revolutionary books? To take God out of everything?
> *Juan:* I know what I saw. There was no god out there. (392)

Fourth, in reaction to Dolores's memories of Cerezita, Juan retells the final scene of *Heroes and Saints*, not from the view of El Pueblo, where Cerezita triumphs in her final act, or from the view of the Chicana newscaster, who is "converted" by Cerezita's martyrdom, but from his own view alongside her: with the bullets and the blood.

> *Juan:* I see Cerezita. (Pause) Someone had torn the cloth from her head. And they had stuck her . . . the head . . . onto a thick grapevine post—
> *Amparo:* ¡Ay, Dios!
> *Juan:* They had forced the post through her mouth and had hung the veil like a sign around her neck, and on it, in blood . . . her blood, they had written THOU ARE WRETCHED." (Pause) And then I understood . . . How profoundly those men . . . with all their land and all their power . . . hated us. And I knew they would do anything not to know their hate was fear. (Pause) And I knew I would never be afraid again. Not even of God. (392–393)

Finally, Dolores's husband, who was absent throughout *Heroes and Saints* and who had been absent since Cerezita's infancy, has rejoined the family in *Watsonville,* as if he had never been gone at all. However, he remains the *cabrón,* the good-for-nothing husband who doesn't work, doesn't support his family, and takes the joy out of Dolores's life. In her words, "You make everything ugly. *Lo peor posible*" (348).

Milagros y Milagros

When Juan Cunningham goes to the diocese monsignor to solicit the church's support of the Watsonville strikers and their Holy Tree, he meets with disbelief and disinterest. The audience is not surprised by this outcome, for we can see that Moraga is referencing the apparitions of La Virgen de Guadalupe in 1531. When the Indian Juan Diego went to the archbishop of New Spain to tell him of the apparition, he was first driven away and later met with doubt and suspicion. The popular ways in which this story has come down emphasizes the split between the colonial church and *la gente del pueblo*—between the rich and the poor, between the colonizers and the colonized. Juan Cunningham—the new mestizo—goes to the monsignor but is met with doubt and suspicion. This also further ties the apparition of La Virgen on the Holy Tree to the original apparition at Tepayac.[31]

That the archbishop was eventually proven wrong—by the miracle of roses for which La Virgen is known—is also part of the telling of this story. We know the monsignor will be proven wrong as well, and the proof comes in the epilogue of the play, when the earthquake (which like the virus knows no prejudice, respects no green card) literally levels the state.

The climax of the play occurs at Act II, scene 10, when Bill 1519 has been made into national law, when Chicanas/os and Mejicanos are denied access to education and social services, even public transportation. While the bill ostensibly separates "illegal" immigrants from "legal" residents and citizens, in daily practice one's access is limited by whether or not the bus driver thinks you look "Mexican" or not. The local union reaches a settlement with the growers that will disenfranchise all the undocumented workers, and the rank and file must decide whether to sign this contract—and thus accept this border within their pueblo—or fight on with a wildcat strike.

Dolores, who has struggled against politics, makes her first political statement to her community:

> They think they can kill la huelga with this law, pero seguimos siendo huelgistas whether we got a union or not. Seguimos siendo americanos whether we got papeles or not. [La Virgen appeared to me porque] Guadalupe es la Emperatriz de América, una América unida. (415)

As the pueblo gets down on their knees to pray, the earth begins to tremble, and women's voices chant the names of the indigenous goddesses of Mexico.

In the same way that Moraga has magnified California Proposition 187 into a national law — a logical extension of the consequences of the anti-immigrant legislation — she magnifies the Loma Prieto earthquake into "the big one" long feared in California, the earthquake that will change life as we know it.

The two official acts of the play are followed by an epilogue.

> A major earthquake, registering seven-point-five on the Richter scale, struck the Central coast of California . . . has left much of San Francisco and Oakland thoroughly devastated. The quake's epicenter was located in the town of Watsonville, which was completely leveled by the quake. Reports just surfacing from the area, however, have confirmed that some ten thousand survivors, mostly Mexican residents, were found gathered together in an oak grove in County Park just outside of town. (416)

Lucha exclaims, "Nobody gives a damn about who's legal or not now. . . . Even those fanáticos fundamentalists right-wingers are scared that all this is a sign from God. Didn't you see the headlines? 'Miracle Tree Saves Mexicans of Watsonville'" (417). At the same time, the Watsonville Chicanas/os and Mexicanos know that this is not the ultimate solution for them and that in fact the tide of public opinion can just as easily turn against them. But this temblor brings clarity about what really matters. La Doña Dolores was been freed from the lifelong burden of her husband, Arturo, who is killed in the earthquake. Though she knows her own death is near, she looks forward to joining her children, Cerezita and Mario, in the afterlife.

Lucha declares her love, her desire for Sonora, in a letter that bridges the gap between the Spanish that we know Lucha speaks and the English in which the play takes place.

> *Lucha:* I want to talk you the way I hear you talk to other womans. Your voice is more low and you forget where go your hands. You laugh more. I want that you forget like that with me, so we can talk with our hearts. I am no a child. I am woman who know what she want. Te quiero . . . No like sisters. With my sister, Isabel, we sleeped together like angels silence. I no notice her there, but I notice you. You touch me and the place stay forever touched. (419)

In April 1996 Moraga discussed Lucha's letter at the University of California, Berkeley, conference "Transformations of Queer Ethnicities: A Conversation with Norma Alarcón and Cherríe Moraga."[32] An earlier draft of the play called for Lucha to declare her lesbianism in Act II, when the play is building toward its climax and when Lucha has articulated how she has changed from a worker to a *huelgista*, to a new citizen-subject (with or without papers). Her declaration at that time would demonstrate that the power of the erotic and the political struggle go hand in hand. During the play's production, Moraga was pressured to move the scene to the epilogue, so that the activist energy would not be curtailed by the lesbian content. That is, to represent lesbianism as the logical result of women's activism would alienate the audience to the "larger" message of the play. This is an example of the complex relationship of Chicana lesbian authors such as Cherríe Moraga to narratives of the Chicano nation — the "larger" message. Moraga is constrained by the narrative that the audience would be alienated, and she responds with a compromise position.

One character conspicuous by his absence in the epilogue is Chente. He is one *vendido* who is never recuperated. This is in contrast to Moraga's recuperation of Ana Perez in *Heroes and Saints*, who ultimately unites with the pueblo: Chente was initially seen as part of the pueblo until he joined the union in its strategy of using immigration status as a wedge to break the strike. The audience knows that, like Don Arturo, Chente has not survived the earthquake because he lacked faith. He put his faith in the union, which "pays his bills" in Lucha's stark assess-

ment, over his faith in his people, or in La Virgen who is the manifestation of Chicano/a-Mexicano faith.

Conclusion

Heroes and Saints and *Watsonville: Some Place Not Here* combine political
call to action with myth, neopagan-Mexican Catholicism, critiques of
sexism, heterocentrism and homophobia, critiques of the conservative
church, and Marxist analysis. Both plays problematize the notion of
a sad or happy ending through their deployment of supernatural and
apocalyptic endings. They return to what we might call "essential"
Chicano/a communities, that is, to working-class communities coming
to political consciousness. And yet they go beyond a strict nationalist
framework, even when self-consciously deploying nationalist strategies.
The use of Mexican religion traditionally suggests a return to nationalism, a return to the strategies of Delano, 1966, and to the origins of the
Chicano/a movement. However, Moraga deliberately deploys Native
American beliefs to problematize the notion of "traditional" religion.
Both texts are queerly marked both through lesbian and gay characters
and through "the use of the erotic."

Thus *Watsonville* makes explicit what disappeared into the subtext
of Nicholasa Mohr's (1983) short story—that politics plays a part in
sexual identity (or vice versa), or perhaps that it *should*. Hilda Hidalgo
articulates how her queer status, the silent subtext of her struggles
against hierarchy, against racism, against sexism, leads her to transcend
borders, to cross over into women of color spaces, like Sonora with her
black, Filipina, and mixed-race feminist community.

These plays are explicitly tied to real political struggles: the fight
against environmental racism in McFarland, California, the Watsonville
strikes of 1985–1987, the ongoing struggle to unionize the strawberry
workers. At the same time they gesture to the long history of Mexican
American women taking action in labor struggles and to women of color
fighting against the discourse that limits "environmentalism" to national
forests and not to working and living conditions or city zoning.[33]

Heroes and Saints and *Watsonville* exist in what Emma Pérez (1999,
127) describes as "the time lag between the colonial and the postcolonial, in a decolonial imaginary reinscribing the old with the new." Like
the shift in vision that I argue occurs in Hilda Hidalgo's oral history and

in the rewriting of Cerezita's death that Moraga enacts in *Watsonville*, these texts choose a path that does not lead back to nationalism but shows a consciousness of the limits of that nationalism and the need for different kinds of strategies, different endings. One can read them as a straight return to nationalism, but to do so, I believe, misses the transformative power of the texts, as they move Chicana lesbian literature into the new millennium.

CHAPTER 8

Conclusion:
With Her Machete in Her Hand

Con su pluma en su mano
Con paciencia y sin temor
Escribió muchas verdades
Y respeto nos ganó.
—TISH HINOJOSA (1995)

"With His Pistol in His Hand"

Ramón Saldívar (1990) contends that to fully appreciate Chicano/a fiction, it is necessary to examine its genealogy, in particular, its relationship to the discursive erasure of Mexican Americans from the history of the American West. Saldívar observes that such texts "signify the imaginary ways in which historical men and women live out their lives." In other words, Chicano/a narrative imagines histories of Mexican Americans, histories that have not made it into the official version of "how the West was won." Saldívar takes as his originary model of Chicano/a narrative, Américo Paredes's 1958 text, *"With His Pistol in His Hand,"* a historical, folkloric, and anthropological study of the *corrido* in general and *El Corrido de Gregorio Cortez* in particular. Paredes identifies the work of the *corrido* as constructing alternative heroes, Mexican heroes, in the history of the Southwest:

> *Corrido*, the Mexicans call their narrative folk songs, especially those of epic themes, taking the name from *correr* which means "to run" or "to flow," for the *corrido* tells a story simply and swiftly, without embellishment. (1958, xi)

José Limón describes Paredes's work as follows:

> [It is a] study of the life, legend and corpus of ballads generated by the activities of one individual, Gregorio Cortez. Until June 12, 1901, Cortez was a rather ordinary Mexican-American in Texas, an agricultural laborer like so many others, who, from his own perspective, was witnessing the intensification of Anglo-American and capitalist domination of Texas, including the predominantly Mexican-American region of south Texas. . . . [This often] took the form of class and racial subordination, the latter evidenced in the rough and ready lynching "justice" often administered to Mexican-Americans accused of crimes. (1994, 79)

On that summer day in 1901, Sheriff Morris of Karnes County visited the home of Gregorio Cortez to question him and his brother Romaldo about a stolen horse. The sheriff spoke no Spanish. He was accompanied by a translator whose command of the language was not sufficient to the task. At one point the sheriff said he was going to arrest Cortez, who replied that he had done nothing for which he could be arrested. The translator rendered this as "No man can arrest me." Perceiving this as a threat, the sheriff fired on Romaldo Cortez, and Gregorio shot the sheriff. Cortez escaped on horseback and "was chased by hundreds of men, and in one or two cases, posses . . . of three hundred men were reported scouring the countryside" (Paredes 1958, 114). One of the many variants of Cortez's legend says that he could have escaped to Mexico but turned back when informed that his family had been imprisoned and that many of the Texas-Mexicans who had aided him on his journey had been harshly punished.[1] After a series of trials, Cortez was acquitted of the murder of Sheriff Morse but convicted of the murder of Sheriff Glover of Gonzales, Texas. Gregorio Cortez was sentenced to life in prison. In July 1915 he was pardoned by Texas governor O. B. Colquitt. Cortez died in 1918, at the age of forty-three.

The Ballad of Gregorio Cortez emphasizes the hero's quiet dignity in the face of injustice, the way in which his struggle symbolizes the struggle of all Texas-Mexicans, and his ability to outwit his pursuers.

Decía Gregorio Cortez	Then said Gregorio Cortez,
con su pistola en la mano:	With his pistol in his hand,
¡Ah, cuánto rinche montado	"Ah, so many mounted Rangers
para un solo mexicano!	Just to take one Mexican!"[2]

Saldívar (1990) argues that *The Ballad of Gregorio Cortez* is emblematic of later Chicano/a literature. However, his discussion shows that contemporary Chicano/a authors speak of being moved, not only by the ballad itself, but also by Paredes's analysis of the significance of *The Ballad of Gregorio Cortez* for Mexico-Texans of the greater border region. Indeed, Limón (1994, 82) has posited that "Mr. Paredes and his book became like a *corrido* and its hero for a new generation of Chicano/a social activists of the sixties, who recognized the legendary fighting qualities of the two men, [Gregorio] Cortez and [Américo] Paredes."[3]

"On the Lower Border of the Rio Grande," says Paredes (1958, 241), "a ballad community much like those of medieval Europe existed during the nineteenth and the early part of the twentieth century." The *corrido* form is a Spanish ballad of varying length, composed of eight-syllable quatrains in an *abcb* rhyme pattern. "Not typically a form of personal narrative, . . . the *corrido* instead tends to take a transpersonal third-person point of view representing the political and existential values of the community as a whole" (Saldívar 1990, 32). Paredes (1958, xxi) pointed out that the *corrido* was a genre written and performed by men: "Men were the performers, while the women and children participated only as audience."

Herrera-Sobek's Feminist Perspective

This is not to say that women were not represented in the *corridos*. In her study, *The Mexican Corrido: A Feminist Analysis* (1990), based on more than three thousand *corridos*, María Herrera-Sobek explores five major female archetypes in the *corrido*: the Good Mother, the Terrible Mother, the Virgin of Guadalupe, The Lover — both faithful and treacherous — and the Soldadera. Most of these archetypes represent both positive (Good Mother, Virgin of Guadalupe, Faithful Lover) and negative (Terrible Mother, Treacherous Lover) examples of feminine behavior. The final one, however, reconfigures "positive female behavior" to include political agency in the form of armed struggle for the revolution. Herrera-Sobek demonstrates that the representation of *soldaderas* takes three forms: those based on historical figures, those that romanticize the soldadera into a love-object, and those in which the *soldadera* is raised to larger-than-life dimensions. In all, the valorization of the *soldadera* praises the woman who goes beyond traditional gender roles.

Nevertheless, Herrera-Sobek's study demonstrates that in the *corrido* both traditional and nontraditional gender roles are predicated on an assumption of heterosexuality.

"Delgadina"

In her article "Sexuality and Discourse: Notes from a Chicana Surivivor," Emma Pérez turns her attention to "Delgadina,"[4] a *corrido* that centers on a female protagonist who fits none of the archetypes discussed above. This song, the *corrido* or romance of Delgadina, tells the daughter's story, and it is not a happy one.

One day Delgadina's father looks at her with lust in his eyes. He commands her to be his woman. She refuses, saying it would be a sin against God and against the Blessed Virgin, as well as a crime against her own mother and her siblings. Her refusal enrages the father, who locks her in a tower. His intention is that she suffer the torments of hunger and thirst until she gives herself to him.

From the window of her tower, Delgadina spies other members of the family and begs for their help, asking them to bring her water lest she die. Each family member refuses to help her, fearing the father's retribution. At last, she asks her father for water. He commands that she be released from the tower and given water immediately, but when the water arrives, Delgadina is already dead.

This *corrido* dates at least from the 1492 expulsion of the Jews from Spain. Its variants can be found throughout the Ladino- and Spanish-speaking world.[5] Herrera-Sobek (1986) argues that the song illustrates the power of patriarchy, which places the daughter in an impossible double bind. If she submits to the father's desire for her, she will be damned. If she refuses, she will surely die. In Pérez's (1991, 171) terms, the *corrido* "symbolizes a daughter's painful entrance into the law of the father."

> ["Delgadina"] does not just pass down the incest taboo to warn against it. The song tells us about a young woman's death when she challenges the sexual law of the father. She cannot, however, break from the law, happy and free to join with women who believe her, or a community who will allow her to be. There is no such community. (Pérez 1991, 172)

Pérez is not only identifying the sexual politics in the original *corrido*. She also takes issue with the theatrical production of "Delgadina" by Luis Valdez (1981, adapted for television 1987). *Corridos*, a musical theater piece, situates Mexican *corridos* as essential to Mexican and Chicano/a culture. While most of the *corridos* performed in the play are from the Mexican Revolution, Valdez decides to set "Delgadina" during the Porfiriato, a gilded age for the Mexican elite. Valdez's narrator invites the audience to view this "peep show," and thus, like the father, the narrator and the audience gaze at Delgadina with desire.

Valdez also compromises the "purity" of Delgadina, in a scene in which she is dancing in her transparent nightgown. She is unaware of the father's gaze, but she knows she is not supposed to be dancing. Visually, the scene is stunning: Delgadina is played by Eveyln Cisneros of the San Francisco Ballet Company. The forbidden dance makes the most of the dancer's ability. However, this scene in effect blames the daughter for inciting her father's desire.

As Pérez (1991, 115) points out, while "Delgadina" incites sympathy for Delgadina, the patriarchal structure that permits her victimization "is not blamed. . . . It is left intact."

Pérez turns her attention to the message the song conveys:

The *corrido* of Delgadina, however[,] is male fantasy, its construction reified. For it is through Delgadina that patriarchy owns is power, its knowledge; it is through patriarchy that women's desire is silenced. . . . ["Delgadina"] also critiques a dominant, all-encompassing patriarchal 'order of things' that demands disclosure. (1999, 116, 122)

In both "Sexuality and Discourse" and *The Decolonial Imaginary*, Pérez argues for the subjectivity of the daughter, even as she acknowledges that certain narratives leave her no room for survival. Given the significance assigned the *corrido* form, as the form from which Chicano/a narrative derives, Pérez's critique of "Delgadina" shows that the *corrido* not only makes women invisible, it calls for their inevitable death.

"La historia de una marimacho"

Gloria Anzaldúa's short story "La historia de una marimacho" is about two women who leave home and family to love one another and create a life together (see chap. 6). The *corrido* ending of the story shifts from first to third person and flattens the complexity of the two women's relationship. Like the *corrido* form itself, the *marimacha's corrido* valorizes the "masculinist" exploits of taming the father and shaming the machos. In one sense, Anzaldúa's *corrido* constitutes a metacritique of both *The Ballad of Gregorio Cortez* and *"With His Pistol in His Hand,"* which similarly minimizes the complexity of Texas-Mexican border culture in favor of the masculine hero and the narrative form that renders women as neither participants nor heroes in Mexican American history but only its audience.

At the same time, Anzaldúa's story creates the alternatives that Emma Pérez calls for in her discussion of "Delgadina": the possibility of breaking free from the law of the father, "happy and free to join with women who believe her, or a community who will allow her to be" (1991, 172). In "La historia de una marimacho," Anzaldúa creates community for her female characters, who ultimately refigure the family so that it is not subject to the law of the father; instead the father must learn to live by new rules.

"Con su pluma en su mano"

I began this chapter with Tish Hinojosa's *corrido* "Con su pluma en su mano" from her 1995 collection, *Fronteras*. Hinojosa is playing with the form of the *corrido* and with traditional definitions of the hero. "Con su pluma en su mano" is a tribute to Américo Paredes, to his construction of Mexican American history and his commitment to Tejano music and folklore. José David Saldívar examines Hinojosa's traditionalist *corrido* thus:

> Like all serious *corrido* composers, Hinojosa begins her song by asking her audiences's permission to sing *"sin tristeza ni maldad"* (without sadness or malice) about Paredes's place in the U.S.-Mexico borderlands. Her opening stance lets her audience know that the central issue of her *corrido* is the life history of a U.S.-Mexico border intellectual. With this appropriate beginning, the singer then presents what Paredes [1958] himself called "a counterpointing of rhythms," "high register singing," and "rigor." (1997, 209)

Throughout her *corrido,* Hinojosa uses traditional poetic language to compare Paredes conterdiscourse to the border itself. . . . Of particular

interest in Hinojosa's *corrido* is the singer's self-reflexiveness. Through
her formal opening and closing of the song, the *corrido* flows from the
social and back again, through its references to her communal audience. Hinojosa's *corrido*, like the classic *corridos* of the U.S.-Mexico
border conflict and the Mexican Revolution, functions as a repositor of
the historical data for a public that has not had access to the emergent
counterdiscourses produced by Paredes in the academy. Unlike the
classic *corridos*, however, Hinojosa in her *despedida* (farewell) offers her
listeners neither the portrait of the male hero nor a character similar to
what María Herrera-Sobek calls "the *canción de gesto*" or song of anger
(199, xiii). Instead Hinojosa's border ballad salutes Paredes the U.S.-
Mexico border writer, singer, and radio disc jockey who passes down
the long *corridos* of struggle contained in folklore. (1997, 190–191)

Saldívar concludes with the final verse of the song but misses the im-
portant gender interventions that Hinojosa herself is making in both
her song and, specifically, in that verse. Recall that Paredes, Ramón
Saldívar, Renato Rosaldo, José Limón, and José David Saldívar are
all defining the *corrido* as a masculinist narrative of male heroes. To read
"Con su pluma en su mano" only as a traditional-style *corrido* about
Paredes the intellectual ignores the Chicana feminist implications of
Hinojosa's work. Though couched in polite and deferential language,
Hinojosa's *corrido* is also challenging the masculinist construction of the
form: she is a Chicana singer and songwriter and describes herself as
"una alumna de don Américo," which could be translated as "a student
of Paredes." However, Hinojosa's use of the feminine *alumna* is significant. The Chicano scholars I name above could be described as *alumnos
de don Américo*, the students, the alumni of the Paredes school of Chicano
studies. Hinojosa sets herself apart as *una alumna*, a female student who
appreciates the gender dynamics in play. *Con su guitarra, con su pluma
en la mano*, with her guitar and her pen in her hand, *con paciencia y sin
temor*, with patience and without fear, Hinojosa both acknowledges and
challenges the masculinist *corrido*. Her tribute articulates the Chicana
alumna position. Like Gloria Anzaldúa's "La historia de una marimacho" and indeed like the authors I have discussed, this song is also a
shout-out to Chicanas. My work here also points to the importance of
these writers in forging new Chicana subjectivities, ones that acknowledge queer desire as always-already present in Chicano/a communities,
both historically and in their contemporary formation.

APPENDIX

Toward a Chronological Bibliography of Chicana Lesbian Fictions, 1971–2000

This study primarily discusses Chicana writers. However, I find it impossible to discuss them without also discussing relevant works by other Latina writers. The symbol (++) denotes authors who are Latina but not Chicana.

1971

Portillo [Trambley], Estela. "The Day of the Swallows." *El Grito* 4, no. 3 (Spring): 4–47. Reprinted in *Contemporary Chicano Theater,* (1976); *The Woman That I Am: A Woman of Color Anthology* (1994).

1980

Morena, Naomi Littlebear. *Survivors: A Lesbian Rock Opera.* Excerpt reprinted as "Coming Out Queer and Brown" in *For Lesbians Only: A Separatist Anthology,* 345–347. London: Onlywomen Press, 1988.

1981

Carrillo, Jo. "María Littlebear." In *Lesbian Fiction: An Anthology,* edited by Elly Bulkin, 17–23. Watertown, MA: Persephone Press.
Gámez, Rocky. "From *The Gloria Stories.*" *Conditions* 7: 50–56. Reprinted in *Cuentos: Stories by Latinas* (1983); *Wayward Girls and Wicked Women* (1986); *Women on Women* (1990); *Persistant Desire: A Femme-Butch Reader* (1992).
Ortiz Taylor, Sheila. "All Things Being Equal." *Christopher Street* (November).
———. "With Friends Like These." *Lesbian Voices* (Fall).
———. "A Friend of the Family." *Focus: A Journal for Lesbians* (September–October).

Villanueva, Alma Luz. "Golden Glass." *Bilingual Review* 8, nos. 2–3 (May–December): 70–72. Reprinted in *Hispanics in the United States,* vol. 2 (1982); *Growing Up Latino* (1993).

1982

Anzaldúa, Gloria. "El Paisano Is a Bird of Good Omen." *Conditions* 8 (Spring): 28–47. Reprinted in *Cuentos: Stories by Latinas* (1983).
Ortiz Taylor, Sheila. *Faultline*. Tallahassee, FL: Naiad Press.
++Paz, Juana Maria. "Frankly My Dear . . . I'm Eating." *Common Lives/Lesbian Lives*, a lesbian quarterly 6 (Winter): 53–65.

1983

Gámez, Rocky. "Doña Marciana Garcia." In *Cuentos: Stories by Latinas*, edited by Alma Gomez, Cherríe Moraga, and Mariana Romo-Carmona, 7–15. New York: Kitchen Table/Women of Color Press.
++Mohr, Nicholasa. "An Awakening . . . Summer 1956." *Revista Chicano-Riqueña* 11, nos. 3–4 (Fall): 107–112. Volume reprinted as *Woman of Her Word: Hispanic Women Write,* edited by Evangelina Vigil (Houston: Arte Público, 1987).
Moraga, Cherríe. *Loving in the War Years: Lo que nunca pasó por sus labios*. Boston: South End Press.

1984

Cisneros, Sandra. *The House on Mango Street*. Reprint New York: Vintage, 1991.
Villanueva, Alma Luz. "The Ripening." *Bilingual Review* 11, no. 2 (May–August): 78–88.

1985

Anzaldúa, Gloria. "People Should Not Die in June in South Texas." In *My Story's On! Ordinary Women/Extraordinary Lives: An Anthology,* edited by Paula Ross. Berkeley, CA: Common Differences Press. Reprinted in *My Father's Daughter: Stories by Women* (1990); *Growing up Latino* (1993).
Ortiz Taylor, Sheila. *Spring Forward/Fall Back*. Tallahassee, FL: Naiad Press.

1986

de la Peña, Terri. "Once a Friend" and "A Saturday in August." Third Prize in University of California, Irvine, Chicano Literary Competition. Published 1989.

Moraga, Cherríe. *Giving Up the Ghost: Teatro in Two Acts*. Los Angeles: West End Press.
++Obejas, Achy. "Polaroids." *Third Woman* 3 (1–2): 49–54.

1987

Cenen. "The Love Making." In *Compañeras: Latina Lesbians — An Anthology*, edited by Juanita [Díaz] Ramos, 141–143. New York: Latina Lesbian History Project.
Chavez, Denise. *The Last of the Menu Girls*. Houston: Arte Público.
++Hidalgo, Hilda. "El ser yo no es un lujo." In *Compañeras: Latina Lesbians — An Anthology*, edited by Juanita [Díaz] Ramos, 72–76. New York: Latina Lesbian History Project.
++Ramos, Juanita [Díaz], ed. *Compañeras: Latina Lesbians — An Anthology*. New York: Latina Lesbian History Project. Reprint New York: Routledge, 1994.

1988

Gámez, Rocky. "A Baby for Adela." In *Politics of the Heart: A Lesbian Parenting Anthology*, edited by Sandra Pollack and Jeanne Vaughn, 100–110. Ithaca, NY: Firebrand Books.
Latimore, Jessie [pseudo.]. *High Contrast*. Tallahassee, FL: The Naiad Press.
Morena, Naomi Littlebear. "Coming Out Queer and Brown." In *For Lesbians Only: A Separatist Anthology*, 345–347. London: Onlywomen Press.
Otero, Rosalie. "Amelia." In *Voces: An Anthology of Nuevo Mexicano Writers*, edited by Rudolfo Anaya, 7–18. Albuquerque: El Norte.
Villanueva, Alma Luz. *The Ultraviolet Sky*. Tempe, AZ: Bilingual Press/Editorial Bilingue. Reprint New York: Anchor Books, 1993.

1989

Alarcon, Norma, Ana Castillo, and Cherríe Moraga, eds. *The Sexuality of Latinas* [special issue]. *Third Woman* 4. Reprint Berkeley: Third Woman Press, 1993.
Anzaldúa, Gloria. "La historia de una marimacho." *Third Woman* 4: 64–68.
———. "Lifeline." In *Lesbian Love Stories*, edited by Irene Zahava. Freedom, CA: Crossing Press.
de la Peña, Terri. "La Maya." In *Intricate Passions*, edited by Tee Corinne, 1–10. Austin: Banned Books.
———. "Once a Friend." In *The One You Call Sister*, edited by Paula Martinac, 49–62. San Francisco: Cleis Press.
———. "Tortilleras." In *Lesbian Bedtime Stories*, edited by Terry Woodrow, 83–92. Willits, CA: Tough Dove Books.
del Fuego, Laura. *Maravilla*. Encino, CA: Floricanto Press.

Gámez, Rocky. "A Slow, Sweet Kind of Death." In *Intricate Passions*, edited by Tee Corrinne, 65–74. Austin: Banned Books.
Moraga, Cherríe. "Shadow of a Man" [excerpt]. *Out/Look* (Summer): 46–51.

1990

Anzaldúa, Gloria. "She Ate Horses." In *Lesbian Philosophies and Cultures*, edited by Jeffner Allen, 371–388. Albany: State University of New York Press.
Córdova, Jeanne. *Kicking the Habit*. Los Angeles: Multiple Dimensions.
de la Peña, Terri. "Blue." In *Riding Desire*, edited by Tee Corrinne, 149–153. Austin: Banned Books.
———. "Labrys." In *Word of Mouth*, edited by Irene Zahava, 31. Freedom, CA: Crossing Press.
———. "Mariposa." In *Lesbian Bedtime Stories 2*, edited by Terry Woodrow, 7–19. Willits, CA: Tough Dove Books.
———. "Tres Mujeres." *Frontiers* 11 (1): 60–64.
Escamill, Edna. "Cajitas, an excerpt from the novel *Daughter of the Mountain*." *Puerto del Sol* 25 (1–2): 217–222.
Gámez, Rocky. "A Matter of Fact." In *Riding Desire*, edited by Tee Corrinne, 36–43. Austin: Banned Books.
Moraga, Cherríe. "La Ofrenda." *Out/Look* 10 (Fall): 50–55. Reprinted in *Chicana Lesbians: The Girls Our Mothers Warned Us About* (1991); *An Intimate Wilderness* (1991); *on our backs* (n.d.); *Women on Women 2* (1993).
———. 1990. *The Shadow of a Man*. Produced by BRAVA! for Women in the Arts and the Eureka Theatre Company in San Francisco, November. Reprinted in *Shattering the Myth* (1992); *Heroes and Saints & Other Plays* (1994).
Ortiz Taylor, Sheila. *Southbound*. Tallahassee, FL: Naiad Press.
Palacios, Monica. "La Llorona Loca: The Other Side." In *Lesbian Bedtime Stories 2*, edited by Terry Woodrow, 174–177. Willits, CA: Tough Dove Press. Reprinted in *Chicana Lesbians: The Girls Our Mothers Warned Us About* (1991).
++*Yo, la peór de todas*. Dir. María Luisa Bemberg. Screenplay María Luisa Bemberg and Antonio Larreta. Adapted from *Las trampas de fe* by Octavio Paz. 105 min. GEA Cinematografica, Buenos Aires. Dist. First Run/Icarus Films.

1991

Anzaldúa, Gloria. "Ms. Right, My True Love, My Soul Mate." In *Lesbian Love Stories*, vol. 2, edited by Irene Zahava, 184–188. Freedom, CA: Crossing Press.
de la Peña, Terri. "Beyond El Camino Real." In *Chicana Lesbians: The Girls Our Mothers Warned Us About*, edited by Carla Trujillo, 85–94. Berkeley: Third Woman Press.
———. "Desert Quartet." In *Lesbian Love Stories*, edited by Irene Zahava, 154–161. Freedom, CA: Crossing Press.
———. "Mujeres Morenas." In *Lesbian Love Stories*, edited by Irene Zahava, 85–93. Freedom, CA: Crossing Press.

Escamill, Edna. *Daughter of the Mountain*. San Francisco: Aunt Lute Books.
———. "The Saga of pan birote y los tres chilis." *Saguaro Literary Journal* 7: 41–47. Reprinted in *Pieces of the Heart* (1993); *The Storyteller in Nike Airs and Other Barrio Stories* (1994).
++Gomez-Vega, Ibis. *Send My Roots Rain*. San Francisco: Aunt Lute Foundation.
Palacios, Monica. 1991. "Personality Fabulosa." *Out/Look* 4 (2): 32–37.
Pérez, Emma. "Gulf Dreams." In *Chicana Lesbians: The Girls Our Mothers Warned Us About*, edited by Carla Trujillo, 96–108. Berkeley: Third Woman Press.
Trujillo, Carla, ed. *Chicana Lesbians: The Girls Our Mothers Warned Us About*. Berkeley: Third Woman Press, 1991.

1992

Anzaldúa, Gloria. "Ghost Trap." *New Chicana/Chicano Writing 1*, edited by Charles Tatum, 40–42. Tucson: University of Arizona Press. Reprinted in *Currents from the Dancing River: Contemporary Latino Fiction, Nonfiction, and Poetry* (1994).
———. "Puddles." *New Chicana/Chicano Writing 1*, edited by Charles Tatum, 43–45. Tucson: University of Arizona Press. Reprinted in *Currents from the Dancing River: Contemporary Latino Fiction, Nonfiction, and Poetry* (1994).
de la Peña, Terri. *Margins*. Seattle: Seal Press.
———. *Territories*. Winner of the 1992 Chicano/Latino Literary Contest (Short Story Collection). See Works in Progress, below.
Escamill, Edna. "Black Orchid." *Sinister Wisdom* 47 (Summer–Fall): 78–81. Reprinted in Escamill, *The Storyteller with Nike Airs and Other Stories of the Barrio* (1994).
Esquibel, Catrióna Rueda. "La Karla." *Amor picante pero sabroso*. Produced by the Latina Lab of Su Teatro, at the Eulipons Theatre, Denver, CO.
Gaspar de Alba, Alicia. "Cimarrona." In *With-out Discovery: A Native Response to Columbus*, edited by Ray Gonzalez, 91–112. Seattle: Broken Moon Press.
———. "Excerpts from the Sapphic Diary of Sor Juana Inés de la Cruz." *Frontiers* 12 (3): 171–179. Reprinted in *Tasting Life Twice: Lesbian Literary Fiction by New American Writers* (1995).
———. "Juana Inés." *New Chicano/Chicano Writing 1*, edited by Charles Tatum, 1–15. Tucson: University of Arizona Press. 1–15. Reprinted in *Growing Up Chicana/o* (1993).
Moraga, Cherríe. *Heroes and Saints*. Reprinted in *Heroes and Saints & Other Plays* (1994).
Villanueva, Alma Luz. "People of the Dog." In *Mirrors beneath the Earth: Short Fiction by Chicano Writers*, edited by Ray Gonzalez, 55–58. Willimantic, CT: Curbstone Press. Reprinted in *Weeping Woman: La Llorona and Other Stories* (1994).

1993

Anzaldúa, Gloria. *Friends from the Other Side/Amigos del otro lado*. San Francisco: Children's Book Press.

Castillo, Ana. *So Far from God*. New York: Norton.

Forte-Escamilla, Kleya [Edna Eocamill]. *Mudu: An Erotic Novel*. Toronto: Sister Vision/Black Women and Women of Colour Press.

Gaspar de Alba, Alicia. *The Mystery of Survival and Other Stories*. Tempe, AZ: Bilingual Press/Editorial Bilingüe.

++Gomez, Marga. *Memory Tricks*. Teatro.

Villanueva, Alma Luz. "Her Choice." In *Infinite Divisions: An Anthology of Chicana Literature*, edited by Tey Diana Rebolledo and Eliana S. Rivero, 337–340. Tucson: University of Arizona Press.

1994

++*Brincando el charco: Portrait of a Puerto Rican*. Dir. and screenplay by Frances Negron-Muntaner. 55 min. 35mm and VHS. Dist. Women Make Movies.

++*Carmelita Tropicana: Your Kunst Is Your Waffen*. Dir. Ela Troyano. Screenplay by Carmelita Tropicana [Alina Troyano] and Ela Troyano. Music by Fernando Rivas. Dist. ITVS. First Run/Icarus Films.

de la Peña, Terri. *Latin Satins*. Seattle: Seal Press.

Forte-Escamilla, Kleya. *The Storyteller with Nike Airs and Other Barrio Stories*. San Francisco: Aunt Lute Foundation.

Garcia, Angela. "Yo, yo." In *Beyond Definition: New Writing from Gay and Lesbian San Francisco*, edited by Marci Blackman and Trebor Healey. San Francisco: Manic D Press.

Gaspar de Alba, Alicia. "Malinche's Rights." In *Currents from the Dancing River: Contemporary Latino Fiction, Nonfiction, and Poetry*, edited by Ray Gonzalez. New York: Harcourt Brace. 261–266. Translation of 1993 "Los derechos de la Malinche," *The Mystery of Survival and Other Stories*, 47–52.

++Gomez, Marga. *Marga Gomez Is Pretty, Witty, and Gay*. Teatro.

Moraga, Cherríe. *Heroes and Saints & Other Plays*. Boston: South End Press.

++Obejas, Achy. *We Came All the Way from Cuba So You Could Dress Like This?* Pittsburgh and San Francisco: Cleis Press.

Villanueva, Alma Luz. "Maya [from Dream]." In *Currents from the Dancing River: Contemporary Latino Fiction, Nonfiction, and Poetry*, edited by Ray Gonzalez, 275–291. New York: Harcourt Brace.

———. *Naked Ladies*. Tempe, AZ: Bilingual Review Press/Editorial Bilingüe.

———. *Weeping Woman: La Llorona and Other Stories*. Tempe, AZ: Bilingual Review Press/Editorial Bilingüe.

1995

Anzaldúa, Gloria. *Prietita and the Ghost Woman/Prietita y La Llorona*. San Francisco: Children's Book Press.

Chavez, Denise. *The Face of an Angel*. New York: Warner Books.

++Gomez, Marga. *A Line around the Block*. Teatro.

1996

de la Peña, Terri. "Caballito del Diablo." In *Out for More Blood*, edited by Victoria Brownworth and Judith M. Redding, 137–148. Chicago: Third Side Press.
———. "Refugio." In *Night Bites: Vampire Stories by Women*, edited by Victoria Brownworth, 165–178. Seattle: Seal Press.
Moraga, Cherríe. *Watsonville: Some Place Not Here*. Dir. Amy Mueller. Brava Theater Center, San Francisco.
++Obejas, Achy. *Memory Mambo*. San Francisco: Cleis Press.
Ortiz Taylor, Sheila. *Imaginary Parents*. Art by Sandra Ortiz Taylor. Albuquerque: University of New Mexico Press.
Pérez, Emma. *Gulf Dreams*. Berkeley: Third Woman Press.

1997

++Lopez, Erika. *Flying Iguanas: An Illustrated All-Girl Road Novel Thing*. New York: Simon & Schuster.
———. *Lap Dancing for Mommy: Tender Stories of Disgust, Blame and Inspiration*. Seattle: Seal Press.

1998

++Levins Morales, Aurora. *Remedios: Stories of Earth and Iron from the History of Puertorriqueñas*. Boston: Beacon Press.
++Lopez, Erika. *They Call Me Mad Dog! A Story for Bitter, Lonely People*. New York: Simon & Schuster.
Ortiz Taylor, Sheila. *Coachella*. Albuquerque: University of New Mexico Press.

1999

Alderete, Pat. "Fire." *Hers3: Brilliant New Fiction by Lesbian Writers*, edited by David Wolverton and Robert Drake, 147–151. Boston: Faber and Faber.
de la Peña, Terri. *Faults*. Boston: Alyson Press.
Gaspar de Alba, Alicia. *Sor Juana's Second Dream*. Albuquerque: University of New Mexico Press.
Limón, Graciela. *The Day of the Moon*. Houston: Arte Público.
Montes, Amelia. "While Pilar Tobillo Sleeps." *Hers3: Brilliant New Fiction by Lesbian Writers*, edited by David Wolverton and Robert Drake, 9–21. New York: Faber and Faber.
Pendleton Jimenez, Karleen. "The Lake at the End of the Wash." *Hers3: Brilliant New Fiction by Lesbian Writers*, edited by David Wolverton and Robert Drake, 177–181. New York: Faber and Faber.
Murray, Ixta Maya. *Locas*. New York: Grove Press.

2000

++Alvarez, Julia. *In the Name of Salomé.* New York: Penguin Putnam.

Montes, Amelia de la Luz. "R is for Ricura." In *Circa 2000: Lesbian Fiction at the Millenium,* edited by David Wolverton and Robert Drake, 160–176. New York: Alyson.

Moraga, Cherríe. "Heart of the Earth: A Popol Vuh Story." In *Puro Teatro: A Latina Anthology,* edited by Chela Sandoval-Sánchez and Nancy Saporta Sternbach. Tucson: University of Arizona Press.

———. *The Hungry Woman/A Mexican Medea.* In *Out of the Fringe: Contemporary Latina/Latino Theatre and Performance,* edited by Caridad Svich and María Teresa Marrero, 289–363. New York: Theatre Communications Group.

———. *Watsonville: Some Place Not Here . . .* In *Plays from the South Coast Reportory: Hispanic Playwright's Project,* edited by David Alfaro. New York: Broadway Play Publishing.

Palacios, Monica. *Greetings from a Queer Señorita.* In *Out of the Fringe: Contemporary Latina/Latino Theatre and Performance,* edited by Caridad Svich and María Teresa Marrero, 365–391. New York: Theatre Communications Group.

———. "Describe Your Work." In *Puro Teatro: A Latina Anthology,* edited by Chela Sandoval-Sánchez and Nancy Saporta Sternbach, 281–284. Tucson: University of Arizona Press.

++Troyano, Alina, et al. *I, Carmelita Tropicana: Performing between Cultures.* Boston: Bluestreak/Beacon.

Notes

Prologue

1. The Book Garden is a women's bookstore in Denver. Mama Bear's was a women's bookstore in Berkeley. Sisterhood Books was a women's bookstore in West Hollywood. Old Wyve's Tales was a women's bookstore in San Francisco. A Different Light is a gay and lesbian bookstore with branches in Los Angeles, San Francisco, and New York.

2. De la Peña 1989a.

3. Maya: Terri de la Peña, 1989a. Gloria: Rocky Gámez, 1983a, 1988, 1989. Josefa: Estela Portillo [Trambley], 1971. Catalina de Erauso, 1626. Xochitl: Alicia Gaspar de Alba, 1993d. Juana: Gaspar de Alba, 1999. Concepcíon: Gaspar de Alba, 1992a. Unnamed lover and unnamed beloved, Emma Pérez, 1996. Chulita: Edna Escamill [Kleya Forté-Escamilla], 1992. Esmeralda: Ana Castillo, 1993. Lucha: Cherríe Moraga, 1996. René: de la Peña, 1992. Sirena: Dolissa Medina, ca. 1995. Sinvergüenza: tatiana de la tierra is planning an anthology of Latina lesbian erotica titled *Las Sinvergüenzas*.

4. Nestle 1992.

5. Anzaldúa 1989; Gaspar de Alba 1993d; de Erauso 1626.

6. "In the Shadow of the Alamo" is an earlier title for Pérez's *Blood Memory, or, Forgetting the Alamo*. "Shadow of a man": Moraga 1991. "Someplace not here," Moraga 1996.

7. Machetes: Anzaldúa 1989. Tarot cards: Gaspar de Alba 1993d. Black orchids: Escamill 1992. Size-nines: Castillo 1996.

8. In 1991 there was speculation about whether *Margins* (de la Peña 1992) or *Gulf Dreams* (Pérez 1996) would appear in print first: which would be "the first Chicana lesbian novel"? In general, I avoid the canonical practice of naming "the first," but in this case I feel it is important to remind readers of Ortiz Taylor's much earlier novel and its sequel, *Southbound* (1990). Ortiz Taylor's third novel in the trilogy about the Chicana lesbian professor Arden Benbow, *Extranjera*, is currently in press.

Introduction

1. See R. Rodriguez 1998.

2. Using *This Bridge* as the starting point in the chronology of writings by women of color is also a point of contention, as Nancy Luna Jiménez brought to my attention in 1992. See also L. E. Pérez 1999.

3. Here and throughout, I am indebted to Luz Calvo (2000, 2001), Emma Pérez (1999), and Teresa de Lauretis (1994) for the significance of primal scenes and primal fantasies for Chicana lesbian cultural production.

4. In 2001 López's digital mural *Our Lady* was featured at the Museum of International Folk Art in Santa Fe, New Mexico. Like the representations of La Virgen de Guadalupe by Yolanda López and Éster Hernández in the 1980s and 1990s, *Our Lady* was critiqued as "blasphemous" and insulting to the culture of [orthodox Catholic] Chicano/as, especially by the archbishop of New Mexico, who called for its removal. For a chronology of the protests, see the Alma López website. Calvo (2004) provides a semiotic analysis and cultural contextualization of the blasphemy/censorship controversy.

5. "My silences have not protected me. Your silence will not protect you" (Lorde 1977).

6. Lorde spoke this phrase often. It has been reprinted in different essays (1978, 1982).

7. "Con su pluma en su mano"—With [her/his] pen in [her/his] hand. The phrase is Tish Hinojosa's. While Hinojosa is paying tribute to the Chicano scholar Américo Paredes, her song demonstrates that Chicana creativity puts Chicanas back in forms that are traditionally represented as masculinist. See chapter 9.

Chapter 1

1. Vol. 11, nos. 3–4. Now the *Americas Review*.

2. It's tempting to excuse this oversight precisely because this was a ground-breaking collection. However, it's important to remember that this volume was published two years after *This Bridge Called My Back* and the same year as *Cuentos* (see below).

3. Ironically, *Voces* did include a short story with a lesbian theme: Rosalie Otero's *Amelia*.

4. "Childhood Recaptured," "Our Families," "Our Neighbors," and "Our Landscapes." Other sections include "Tradición oral y memorate," on oral traditions and *memorate*—popular recollections of real-life events—and "Las mujeres hablan."

5. However, several of the contributions do allow for a lesbian reading, including Denise Chávez's "Love Poem," Margo Chávez's short story "Je reviens," and María Dolores Gonzales's *Self-Portrait*.

6. Which begs the question of whether they identified as lesbians at that time.

7. *Infinite Divisions* and *Women Singing in the Snow* are actually companion pieces for Tey Diana Rebolledo. *Infinite Divisions* is a compilation of Chicana literature that

fits Rebolledo's critical models. Much of the editorial introduction to *Infinite Divisions* is repeated and expanded in Rebolledo's critical volume, *Women Singing in the Snow*.

8. See also my discussion of Rebolledo's *Women Singing in the Snow*, below.

9. In a 1995 interview, Bernice Zamora takes exception to an (unnamed) critic who "made an innuendo that I was a lesbian" (Li 1995, 298).

10. See Appendix.

11. "La Ofrenda" is one of the most widely reprinted stories in Chicana lesbian fiction. See Appendix for full publication information.

12. While all of de la Peña's stories deal with Chicana characters, with the exception of "Tres mujeres," all of her short stories have been published in lesbian journals and anthologies. "Tres mujeres," which was published in *Frontiers* 11, a special issue on Chicanas, is not explicitly lesbian.

13. Before completing her first novel, *Margins*, de la Peña, published stories — "Mujeres morenas" and "Tortilleras" — featuring the main characters from the novel, although only "Mujeres Morenas" was included in *Margins*. In addition, de la Peña's fiction constructs a community of Chicana lesbian characters from the greater Los Angeles area.

14. María Herrera-Sobek, in a review blurb from the back cover of the book.

15. Rebolledo is by no means alone in this. For a discussion of the erasure of Anzaldúa's lesbianism, see D. González 1998.

16. In her 1998 essay, "Chicanas Theorize Feminism," the psychologist Aída Hurtado uses "sitios y lenguas" as her organizing theme, divorcing it from its lesbian beginnings. She does not trace the term to "Sexuality and Discourse" but rather to Pérez's essay "Irigaray's Female Symbolic." This later essay was originally published in 1994, although Hurtado dates it as 1997, the year that "Irigaray's Female Symbolic" was being reprinted in *Living Chicana Theory*.

17. De la Peña herself has written "nameless" characters in her short fiction an reserves the right to give her Chicana characters "American" names (e.g., Jessica).

18. This phrase is Caroline Allen's from *Following Djuna: Women Lovers and the Erotics of Loss*, in which she argues for a genealogy of lesbian literature beginning not with Radclyffe Hall's *The Well of Loneliness* but with Djuna Barnes's *Nightwood*. Although Allen's study was published before *Gulf Dreams*, Allen's phrase succinctly captures the dynamics of the relationship between the narrator and the young woman in Pérez's novel. See chapter 5 for further discussion of *Gulf Dreams*.

Chapter 2

1. In *La Malinche in Mexican Literature* (1991), Sandra Messinger Cypess demonstrates that the representation of La Malinche as traitor is a product of the Mexican nationalist period. From the colonial period to the nationalist period, La Malinche was held in high regard.

2. See Cotera 1977; C. E. Orozco 1986; Pesquera and Segura 1993. All are reprinted in Alma M. García (1997).

3. *Hungry Woman/Mexican Medea* is a rich text that allows for many different

meanings, and those meanings my shift over time. The first staged reading of the play was held in 1995. In the 2000 and subsequent publications, Moraga dedicates the play to the memory of native/Chicana/two-spirit artist and activist Marsha Gomez, who was killed by her son, Mekaya, in 1998. Whereas I draw from the discussions of Ana Cardona in my reading of the play, when read in relation to Gomez, the powerful emotions of the play would give a very different reading.

Chapter 3

1. Throughout this chapter, I mark the definite article in the phrase "'the' Aztec Princess," following Norma Alarcón's "Chicana Feminism: In the Tracks of 'the' Native Woman" (1990, 1998). Alarcón challenges the anthropological construction of native women as interchangeable (there is really only one native woman for whom all others are mere individual types) and Mexican nationalist constructs — such as Octavio Paz's "Hijos de la Chingada"—which attribute the Spanish conquest of the Americas to the compliance of native women, embodied in the person of Malinalli Tenepal and carried on as an "original sin" by all Mexican (and by extension Chicana) women. At the same time, Alarcón marks Chicana feminism's efforts to move beyond a nationalist construction of "La Chicana," which elides difference in favor of an imaginary unified subject, always already inscribed in relation to "El" Chicano/a.

2. Other variations of this myth suggest that Popocatépetl was not from a rival tribe but of "plebeian" origin. Pérez-Torres's retelling of this myth indicates that Popo is "guarding [Ixta's]pregnant body" (1995, 191). I have omitted the reference to the pregnancy in the quote above because I have not found it elsewhere and also because the paintings themselves give no indication of pregnancy. At the same time, this variation could serve to additionally mark the Aztec Princess as a sexual body: she is no virgin princess.

3. For further discussions of Native American women in the Anglo-American imaginary, see Green 1975; Dearborn 1986; Fiedler 1968.

4. See Cypess 1991, chaps. 1–3.

5. My thinking on this topic was originally influenced by Aureliano DeSoto. In his unpublished essay (1994), DeSoto discusses these calendars and the ways in which they evoke a pastoral Mexico for Chicana and Chicano/a viewers. Additional suggestions of images and sources have come from Keta Miranda, Luz Calvo, W. Phil Rodriguez, Maylei Blackwell, Shifra Goldman, Ondine Chavoya, and Eleanor Esquibel.

6. I have attempted to standardize the spellings Popocatépetl and Ixtacihuátl. Although the nicknames Ixta, Ixtli, and Mixtli are interchangeable, to avoid confusion I use Ixta throughout.

7. Because the Aztec themes of the calendars is well established, the imitation of Helgueran themes by other Mexican calendar artists may be largely pragmatic: the Mexican calendar publisher Calendarios Landín holds the copyright to Helguera's work, and thus to be competitive, other publishers must supply native themes by different artists.

8. For a discussion of Mexican calendar art and Chicano/a lived space, see Ybarra-Frausto 1986.

9. Elsewhere (Esquibel 2003b), I focus on three of Helguera's paintings from his series on Ixtacihuátl and Popocatépetl (*La leyenda de los volcanes, Grandeza azteca,* and *Amor indio*). Here I limit my discussion to *Amor indio* but acknowledge that it is part of a larger group of paintings.

10. See Pérez-Torres 1994 for a discussion of this poem as lesbian representation.

11. Ixta is dressed — or undressed — in a similar fashion in another of Helguera's paintings, *Gesto azteca*.

12. An earlier version of this essay was presented at the "New Perspectives in Chicana/Chicano/a Studies" conference at UCLA in spring 1997. At that time, the eminent art historian Shifra Goldman suggested that I look to the work of Saturnino Herrán as the inspiration for Helguera's calendars. Herrán was an artist of the revolution whose work valorized indigenous subjects. What I did not expect to find was that the chain of signification between Herrán, Helguera, and Terrill is actually a circle. Although the androgyny of Herrán's male figures was quite common for his period, when viewed through the lens of Joey Terrill's work, it is unexpectedly queer. Herrán's work could be retitled "Aztec Drag Queens" and easily become a cult symbol of queer Xicanísmo. It is perhaps this element that most clearly relates to Helguera's Ixta and Popo series. One sees a fetishization of the male Aztec figure that is not hypermasculine but instead more like the representations of Ixta.

13. Starting in the 1990s and continuing into the present, hundreds of women have been murdered in Juárez and Chihauhua city in Mexico. The Juárez murders have drawn the attention of Mexicana and Chicana feminists; they have challenged local police and governmental inaction, as well as efforts to dismiss the victims as prostitutes. In 2003, during *los días de los muertos*, the Chicano Studies Research Center at the University of California, Los Angeles, along with Amnesty International, hosted a conference organized by Alicia Gaspar de Alba titled "The Maquiladora Murders, or, Who Is Killing the Women of Juárez." The conference featured *testimonios*, activism, scholarship, creative writing, and memorials. *Chicana/Latina Studies: Journal of Mujeres Activas en Letras y Cambio Social* 4 (1) focuses on the murders and includes works by Alicia Schmidt-Camacho, Gaspar de Alba, Claudia Rodriguez, Evangelina Arce, Elena Poniatowska, Alma Lopez, and Favianna Rodriguez, among others.

14. Or folks who call themselves by that name when they come together for certain social or political goals.

15. In fact, reading the erotica becomes a prelude to a sex scene between Jessica and her friend and housemate Chic Lozano, whom Jessica sees as "a modern-day Chac-Mool, offering herself" (95). Interestingly, Adriana Carranza appears briefly in *Latin Satins* when Jessica's band performs at a lesbian bar in L.A. to an audience full of Chicana lesbians: "Jessica recognized many familiar faces: Toni Dorado, Alicia Orozco, Marti Villanueva, Monica Tovar, Adriana Carranza, Jen Avila, Pat Ramos, Veronica Melendez, and René Talamantes" (250). All are characters from de la Peña's short stories (1989b, 1989c, 1991a, 1989a, 1990c, respectively) and her first novel, *Margins* (1992).

16. Castañeda is discussing nineteenth-century historiographic texts of the American West.

17. "The Scholar and the Feminist IX" conference, held April 24, 1982. Proceedings published in Vance 1984. See also the coverage of the conference in *off our backs*, April–October 1982.

18. Fran Moira's coverage of "A Speak-Out on Politically Incorrect Sex," which included names of panel attendees.

Chapter 4

1. For example, Paz envisions the colonial primal scene (to use Calvo and Pérez's term) as the Spaniard having sex with a native woman, here embodied in the figure of Malintzin Tenepal (La Malinche), Cortés's native translator. According to Paz, all of Mexico acknowledges that La Malinche is "La Chingada," literally, "the fucked woman." Almost every Chicana feminist in academia has had to contend with Paz's discussion of "Los Hijos de la Chingada."

2. See, for example, Propper 1982; Freedman 1996.

3. It should be noted, however, that a lack of facts and documents regarding the natural father of Juana Inés (whom, in all likelihood, she never knew) does not keep Paz from spending most of two chapters speculating on what Juana must have felt for her absent father and how she must have resented her mother for his absence and for later taking another lover.

4. In fact, we see again Paz's pet theory, the "Oedipus Conquest Complex." (The term is Pérez's. See Pérez 1991, 1999; Calvo 2001.)

5. See Judith C. Brown's *Immodest Acts*, an account of Benedetta Carlini (1590–1661), a nun who engaged in sexual intercourse with one of her co-sisters; the history of Catalina de Erauso (1592?–1650); Israel Burshatin's and Sherry Velasco's work on Eleno/a de Céspedes (1545?–1588); and, of related interest, Jesús Fernández Santos's *Extramuros*, a lesbian novel about nuns during the Spanish Inquisition (seems to combine elements of Benedetta Carlini and Magdalena de la Cruz [d. 1560]).

6. See Bhaba 1994, 67.

7. I am interested in the questions and contradictions raised by Gaspar de Alba's critical analysis of Sor Juana's privileged position, not out of a desire to police the boundaries of mestizaje but because I think it provides an important context for reading her short story "Cimarrona."

8. These terms refer to *castas*, racially mixed subjects of New Spain. While there are more than fifty terms to describe precise racial mixture, these three are the most widely used. *Mestiza/o* refers to the offspring of Spaniards and Indians, *mulata/o* to the offspring of a Spaniards and Africans, and *zamba/o* to the offspring of Indians and Africans. Set against these are the *peninsulares* (or *gachupines*) and the *criollos*, the "racially pure" subjects of New Spain. *Peninsulares* were born in Spain; *criollos* were born in New Spain, of Spanish parents. *Peninsulares* held all high positions in the ruling hierarchy, a fact that was bitterly resented by the *criollos*.

9. Similar arguments have been made in relation to Emily Dickinson and her retreat from society.

10. Gaspar de Alba is arguing against Octavio Paz in particular. It is possible that Portillo would have been influenced by Paz: his biography, *Sor Juana Inés de la Cruz, o, las trampas de fé,* was first published in 1982, and Portillo's play was published the following year. However, it is more likely that Portillo wrote her play and saw it performed much earlier than 1983.

11. Elsewhere, the dramatist and essayist Cherríe Moraga has criticized Portillo for the overdetermined heterocentrism in her work, as well as for the ways in which her female protagonists are continually seeking paternal approval. See "The Obedient Daughter," Moraga's 1989 review of Portillo's novel *Trini.*

12. Portillo never describes Andrés or Slave Juana in racial terms. However, since the character Slave Juana appears to be based on Juana de San José, I have assumed that both characters are of African descent.

13. While Paz makes reference only to *criollos,* mestizos, and Indians in his narrative, Portillo, through the character of Father Antonio, deliberately and consistently marks a more racially complex Mexico, from the Indian villages in the mountain to "zambo slaves living in the hovels behind the rich men's house" (178).

14. I have altered this passage slightly for continuity. The final sentence actually comes earlier in Sor Juana's speech.

15. See Paz 1988, 504–508.

16. See also Mieka Valdez's rendering of Sor Juana and the vicereina in *Jotas in 'da Hood.* Valdez has conducted interviews with members of the Mexican lesbian organization El Closet de Sor Juana. *Jotas* is an altar to queer Xicanísma that lays claim to Sor Juana, representing her and the condesa through allusions to both Frida Kahlo's *Two Fridas* as well as to the anonymous portrait *Gabrielle d'Estree and One of Her Sisters at Bath.*

17. See note 2 above regarding "racial" categorizations in New Spain.

18. See also Gaspar de Alba 1999, 33.

19. At the end of the term of the Marques de Mancera in 1674, Fray Payo Enríquez de Rivera, archbishop of Mexico, was named viceroy. He was succeeded by Tomas Antonio de la Cerda, Marques de la Laguna, in 1680. His wife, María Luisa, Condesa de Paredes, was thus the next vicereina after Leonor Carreto.

20. Concepción is a recurring character in Gaspar de Alba's Sor Juana stories. Unlike the other characters mentioned here, Concepción does not appear to be based on a historical figure. In the stories, Concepción is a young *mestiza* novice who waits on Sor Juana. See chapter 4 for my discussion of Gaspar de Alba's "Cimarrona," in which Concepción is the main character.

21. It is important to note that many of the ideas in "Excerpts from the Sapphic Diaries" are pursued further in Gaspar de Alba's novel *Sor Juana's Second Dream* (1999), in which, for example, Juana develops an internal critique about her own attitudes toward Jane.

22. Gaspar de Alba later creates the character of Sor Felipa, a novice whose "swarthy features and ... wealth ... are attributed to a Jewish ancestry" (1999, 134). Sor Felipa tutors Concepción to help her achieve the level of literacy she

will need to serve Sor Juana as secretary. When Felipa becomes ostracized by the anti-Semitism in the convent she escapes the convent and is captured and held by the Tribunal of the Inquisition. Her family history is revealed: of Jewish origin, her family—like all Jewish subjects of Spain—was forced to convert to Catholicism but suspected of continuing to practice the Jewish faith. Her father and brothers "were crucified in their own olive grove, their foreheads branded with a Hebrew symbol [and her] mother took her own life as a result" (144). Felipa dies in the church dungeons—in all probability killed by guards or fellow prisoners—"There was a white crust on her tongue and human feces all over her face." Thus Felipa is another of the women of Sor Juana's era who, because of her race and class, lives a very different life from Sor Juana's gilded cage.

23. The sacking of Vera Cruz from May 17 to May 30, 1683, is briefly mentioned in Paz, 184.

24. Foolish men who accuse/woman for no reason/never seeing your own culpability/for the fault you find. (My translation.)

25. See chapter 4 for a complete discussion of Popocatépetl in the Chicano/Mexican imagination.

Chapter 5

1. See also Farwell 1993, who promotes a metaphoric usage of "lesbian," and de Lauretis 1994, chap. 4, who critiques such a usage at length. By "utopic," I am referring to texts that invoke the idea of lesbianism as an escape from the problems, inequalities, and power dynamics of heterosexual relationships, as if lesbian relationships would somehow be free of these (not to mention passion). Such a romanticization of "lesbian" is curiously akin to fantasies about the convent as just such an escape. See, for example, Alma Luz Villanueva's *Weeping Woman: La Llorona and other Stories* (1994), particularly "El Alma/The Soul, Three" (151–156), and Denise Chávez's *The Face of an Angel* (1995). In the latter, the fantasies of the convent and lesbianism as escapes from heterosexuality are united in the figure of Sister Lizzie (439–446).

2. An excellent case in point is Becky Birtha's "Johnnieruth" (1990), in which the eponymous heroine, a fourteen-year-old African American, constantly resists the gender expectations put on her by her mother and her neighborhood. While walking to church one day, Johnnieruth sees a woman—"this lady . . . She ain't nobody's mama—I'm sure"—who is not all dressed up and on her way to church but who (like Johnnieruth) is dressed comfortably, pleasing nobody but herself. As Johnnieruth turns to watch her walk by, the woman eyes her in recognition (73). Near the end of the story, Johnnieruth sees two women kissing "for a whole long time" (75). Again, they seem to recognize her and she them, and as she bicycles home, thinking about them kissing and then looking at her, she finds herself laughing "for no reason at all" (76).

3. I wish to reiterate that I discuss Chicana lesbian fictions in a Chicana literary context: I do not attempt either a history or a sociological study of Chicana girlhood friendships. Nor do I position these representations of Chicana girlhood

friendships within a universal, and thus problematic, construction of "lesbian" and/ or homosocial relations between women, which would merely inscribe Chicana lesbian fiction in a largely Anglo-American, northern European "tradition." While the characters or the texts themselves often construct Chicana sexuality against Mexicana and Anglo-American sexuality, with the former seen as more restrictive and the latter as less restrictive (see notes 15 and 21), I urge the reader to avoid slipping from the literary to the sociological: these texts represent stories Chicanas tell about themselves and their communities that may or may not have anything to do with the material social conditions of (sexual) lives. Indeed, any sociological statement about Chicana (or Mexicana, or Anglo) sexuality per se would flatten the heterogeneous, historically embedded, and conflictive ways in which sexuality is constructed in diverse Chicana/o communities. At the same time, however, the stories themselves become part of the material social conditions, so that even while arguing against slippage, I acknowledge the overlap.

4. I have deliberately chosen not to include comparable works that focus exclusively on adult friendships or adult sexual relationships, such as Estela Portillo Trambley's *Day of the Swallows* (1976), Sheila Ortiz Taylor's *Faultline* (1982), Ana Castillo's *The Mixquiahuala Letters* (1992), and Jeanne Córdova's *Kicking the Habit* (1990), to name but a few. Laura del Fuego's novel *Maravilla* (1989) could easily be included in the current study, as could short stories by Alma Luz Villanueva and Helena María Viramontes, which I hope to discuss in the future.

5. Rebolledo (1995, 199) mentions de la Peña only briefly: "The 1990's has brought forth a variety of *lesbian* novels and other creative materials about *lesbian* consciousness, including *Margins* by Terri de la Peña."

6. Rosaldo mistakenly identifies Esperanza's mother as supplying the shoes.

7. "Not a girl, not a boy, just a little baby" is one of the jump rope rhymes Nenny chants.

8. This is not to suggest that wanting to be *like* Sally is wholly divorced from wanting to be *with* Sally. I develop this more in relation to Rocío in *The Last of the Menu Girls*, below.

9. The phrase "justo y necesario" comes from the Catholic mass in Spanish. In English, it would be equivalent to just, right, or righteous and needful, although in the English-language mass, the equivalent of "Es justo y necesario" is "It is right."

10. See also Herrera-Sobek (1987), who recognizes that Esperanza's lament "is directed not only against Sally the silent interlocutor but at the community of women." Because Herrera-Sobek is discussing "Red Clowns" without reference to the other Sally stories, she minimizes the significance of Esperanza's relationship to Sally.

11. "Sally," "What Sally Said," "The Monkey Garden," "Red Clowns," and "Linoleum Roses" appear as numbers 32, 37, 38, 39, and 40, respectively.

12. The line actually reads, "For the ones I left behind. For the ones who cannot out." Yvonne Yarbro-Bejarano (1987, 143), reading from the first edition, gives the last line as "For the ones I left behind. For the ones who cannot get out." One could interpret "For the ones who cannot out," which appears in the second revised edition (Arte Público, 1988), as a printing error, with the verb accidentally omit-

ted. However, it seems likely that such an error would have been caught in the 1991 Vintage/Random House edition. I prefer to believe that Cisneros intentionally changed the line when she revised the manuscript in 1988, leaving the gap to be bridged by the reader.

13. "Willow Game" appeared in *Nuestro* (1982), "Evening in Paris" in *Nuestro* (1981), "The Closet" in the *Americas Review* (1986), and "Space Is Solid" in *Puerto del Sol* (1986).

14. Rosaldo's term for this connection is *matrimony*, used here as the female equivalent of *patrimony*, and thus matrilineal heritage. By choosing a term that already signifies the institution of heterosexual marriage, Rosaldo embeds a heteronormative understanding of women in general and of Rocío in particular.

15. There is an implication, however, that in Rocío's community Chicanas do not get abortions either.

16. Interestingly, Bertha, the "female" lesbian, never appears, although "Esperanza the dyke" (32) figures prominently in the ninth and eleventh sections of the story.

17. "His father was a [Seventh Day] Adventist" (my translation). That is, being from a strict religious background, he is unlikely to do such things as Rocío imagines.

18. The Los Angeles stories are "La Maya" (1989a), "Once a Friend" (1989b), "A Saturday in August" (1989c), "Tortilleras" (1989d), "Blue" (1990a), "Labrys" (1990c), "Mariposa" (1990b), "Beyond El Camino Real" (1991a), "Desert Quartet" (1991b), and "Mujeres Morenas" (1991c). Indeed, many of the characters from these stories and those from *Margins* appear in a community scene at the end of de la Peña's second novel, *Latin Satins* (1994, 250).

19. These works draw certain essentialized notions of identity and race in their idealized depictions of Chicana/Chicana relations. This is somewhat self-consciously done, since de la Peña is working in a publishing realm in which the majority of representations are of Anglo/Anglo lesbian couples, or, more infrequently, an Anglo woman with a woman of color. Indeed, a favorable but rather uninformed review of *Margins* in the *Advocate* explains that "the spectrum of lesbian literature includes so few Latina voices" because of "the dominance of the Catholic church" (Wolverton 1992, 40).

20. Closeted lesbians and bisexuals alike are represented as unhealthy partners.

21. Veronica's married (heterosexual) sister, Angela, does not appear in the novel. Like Joanna, Veronica's sister-in-law Connie died young and thus has assumed the sexual innocence of "an angel." This sexual innocence is limited to Chicanas, for Veronica's new sister-in-law, Joyce, an Anglo, is demonstrably passionate with her husband.

22. A view to which Veronica, Lucy, and indeed the Catholic church subscribe.

23. Lucy may again be echoing the Catholic church's judgment that while one does not choose to be a homosexual, one can—and should—refrain from acting on homosexual impulses.

24. This is the most basic outline of the novel. Structurally, there is also a second narrative, of memory, which produces abrupt images of molestation and sexually motivated violence directed against the narrator, as well as images of her turning violence against herself.

Chapter 6

1. My title situates my work in the genealogies of Chicana and Latina Lesbian writing. I call these histories "shameless"—whether or not they deal with explicit sexuality—because telling these stories is not only a political act but one which marks the writer as *una sinvergüenza*, a woman who knows no shame. "Shameless" is also inspired by the editorial work of tatiana de la tierra, whose most recent project, an anthology of Latina lesbian erotica, is titled *Las Sinvergüenzas*. De la tierra has played an important role in the publication and circulation of Latina lesbian writing. From 1991 to 1994 she was on the editorial board of *esto no tiene nombre*, a Latina lesbian magazine headquartered in Miami. On her own, de la tierra edited *conMoción* from 1995 to 1996. Both of these *revistas* published new writings by Latina lesbians, many of whom had never before appeared in print. At the same time, they included essays by, interviews with, and reviews of the works of more established writers, such as Cherríe Moraga, Gloria Anzaldúa, Luz Maria Umpierre, Achy Obejas, and Terri de la Peña.

2. "Talking Race, Talking Sex" syntactically invokes Gloria Anzaldúa's 1990 anthology, *Haciendo Caras: Making Face, Making Soul*, but more specifically, it marks the ways in which Chicana lesbian fictions that choose a historical setting simultaneously depict the race/class positions of Chicanas/os in the Southwest and articulate lesbian subjectivities.

3. Antonia Castañeda, "Memory, Language and Voice of Mestiza Women on the Northern Frontier" (1993a); Clara Lomas, "The Articulation of Gender in the Mexican Borderlands"; Amelia M. de la Luz Montes, "Rewriting the Present"; Rosaura Sánchez, "Nineteenth-Century Californio Narratives."

4. Alicia Gaspar de Alba and Aurora Levins Morales have made convincing arguments to recognize Sor Juana Inés del Cruz (1651?–1695) and "La Monja Alférez" (the Lieutenant Nun) Catalina de Erauso (1592?–1650) as Chicana lesbians. See Gaspar de Alba 1998, 1999; Levins Morales 1998.

5. Or perhaps queer novels about historical Chicanas. Limón, *The Day of the Moon*; Gaspar de Alba, *Sor Juana's Second Dream*; Montes, "As If in a Photographic Instance" (in progress); and Pérez, "Blood Memory: Forgetting the Alamo" (in progress).

6. Persephone Press was the original publisher of *This Bridge Called My Back: Writings by Radical Women of Color* (1981). According to Moraga and Anzaldúa, the first edition of *This Bridge* "had already gone out of print" when the press went out of business. It would be a safe assumption that Bulkin's anthology likewise was out of print even before 1983. See Moraga and Anzaldúa 1983, publishing note.

7. I.e., not working.

8. In "The Widowed Women of Santa Fe" (1990), González argues that Hispanic cultures have a larger percentage of single women than do Anglo societies, and that such women are more likely to be incorporated into family groups.

9. *Tortillera*, or tortilla maker, is a slang term for lesbian. (When you make tortillas, you slap your hands together back and forth: this can be read as a representation of tribadism.)

10. See also chapter 5 which shows how the "official discourse" of an obituary can erase a lesbian relationship. In her short story "Se le murió," GVR (a

pseudonym) demonstrates that lesbian relationships are glossed over at the death of one partner, precisely when the other partner is most in need of support.

11. Anzaldúa uses "marimacho" in the title, perhaps to emphasize the heroine's butch identity. Current usage is "marimacha," which I use when referring to the butch character.

12. Norma Alarcón's Third Woman Press now publishes the Mujer Latina series, the latest volume of which is Carla Trujillo's 1999 anthology, *Living Chicana Theory*.

13. The other is Adela Alonso's short story "Virgencita, danos chance" (1989).

14. In García's short story "Yo yo," the narrator chooses an outfit to visit her grandmother:

I've picked through [the clothes] a dozen times, dressing and undressing, studying myself in the mirror. With each try I see her, Marimacha. That's what I was called growing up. Marimacha: Macho María. (1994, 39)

15. The macha raised up her machete
    That day in San Juan Puñacuato.
    Don Rafo's fingers fell to the ground
    And his courage ran to the hills.

    Today you can still hear it said
    By the people of San Juan Puñacuato
    That a man is not worth a damn
    And huevos do not make the macho.

16. "What can we do, two women, without money, without friends, without land?"

17. My argument here is limited to this "La historia de una marimacha." In another context, Anzaldúa asserts:

As a mestiza I have no country, my homeland cast me out; yet all countries are mine because I am every woman's sister or potential lover. As a lesbian I have no race, my own people disclaim me; but I am all races because there is the queer of me in all races. ([1987] 1999, 102)

18. This has colonialist implications as well. For instance, describing the father after he is maimed, the marimacha says, "Parecía indio con su paño doblado alrededor de la cabeza tapando el agüjero que más antes fue su oreja"—the father, like the Indian men, is emasculated (67).

19. "I would not trade one second of my life with her, not for gold or silver."

20. "Our love is strong, papi, just like yours for mama. No love is cheap, not even the love of one woman for another."

21. "For you life is a struggle. . . . But . . . I am fearful."

22. "Our life is not going to be easy."

23. "Life is dangerous to all, rich or poor, man or woman."

24. "Yes, but it's more of a danger for women, and most of all to women like us."

25. See Gómez, Moraga, and Romo-Carmona 1983; Carter 1989; Holoch and Nestle 1990; Nestle 1992.

26. Bannon [1957] 1983c.

27. Neither Yvonne Keller nor the librarians at the lesbian pulp fiction archives at Duke University have been able to identify the title *Shadow of a Woman*. It may be a transposition of Bannon's *Women in the Shadows* (1959), or, as Keller has suggested, it may refer to a different pulp novel that we are unable to identify precisely because lesbian pulp fiction, in spite of its immense popularity, was an illegitimate form of discourse.

28. Bannon [1962] 1983a.

29. Bannon [1960] 1983b.

30. Claire Morgan [Patricia Highsmith] 1952.

31. Ann Aldrich [Marijane Meaker] 1960.

32. Aldrich 1958.

33. For a discussion of the trend in the late 1960s and early 1970s to make butch lesbians more assimilable, see Case 1989. In particular, Case argues that the lesbian organization Daughters of Bilitis actively discouraged butch identity. In their history of the Daughters of Bilitis, Del Martin and Philips Lyon (1991, 77) give a decidedly ageist and classist dismissal of butch-femme roles: "The minority of Lesbians who still cling to the traditional male-female or husband-wife pattern in their partnerships are more than likely old-timers, gay bar habituées or working class women. The old order changeth, however, and . . . the number of Lesbians involved in butch-femme roles diminishes."

34. Keller (1997, 44) describes these reprints as "re-vamped pulps."

35. I rely here on Keller's (1997, 46) classification.

36. Lee Lynch, "I read every one of these mass-market paperbacks I could get my hands on, always hungry for my life in literature" (1990, 40–41). Quoted in Keller 1997, 1.

37. Carla F. Scott (1993) discusses the portrayal of racism in Greenwich Village in Audre Lorde's *Zami*. Scott examines the ways in which the character Audre recognizes and names the manifestations of racism and exclusion in carding practices at the girl bars, which her white friends simply do not see. When Audre persists, the other women attempt to erase the specificity of racism toward blacks by invoking the narrative "all lesbians are discriminated against."

38. Rocky does not include Rosita Vargas, or for that matter, Adela, in her reckoning.

Chapter 7

1. See Pérez-Torres 1995, especially chap 3, "The Reformation of Aztlán."

2. "Que mueran los gachupines y que viva la Virgen de Guadalupe . . ."— the cry for independence issued by Father Hidalgo in the town of Dolores, Guanajuato.

3. *El Plan* evinces revolutionary energy that is similar to that in the Declaration of Independence, which proclaims the unalienable rights of the universal "man,"

while in the case of *El Plan* it is the rights of the bronze people, the bronze nation, that are articulated.

4. See my argument about "La Malinche" in chapter 3.

5. See also Emma Pérez's *Gulf Dreams,* which points out serious contradictions in the romanticized notion of "the Chicano community": in a highly publicized rape case, the defense lawyer for five men accused of raping a young woman disregards the actual rape of a Chicana by Chicanos and instead argues that the trial itself is a manifestation of racism against the Chicanos. This (nationalist) defense completely erases the young woman and the violence done to her. Pérez further highlights the sentimentalizing images of the Chicano/a family so prevalent in Chicana and Chicano writing in the way that she problematizes memory in the novel. As a child, the narrator experiences her grandmother as always disapproving, suspicious, rigid, and overly critical. When reflecting back on her family from adulthood, the narrator chooses instead an image of her grandmother making tortillas, thus admitting to her own sentimentalizing.

6. Hidalgo is also clearly alluding to Audre Lorde's "Poetry Is Not a Luxury."

7. See Hidalgo, below.

8. This and other translations of Hidalgo are my own.

I began to walk and after a while went into this place to have a soft drink. When I asked for a Pepsi-Cola, the man who worked there pointed out a sign which said "No Niggers, No Mexicans, No dogs," that is, that they did not permit blacks, mejicanos or dogs. My first impression was that I was not any of those things. But this impression lasted only a fraction of a second, and then I realized that yes, *I was all of those things and more.* I felt a tremendous fury and thought: "You will serve me." I think that the gentleman read the expression on my face, because he served me the Pepsi-Cola. I took the drink, and with all the fury that I had, broke the full bottle against the counter and left a half dollar.(Emphasis added)

9. She begins by relating her decision to leave the convent in Puerto Rico:

Pero llegó el momento en que me dije: "Bueno Hilda, tú no puedes vivir bajo el código de la Iglesia," aunque sin decirme en ese momento: "Hilda, tú eres lesbiana." Fue entonces cuando me salí del convento.

But there came a moment in which I said to myself: "Well, Hilda, you cannot live under the code of the Church, although *without saying to myself,* "Hilda, you are a lesbian." It was then that I left the convent. (72; emphasis added)

She foregrounds her sexuality, her inability to live as a lesbian in the church, and her decision to leave Puerto Rico. Although the "moment" she decides to leave the convent is clearly affected by her sexuality, it is not solely an instance of lesbian identification.

Following the confrontation, "Hidalgo" wanders the streets for several hours before catching the first bus out of Texas. She joins another friend in Washington, D.C., and becomes active in the black Civil Rights movement, noting that, because of the racism in the Puerto Rican community, she was the only Puertorriqueña to become involved.

10. McFarland, California.

11. Works such as *The Shrunken Head of Pancho Villa* (1967), *Salt of the Earth* (1953), and *Mi Familia* (1994) privilege the heteronormative family with a male breadwinner.

12. As a *comadre*, Amparo is Dolores's refuge. See my discussion of *comadrazgo* in chapter 5.

13. See de Lauretis 1994, chapter 5, "The Lure of the Mannish Lesbian." Although de Lauretis argues earlier that "it takes two women, not one, to make a lesbian" (283), her argument is that lesbianism is distinguished from feminist identification through sexual desire. Moraga literally challenges de Lauretis's terms, that the subject and the object of her desire "are both female-embodied" (284) through her creation of Cerezita, who is not female embodied but who nevertheless desires the female body through the sexual act.

14. See Luz Calvo's (2000) discussion of the semiotics of *la marimacha*.

15. Like Pilar in "La Maya" (see chap. 3), Freddie is the authentic indigenous Mexican, whom both Mario and Cerezita refer to as "the Mayan god."

16. In the real McFarland.

17. *Heroes and Saints* also allows for the possibility that Dolores's husband has had male lovers, but this possibility is disallowed in *Watsonville*.

18. See also Ruíz 1987; Soldatenko 2002; Zavella 1987.

19. These political situations of the 1980s were also clearly inspired by the U.S.-supported Chilean coup in 1973 and U.S. efforts in Latin America to suppress socialism in favor of pro-American dictatorships.

20. Based on the community of East Palo Alto, California.

21. An exploration of lesbian themes and representation in the death of Selena and the subsequent trial of Yolanda Saldívar.

22. See the 1985 documentary by the Cannery Workers Organizer's Project, *Sí Se Puede*.

23. See also "María Littlebear" in chapter 6, for a discussion of how a similar apparition in Holman, New Mexico, plays out in the racial economy of the 1940s. For more on the apparition of La Virgen, see René Moreno's video, *The Holy Tree*.

24. For a discussion of Proposition 187 and a semiotic analysis of the realms of representation, see Calvo 2001.

25. See Lora Romero's "When Something Goes Queer" and the historical accounts in Alma Gómez's collection, *Chicana Feminist Theory*.

26. "Chente," a nickname for Inocente, is semantically tied to Chencho or Inocencio, the rapist in Emma Pérez's *Gulf Dreams* (see chap. 5).

27. In *Salt of the Earth*, Ramón Quintero becomes discouraged when he hears the mine owners' strategy of "looking at the big picture."

28. Chente is distinct from Ramón Quintero, who labels Salvador Prieto a *vendido* when he catches him scabbing but will not hit him: "I wouldn't dirty my hands on you." Of course, the narrative itself ensures that the audience shares Ramón's judgment of Salvador.

29. See Anonymous 1997; Blackwell 2003; González 1998; Pérez 1994.

30. In this sense, then, Moraga disagrees with Teresa de Lauretis, who argues that it takes two women, not one, to make a lesbian. Cerezita's desire for (her own) lost female body and her close relation to Mario and to queer sexualities seem to reinvent her as queer.

31. That the monsignor is "Hispanic" could refer to the Spanish colonizers or a linkage between the monsignor and the Florida Hispanic Senator "Casanova," the champion of the national bill #1519 (the fictional version of California's Proposition 187). Moraga may also be referring to the University of California Board of Regents' dismantling of affirmative action in 1994. A Latino regent was extremely vocal against "special privileges" for Chicanos "over" other Latinos.

32. In April 1996 Moraga discussed this development at the conference "Transformations of Queer Ethnicities: A Conversation with Norma Alarcón and Cherríe Moraga" (Catrióna Rueda Esquibel, respondent). Queer Ethnic Studies Working Group, Doreen B. Townsend Center for the Humanities, University of California, Berkeley.

33. In the documentary *Chicano Park*, a Chicano/a community protests the city's rezoning of their area to permit heavy industry and salvage, producing the heaviest pollution in a residential area.

Chapter 8

1. Texas law enforcement jailed Cortez's wife, children, mother, sister-in-law, and injured brother, Romaldo (who died in custody). Mexicans suspected of assisting Cortez were lynched, shot, terrorized, and imprisoned.

2. "Ballad of Gregorio Cortez," Variant G, in Paredes 1958, 171–172.

> Then said Gregorio Cortez,
> With his pistol in his hand,
> "Ah, so many mounted Rangers
> Just to take one Mexican!" (Paredes's translation)

3. Robert Young's 1981 film, *The Ballad of Gregorio Cortez*, starring Edward James Olmos, is based on *"With His Pistol in His Hand."*

4. The girl's name is "Delgadina," whose literal translation is "the skinny girl." I also read this to refer to "the skeleton girl," i.e., the daughter who starves to death.

5. Delgadina's story also has several elements in common with the hagiography of Santa Bárbara. This virgin martyr converted to Christianity and refused to marry the man her father had chosen for her. Her father locked her in a tower and ultimately beheaded her. (He was subsequently struck by lightning.) In syncretic Santería, Santa Bárbara symbolizes Changó, the orisha of lightning.

Bibliography

Acuña, Rodolfo. 1988. *Occupied America: A History of Chicanos*. Third ed. New York: Harper & Row.

Alarcón, Norma. 1981. "Hay que inventarnos/We Must Invent Ourselves." *Third Woman* 1 (1): 4–6.

———. 1983. "Chicana's Feminist Literature: A Re-Vision through Malintzin/ or Malintzin: Putting Flesh Back on the Object." In *This Bridge Called My Back: Writings by Radical Women of Color*, edited by Cherríe Moraga and Gloria Anzaldúa, 182–190. New York: Kitchen Table/Women of Color Press.

———. 1989a. "The Sardonic Power of the Erotic in the Works of Ana Castillo." In *Breaking Boundaries: Latina Writings and Critical Readings*, edited by Asunción Horno-Delgado, Eliana Ortega, Nina M. Scott, and Nancy Saporta Sternbach, 94–107. Amherst: University of Massachusetts.

———. 1989b. "Traddutora, Traditora: A Paradigmatic Figure of Chicana Feminism." *Cultural Critique* 13 (Fall): 57–87.

———. 1990. "Chicana Feminism: In the Tracks of 'the' Native Woman." *Critical Studies* 4 (3): 248–256.

———. 2001. "Re: The Need for New Ways of Thinking." Email communication, posted to Professors for Peace discussion list, 09/28/2001, Message no. 546. Cited by permission of Norma Alarcón.

Alarcón, Norma, Ana Castillo, and Cherríe Moraga, eds. 1993. *The Sexuality of Latinas*. Berkeley: Third Woman Press.

Alarcón, Norma, Rafael Castro, Deena Gonzalez, Margarita Melville, Emma Pérez, Tey Diana Rebolledo, Christine Sierra, and Adaljiza Sosa Ridell, eds. 1993. *Chicana Critical Issues: Mujeres activas en letras y cambio social*. Chicana/Latina Studies. Berkeley: Third Woman Press.

Alarcón, Norma, and Cherríe Moraga. 1996. "The Right to Passion-Transformations of Queer Ethnicities." In *The Queer Ethnic Studies Working Group*. Berkeley: Doreen B. Townsend Center for the Humanities, University of California, Berkeley.

Albuquerque Museum, ed. 1994. *Man on Fire: Luis Jiménez/Hombre en llamas: Luis Jiménez*. Albuquerque: Albuquerque Museum.

Alcalá, Rita. 2003. "A Chicana Hagiography for the 21st Century: Ana Castillo's *Locas Santas*." In *Velvet Barrios: Popular Culture and Chicana/o Sexualities*, edited by Alicia Gaspar de Alba. New York: Palgrave/Macmillan.

Aldama, Arturo J., and Naomi H. Quiñonez, eds. 2002. *Decolonial Voices: Chicana and Chicano Cultural Studies in the 21st Century*. Bloomington: Indiana University Press.

Aldama, Frederick Luis. 2002. "Penalizing Chicano/a Bodies in Edward J. Olmos's *American Me*." In *Decolonial Voices: Chicana and Chicano Cultural Studies in the 21st Century*, edited by Arturo J. Aldama and Naomi H. Quiñonez, 78–97. Bloomington: Indiana University Press.

Aldrich, Ann [Marijane Meaker]. 1955. *We Walk Alone: Through Lesbos' Lonely Groves*. Greenwich, CT: Fawcett.

———. 1958. *We, Too, Must Love*. Greenwich, CT: Fawcett Gold Medal.

———. 1960. *Carol in a Thousand Cities*. Greenwich, CT: Fawcett Gold Medal.

Alfaro, Luis. 1998. *Chicanismo*. Produced and directed by Luis Alfaro. PBS Television.

Allen, Carolyn. 1996. *Following Djuna: Women Lovers and the Erotics of Loss*. Theories of Representation and Difference. Bloomington: Indiana University Press.

Almaguer, Tomás. 1991. "Chicano Men: A Cartography of Homosexual Identity and Behavior." *Differences* 3 (2): 75–100.

———. 1994. *Racial Faultlines: The Historical Origins of White Supremacy in California*. Berkeley: University of California Press.

Alurista, F. A. Cervantes, Juan Gómez-Quiñones, Mary Ann Pacheco, and Gustavo Segade, eds. 1976. *Festival de Flor y Canto: An Anthology of Chicano Literature*. Los Angeles: El Centro Chicano, University of Southern California.

Alvarez, Julia. 1995. *In the Time of the Butterflies*. New York: Plume (Penguin Putnam).

———. 2000. *In the Name of Salomé*. New York: Plume (Penguin Putnam).

Anaya, Rudolfo. 1984. *The Legend of La Llorona: A Short Novel*. Berkeley: Tonatiuh-Quinto Sol International.

———. 1994. *Bless Me, Ultima*. Quinto Sol Publications Edition. New York: Warner Books.

———, ed. 1988. *Voces: An Anthology of Nuevo Mexicano Writers*. Albuquerque: University of New Mexico Press.

Anaya, Rudolfo A., and Francisco Lomelí, eds. 1991. *Aztlán: Essays on the Chicano Homeland*. El Norte Press Edition. Albuquerque: University of New Mexico Press.

Anderson, Benedict. 1991. *Imagined Communities*. London: Verso.

André, María Claudia. 2003. "Empowering the Feminine/Feminist/Lesbian Subject through the Lens: The Representation of Women in María Luisa Bemberg's *Yo, la peór de todas*." In *Tortilleras: Hispanic and Latina Lesbian Expression*, edited by Lourdes Torres and Inmaculada Pertusa-Seva, 159–175. Philadelphia: Temple University Press.

Anonymous. [1971] 1997. "El Movimiento and the Chicana." In *Chicana Feminist Thought: The Basic Historical Writings*, edited by Alma M. García, 81–83. New York: Routledge.

Anzaldúa, Gloria. 1983. "El Paisano Is a Bird of Good Omen." In *Cuentos: Stories by*

Latinas, edited by Alma Gómez, Cherríe Moraga, and Mariana Romo-Carmona, 153–175. New York: Kitchen Table/Women of Color Press.

———. 1989. "La historia de una marimacho." *Third Woman* 4: 64–68.

———. 1993a. "Border Arte: Nepantla, Lugar de la Frontera." In *La Frontera/ The Border: Art about the Mexico/United States Border Experience,* edited by Patricio Chavez and Madeleine Grynsztejn, 107–114. San Diego: Centro Cultural de la Raza/Museum of Contemporary Art, San Diego.

———. 1993b. "Chicana Artists: Exploring Nepantla, el Lugar de la Frontera." *NACLA Report on the Americas* 27 (1): 37–43.

———. 1993c. *Friends from the Other Side/Amigos del otro lado.* San Francisco: Children's Book Press.

———. 1995. *Prietita and the Ghost Woman/Prietita y La Llorona.* San Francisco: Children's Book Press.

———. 1998. "To(o) Queer the Writer: Loca, Escritora y Chicana." In *Living Chicana Theory,* edited by Carla Trujillo, 263–276. Berkeley: Third Woman Press.

———. [1987] 1999. *Borderlands/La Frontera: The New Mestiza.* San Francisco: Spinsters/Aunt Lute.

Aparicio, Frances, and Susana Chávez Silverman, eds. 1997. *Tropicalizations: Transcultural Representations of Latinidad.* Re-Encounters with Colonialism. Hanover, NH: University Press of New England for Dartmouth College.

Araujo-Salinas, Laura. 1998. "Loving and Hating with the Same Passion: The Lesbian Consciousness in Roffiel's *Amora* and de La Peña's *Margins.*" Paper presented at the National Association of Chicana and Chicano Studies 25th Annual Conference, México, D.F.

Arrizón, Alicia. 2000. "Mythical Performativity: Relocating Aztlán in Chicana Feminist Cultural Productions." *Theatre Journal* 52: 23–49.

Artenstein, Isaac, dir. 1983. *Ballad of an Unsung Hero.* [Film] Cinema Guild, New York.

———. 1988. *Break of Dawn.* [Film] 1 hr., 40 min. San Diego, CA.

Baca, Jimmy Santiago. 1987. *Martín & Meditations on the South Valley.* New York: New Directions.

Bannon, Ann. [1962] 1983a. *Beebo Brinker.* Tallahassee, FL: Naiad Press.

———. [1960] 1983b. *Journey to a Woman.* Tallahassee, FL: Naiad Press.

———. [1957] 1983c. *Odd Girl Out.* Tallahassee, FL: Naiad Press.

———. [1959] 1983d. *Women in the Shadows.* Tallahassee, FL: Naiad Press.

Barcelo, Margarita Theresa. 1995. "Geographies of Struggle: Ideological Representations of Social Space in Four Chicana Writers." Ph.D. dissertation, University of California, San Diego.

Barnes, Djuna. 1937. *Nightwood.* New York: New Directions.

Barraza, Santa. 2001. *Santa Barraza: Artist of the Borderlands.* Borderlands (Río Grande/Río Bravo). College Station: Texas A&M Press.

Bemberg, María Luisa. 1990. *Yo, la peór de todas.* [Film] GEA Cinematografica, First Run/Icarus Films, New York.

Bergmann, Emilie. 1998. "Abjection and Ambiguity: Lesbian Desire in Bemberg's *Yo, la peór de todas.*" In *Hispanisms and Homosexualities,* edited by Sylvia Molloy and Robert McKee Irwin, 229–247. Durham, NC: Duke University Press.

Bergmann, Emilie L., and Paul Julian Smith, eds. 1995. *¿Entiendes? Queer Readings, Hispanic Writings*. Series Q. Durham, NC: Duke University Press.

Bernal, Martha E., and George P. Knight, eds. 1993. *Ethnic Identity. Formation and Transmission among Hispanics and Other Minorities*. 1st ed. United States Hispanic Studies. Albany: State University of New York Press.

Bethel, Lorraine. 1976. "Conversations with Ourselves: Black Female Relationships in Toni Cade Bambara's *Gorilla, My Love* and Toni Morrison's *Sula*." Unpublished manuscript.

Bhaba, Homi K. 1994a. *The Location of Culture*. London: Routledge.

———. 1994b. "The Other Question: Stereotype, Discrimination and the Discourse of Colonialism." In *The Location of Culture*, 66–84. London: Routledge.

Biberman, H. J. [Herbert J.]. 1953. *Salt of the Earth*. Los Angeles: Voyager Company.

———. 1965. *Salt of the Earth: The Story of a Film*. Boston: Beacon Press.

Birtha, Becky. 1990. "Johnnieruth." In *Breaking Ice: An Anthology of Contemporary African American Fiction*, edited by Terry McMillan, 71–76. New York: Penguin.

Blackman, Inge. 1994. *BD Women*. [Film] 20 min. Women Make Movies, New York.

Blackwell, Maylei. 2003. "Contested Histories: Las Hijas de Cuauhtemoc, Chicana Feminisms, and Print Culture in the Chicano Movement, 1968–1973." In *Chicana Feminisms: A Critical Reader*, edited by Gabriela Arredondo, Aida Hurtado, Norma Klahn, Olga Najera-Ramirez, and Patricia Zavella, 59–89. Durham, NC: Duke University Press.

Boutry, Katherine. 2000. "Black and Blue: The Female Body of Blues Writing in Jean Toomer, Toni Morrison, and Gayl Jones." In *Black Orpheus: Music in African American Fiction from the Harlem Renaissance to Toni Morrison*, edited by Saadi A. Simawe. New York: Garland.

Brady, Mary Pat. 1999. "The Contrapunctal Geographies of *Woman Hollering Creek and Other Stories*." *American Literature* 71 (1): 117–150.

———. 2002. *Extinct Lands, Temporal Geographies: Chicana Literature and the Urgency of Space*. Latin America Otherwise. Durham, NC: Duke University Press.

Brett, Guy. 1990. *Transcontinental: An Investigation of Reality*. London: Verso.

Brice, Jennifer. 1998. "Earth as Mother, Earth as Other in Novels by Silko and Hogan." *Critique* 39: 127–138.

Brice-Finch, Jacqueline. 2001. "Edwidge Danticat: Memories of Maafa." *Macomere: Journal of the Association of Caribbean Women Writers and Scholars* 4: 46–54.

Brincando el charco: Portrait of a Puerto Rican. 1994. Produced and directed by Frances Negrón-Muntaner. Women Make Movies, New York.

Brown, Isabel Zakerzewski. 1999. "Historiographic Metafiction in in the *Time of the Butterflies*." *South Atlantic Review* 64 (2): 98–112.

Broyles-Gonzalez, Yolanda. 1986. "Women in El Teatro Campesino: '¿Apoca Estaba Molacha La Virgen De Guadalupe?'" In *Chicana Voices: Intersections of Class Race and Gender*, edited by Teresa Córdoba, 162–187. Austin: Center for Mexican American Studies.

———. 1989. "Toward a Re-Vision of Chicano Theater History: The Women of El Tearo Campesino." In *Making a Spectacle: Feminist Essays on Contemporary Women's*

Theatre, edited by Lynda Hart, 209–238. Ann Arbor: University of Michigan Press.

———. 1994. *El Teatro Campesino: Theater in the Chicano Movement*. Austin: University of Texas Press.

———. 2001. *Lydia Mendoza's Life in Music/La historia de Lydia Mendoza*. Oxford: Oxford University Press.

Bruce-Novoa, Juan. 1990a. "Canonical and Non-Canonical Literature." In *Retrospace: Collected Essays on Chicano Literature*, 132–145. Houston: Arte Público.

———. 1990b. *Retrospace: Collected Essays on Chicano Literature, Theory, and History*. Houston: Arte Público.

———. 1994a. "Dialogical Strategies, Monological Goals: Chicano Goals." In *An Other Tongue*, edited by Alfred Arteaga, 226–245. Durham, NC: Duke University Press.

———. 1994b. "Sheila Ortiz Taylor's *Faultline*: A Third Woman Utopia." In *Chicana (W)Rites on Word and Film*, edited by María Herrera-Sobek and Helena María Viramontes, 225–244. Berkeley: Third Woman Press.

Buitrón, Robert C.1989a. "Ixta Ponders Leverage Buyout." In *Chicano Art: Resistance and Affirmation*. Los Angeles: Wight Art Gallery, University of California.

———. 1995. "Artist's Statement." In *From the West: Chicano Narrative Photography*, edited by Chon A. Noriega, 24. Seattle: University of Washington Press.

Bulkin, Elly, ed. 1981. *Lesbian Fiction: An Anthology*. Watertown, MA: Persephone Press.

Burgin, Victor. 1982. "Looking at Photographs." In *Thinking Photography*, edited by Victor Burgin, 142–153. London: Macmillan.

Burns, Diane. 1983. "Sure, You Can Ask Me a Personal Question." In *Songs from This Earth on Turtle's Back*, edited by Joseph Bruchac. New York: Greensfield Review Press.

Butler, Judith. 1991. "Imitation and Gender Insubordination." In *Inside/Out: Lesbian Theories, Gay Theories*, edited by Diana Fuss, 13–31. New York: Routledge.

———. 1993. *Bodies That Matter: On the Discursive Limits of "Sex."* New York: Routledge.

Calvo, Luz. 2000. "Impassioned Icons: Alma Lopez and Queer Chicana Visual Desire." Paper presented at the American Studies Association, Detroit, MI.

———. 2001. "Border Fantasies: Sexual Anxieties and Political Passions in the U.S./ Mexico Borderlands." Ph.D. dissertation, University of California, Santa Cruz.

———. 2002. "'Lemme Stay, I Want to Watch': Ambivalence in Borderlands Cinema." In *Latino/a Popular Culture*, edited by Michelle Habell-Pallán and Mary Romero, 73–81. New York: New York University Press.

———. 2004. "Art Comes for the Archbishop: Contemporary Chicana Feminist Struggle." *Meridians: Feminism, Race, Transnationalism*. Middletown, CT: Wesleyan University Press.

Candelaria, Cordelia. 1980. "La Malinche: Feminist Prototype." *Frontiers* 5, no. 2 (Summer): 1–6.

———. 1986. *Chicano Poetry: A Critical Introduction*. Westport, CT: Greenwood Press.

Cantú, Norma. 1995. *Canícula: Snapshots of a Girlhood en la Frontera.* Albuquerque: University of New Mexico Press.

Cantú, Norma, and Ofelia Zapata Vela. 1991. "The Mexican-American Quilting Traditions of Laredo, San Ygnacio, and Zapata." In *Hecho en Tejas: Texas-Mexican Folk Arts and Crafts,* edited by Joe S. Graham, 77–92. Denton: University of North Texas Press.

Cantú, Norma, and Olga Nájera-Ramírez, eds. 2002. *Chicana Traditions: Continuity and Change.* Urbana: University of Illinois Press.

Carby, Hazel V. 1987. *Reconstructing Womanhood: The Emergence of the Afro-American Woman Novelist.* New York: Oxford University Press.

Cardenas de Dwyer, Carlota, ed. 1975. *Chicana Voices.* Boston: Houghton Mifflin.

Carrillo, Jo. 1981. "María Littlebear." In *Lesbian Fiction: An Anthology,* edited by Elly Bulkin, 17–23. Watertown, MA: Persephone Press.

Carter, Angela, ed. 1989. *Wayward Girls and Wicked Women: An Anthology of Stories.* Virago Edition. New York: Penguin.

Case, Sue-Ellen. 1989. "Towards a Butch-Femme Aesthetic." In *Making a Spectacle: Feminist Essays on Contemporary Women's Theatre,* edited by Lynda Hart, 282–299. Ann Arbor: University of Michigan Press.

———, ed. 1990. *Performing Feminisms.* Baltimore: Johns Hopkins University Press.

Castañeda, Antonia I. 1990a. "Gender, Race, and Culture: Spanish-Mexican Women in the Historiography of Frontier California." *Frontiers* 9 (1): 8–20.

———. 1990b. "The Political Economy of Nineteenth-Century Stereotypes of *Californianas.*" In *Between Borders: Essays on Mexicana/Chicana History,* edited by Adelaida R. Del Castillo, 213–236. Encino, CA: Floricanto Press.

———. 1992. "Women of Color and the Rewriting of Western History: The Discourse, Politics and Decolonization of History." *Pacific Historical Review* 21 (3): 501–533.

———. 1993a. "Memory, Language and Voice of Mestiza Women on the Northern Frontier: Historical Documents as Literary Text." In *Recovering the U.S. Hispanic Literary Heritage,* edited by Ramón Gutiérrez and Genaro Padilla, 265–278. Houston: Arte Público.

———. 1993b. "Sexual Violence in the Politics and Policies of Conquest: Amerindian Women and the Spanish Conquest of Alta California." In *Building with Our Hands: New Directions in Chicana Studies,* edited by Adela de la Torre and Beatríz M. Pesquera, 15–33. Berkeley: University of California Press.

———. 1998. "History and the Politics of Violence against Women." In *Living Chicana Theory,* edited by Carla Trujillo, 310–319. Berkeley: Third Woman Press.

———. 2001. "'Que Se Pudieran Defender (So You Could Defend Yourselves)': Chicanas, Regional History and National Discourses." *Frontiers* 22 (3): 166–142.

Castilla, Margarita, Vanessa Cruz, tatiana de la tierra, Patricia Pereira-Pujol, and Lori Cardona. 1993. "Rincón editorial." *este no tiene nombre* 2 (3): 4.

Castillo, Ana. 1992. *The Mixquiahuala Letters.* Bilingual Press/Editorial Bilingüe Edition. New York: Anchor Books.

———. 1993. *So Far from God.* New York: Norton.

————. 1994a. "Ixtacihuatl Died in Vain." In *My Father Was a Toltec and Selected Poems, 1973–1988*, 39–41. New York: Norton.

————. 1994b. *My Father Was a Toltec and Selected Poems, 1973–1988*. New York: Norton.

————. 1996a. "Crawfish Love." In *Loverboys*, 131–134. New York: Norton.

————, ed. 1996b. *Goddess of the Americas*. New York: Riverhead Books.

Cervantes, Lorna Dee. 1981a. "Beneath the Shadow of the Freeway." In *Emplumada*, 11–14. Pittsburgh: University of Pittsburgh Press.

————. 1981b. *Emplumada*. Pittsburgh: University of Pittsburgh Press.

————. 1988. "Bird Ave." In *Chicana Creativity and Criticism: Charting New Frontiers in American Literature*, edited by María Herrera-Sobek and Helena María Viramontes. Houston: Arte Público.

Chabram, Angie. 1991. "Conceptualizing Chicano Critical Discourse." In *Criticism in the Borderlands: Studies in Chicano Literature, Culture, and Ideology*, edited by Héctor Calderón and José David Saldívar, 125–148. Durham, NC: Duke University Press.

Chabram-Dernersesian, Angie. 1992. "I Throw Punches for My Race, but I Don't Want to Be a Man: Writing Us — Chica-Nos/Chicanas — into the Movement Script." In *Cultural Studies*, edited by Lawrence Grossberg, Cary Nelson, and Paula Treichler, 81–95. London: Routledge.

————. 1993. "And, Yes . . . the Earth Did Part: On the Splitting of Chicana/o Subjectivity." In *Building with Our Hands: New Directions in Chicana Studies*, edited by Adela de la Torre and Beatríz Pesquera, 34–56. Berkeley: University of California Press.

Chávez, Denise. 1987. *The Last of the Menu Girls*. Houston: Arte Público.

————. 1988. "Novenas Narrativas." In *Chicana Creativity and Criticism*, edited by María Herrera-Sobek and Helena María Viramontes, 85–100. Houston: Arte Público.

————. 1995. *The Face of an Angel*. New York: Warner Books.

Chávez, John R. 1984. *The Lost Land: The Chicano Image of the Southwest*. Albuquerque: University of New Mexico Press.

Christian, Karen. 1992. "Will the 'Real Chicano' Please Stand Up? The Challenge of John Rechy and Sheila Ortiz Taylor to Chicano Essentialism." *Americas Review* 20, no. 2 (Summer): 89–104.

Chrystos. 1993. *In Her I Am*. Vancouver: Press Gang Publishers.

Cisneros, Sandra. 1991a. *The House on Mango Street*. Arte Público Edition. New York: Vintage.

————. 1991b. *Woman Hollering Creek, and Other Stories*. New York: Random House.

Cliff, Michelle. 1980. *Claiming an Identity They Taught Me to Despise*. Watertown, MA: Persephone Press.

Cobos, Rubén. 1983. *A Dictionary of New Mexico and Southern Colorado Spanish*. Sante Fe: Museum of New Mexico Press.

Cooper Alarcón, Daniel. 1997. *The Aztec Palimpsest: Mexico in the Modern Imagination*. Tucson: University of Arizona Press.

Córdova, Jeanne. 1985. "My Immaculate Heart." In *Lesbian Nuns*, edited by Rosemary Curb and Nancy Manahan, 3–15. Tallahassee, FL: Naiad Press.

———. 1990. *Kicking the Habit: A Lesbian Nun Story*. Los Angeles: Multiple Dimensions.

Corinne, Tee. 1989. *Intricate Passions*. Austin, TX: Banned Books.

———. 1991. *Riding Desire: An Anthology of Erotic Writing*. Austin, TX: Banned Books.

Corona, Mireya. 1996. Review of *Latin Satins*. *conMoción* 2: 13.

Cosme, Rose. 1993. Review of *Margins*. *esto no tiene nombre* 2 (2): 7.

Cotera, Marta P. 1977. *The Chicana Feminist*. Austin, TX: Information Systems Development.

———. 1980. "Feminism: The Chicana and Anglo Versions, a Historical Analysis." In *Twice a Minority: Mexican American Women*, edited by Margarita B. Melville, 217–234. St. Louis: Mosby.

Cruz, Manuel. 1974. "Untitled (Homeboy)." Albuquerque: Social and Public Art Resource Center and University of New Mexico Press.

Curb, Rosemary, and Nancy Manahan, eds. 1986. *Lesbian Nuns: Breaking Silence*. Naiad Edition. New York: Warner Books.

Cypess, Sandra Messinger. 1991. *La Malinche in Mexican Literature from History to Myth*. Texas Pan American Series. Austin: University of Texas Press.

Dash, Julie. 1992. *Daughters of the Dust (Screenplay)*. In *Daughters of the Dust: The Making of an African American Woman's Film*, 73–164. New York: New Press.

Davalos, Karen Mary. 2001. *Exhibiting Mestizaje: Mexican (American) Museums in the Diaspora*. Albuquerque: University of New Mexico.

Davis, Angela Yvonne. 1998. *Blues Legacies and Black Feminism: Gertrude "Ma" Rainey, Bessie Smith, and Billie Holiday*. New York: Pantheon.

de Erauso, Catalina. [1626] 1996. *Lieutenant Nun: Memoir of a Basque Transvestite in the New World*. Translated by Michele Stepto and Gabriel Stepto. Boston: Beacon Press.

de la Cruz, Sor Juana Inés. 1994. *The Answer/La respuesta*. Translated by Amanda Powell. Old Westbury, NY: Feminist Press.

de la Mora, Sergio. 1995. "Giving It Away: *American Me* and the Defilement of Chicano Manhood." Paper presented at Cine-Estudiantil Film Festival, March 7–11, Central Cultura de la Raza, San Diego.

———. 2003. "The Lessons of Chicana Lesbian Fictions and Theories." In *Chicana Feminisms: A Critical Reader*, edited by Gabriela Arredondo, Aida Hurtado, Norma Klahn, Olga Nájera-Ramírez, and Patricia Zavella, 178–184. Durham, NC: Duke University Press.

de la Peña, Terri. 1989a. "La Maya." In *Intricate Passions*, edited by Tee Corinne, 1–10. Austin, TX: Banned Books.

———. 1989b. "Once a Friend." In *The One You Call Sister*, edited by Paula Martinac, 49–62. San Francisco: Cleis Press.

———. 1989c. "A Saturday in August." In *Finding Courage*, edited by Irene Zahava, 141–150. Freedom, CA: Crossing Press.

———. 1989d. "Tortilleras." In *Lesbian Bedtime Stories*, edited by Terry Woodrow, 83–92. Willits, CA: Tough Dove Books.

————. 1990a. "Blue." In *Riding Desire*, edited by Tee Corinne, 149–153. Austin, TX: Banned Books.

————. 1990b. "Labrys." In *Word of Mouth*, edited by Irene Zahava, 31. Freedom, CA: Crossing Press.

————. 1990c. "Mariposa." In *Lesbian Bedtime Stories 2*, edited by Terry Woodrow, 7–19. Willits, CA: Tough Dove Books.

————. 1990d. "Tres Mujeres." *Frontiers* 11 (1): 60–64.

————. 1991a. "Beyond El Camino Real." In *Chicana Lesbians: The Girls Our Mothers Warned Us About*, edited by Carla Trujillo, 85–94. Berkeley: Third Woman Press.

————. 1991b. "Desert Quartet." In *Lesbian Love Stories 2*, edited by Irene Zahava, 154–161. Freedom, CA: Crossing Press.

————. 1991c. "Mujeres Morenas." In *Lesbian Love Stories 2*, edited by Irene Zahava, 85–93. Freedom, CA: Crossing Press.

————. 1992. *Margins*. Seattle: Seal Press.

————. 1993a. "Letter to the Editors." *esto no tiene nombre* 2 (4): 1.

————. 1993b. "Still on the *Margins*." *esto no tiene nombre* 2 (3): 6.

————. 1994a. "Connecting and Forgiving: The Writings of Chicana Lesbians." *Lesbian Review* 1 (2): 27.

————. 1994b. *Latin Satins*. Seattle: Seal Press.

————. 1994c. "Of Cursors and Kitchen Tables." *off our backs* 24, no. 6 (June): 10.

————. 1994d. "Spoken Words." *off our backs* 24, no. 6 (June): 10–11.

————. 1995. "Second Thoughts about Sweaty Pages." *conMoción* 2: 36.

————. 1996. Review of *Gulf Dreams*. *Sojourner* 22: 3.

————. 1999. *Faults*. Boston: Alyson Press.

de Lauretis, Teresa. 1987. *Technologies of Gender: Essays on Theory, Film, and Fiction*. Theories of Representation and Difference. Bloomington: Indiana University Press.

————. 1994. *The Practice of Love: Lesbian Sexuality and Perverse Desire*. Bloomington: Indiana University Press.

————. 1996. "Closing the Gulf between Us." *Lesbian Review of Books* 2 (4): 4.

de Quincey, Thomas. 1882. *The Spanish Nun*. Lovell's Library. New York: Allen Bros.

Dearborn, Mary V. 1986. *Pocahontas's Daughters*. New York: Oxford University Press.

Del Castillo, Adelaida R. 1977. "Malintzín Tenépal: A Preliminary Look into a New Perspective." In *Essays on La Mujer*, edited by Rosaura Sánchez and Rosa Martinez Cruz, 124–149. Los Angeles: University of California, Los Angeles, Chicano Studies Center Publications.

————. 1990. *Between Borders: Essays on Mexicana/Chicana History*. La Mujer Latina Series. Encino, CA: Floricanto Press.

Delgadillo, Theresa. 1998. "Forms of Chicana Feminist Resistance: Hybrid Spiritualities in Ana Castillo's *So Far from God*." *Modern Fiction Studies* 44 (4): 888–916.

DeSoto, Aureliano. 1993. "'There Is No 'There' There': Aztlán, Chicanísmo, and Diasporic Alternatives." Unpublished manuscript.

————. 1994. "Unreconciled Nostalgia: The Invention of 'México' and Cherríe

Moraga's *The Last Generation*." Paper presented at the National Association of Chicano Studies Northern California Regional Conference, University of California, Santa Cruz.

Dewey, Janice. 1989. "Doña Josefa: Bloodpulse of Transition and Change." In *Breaking Boundaries: Latina Writings and Critical Readings*, edited by Asunción Horno-Delgado, Eliana Ortega, Nina M. Scott, and Nancy Saporta Sternbach, 39–47. Amherst: University of Massachusetts Press.

Díaz, Gina. 1998. "Gender Performance in Chicana Lesbian Fiction." Paper presented at the Mujeres Activas en Letras y Cambio Social (MALCS) Summer Institute, University of California, Santa Cruz.

Díaz del Castillo, Bernal. [1632] 1963. *The Conquest of New Spain*. Translated by J. M. Cohen. New York: Penguin Classics. Original in Spanish.

DuBois, Ellen Carol, and Vicky L. Ruíz, eds. 1990. *Unequal Sisters*. New York: Routledge.

Duggan, Lisa. 2000. *Sapphic Slashers: Sex, Violence, and American Modernity*. Durham, NC: Duke University Press.

Dunye, Cheryl. 1996. *The Watermelon Woman*. [Film] First Run Films, New York.

El Norte. 1983. [Film]. Produced and directed by Gregory Nava and Anna Thomas. Frontera Films.

Enloe, Cynthia. 1990. *Bananas, Beaches, and Bases: Making Feminist Sense of International Politics*. Pandora Edition. Berkeley: University of California Press.

Escamill, Edna. 1992. "Black Orchid." *Sinister Wisdom* 47 (Summer–Fall): 78–81. Reprinted in Forte-Escamilla 1994.

Espinosa, Monica. 1994. "The Closet in Denise Chávez's *Last of the Menu Girls*." Paper presented at the 6th European Conference on Latino Cultures in the U.S., Bordeaux, France.

Esquibel, Catrióna Rueda. 1998. "Memories of Girlhood: Chicana Lesbian Fictions." *Signs* 23 (3): 644–681.

———. 1999. "Chicana Lesbian Fictions: Ambivalence, Erotics, and Authenticity." Ph.D. dissertation, University of California, Santa Cruz.

———. 2002. *A Bibliography of Queer Chicana Fictions* [Online]. [Cited 1994, 2003]. Available from www.chicana-lesbians.com.

Faderman, Lillian. 1991. *Odd Girls and Twilight Lovers: A History of Lesbian Life in Twentieth-Century America*. (*Between Men–Between Women*). New York: Penguin.

———. 1995. "What Is Lesbian Literature? Forming a Historical Canon." In *Professions of Desire: Lesbian and Gay Studies in Literature*, edited by George E. Haggerty and Bonnie Zimmerman, 49–59. New York: Modern Language Association of America.

Fanon, Frantz. 1967. *Black Skin, White Masks*. Translated by Charles Lam Markmann. New York: Grove Weidenfeld.

Farwell, Marilyn R. 1993. "Toward a Definition of the Lesbian Literary Imagination." In *Sexual Practice, Textual Theory: Lesbian Cultural Criticism*, edited by Susan J. Wolfe and Penelope Stanley, 66–84. Cambridge, MA: Blackwell.

Feinberg, Leslie. 1993. *Stone Butch Blues*. Ithaca, NY: Firebrand.

Fernández, Roberta. 1989. "'The Cariboo Cafe': Helena Maria Viramontes Discourses with Her Social and Cultural Contexts." *Women's Studies* 17 (1–2): 71–86.

———. 1994. "Abriendo Caminos in the Brotherland: Chicana Writers Respond to the Ideology of Literary Nationalism." *Frontiers* 14 (2): 23–51.

———, ed. 1994. *In Other Words: Literature by Latinas of the United States*. Houston: Arte Público.

Fernández, Salvador C. 2003. "Coming-out Stories and the Politics of Identity in the Narrative of Terri de la Peña." In *Tortilleras: Hispanic and Latina Lesbian Expression*, edited by Lourdes Torres and Inmaculada Pertusa-Seva, 68–80. Philadelphia: Temple University Press.

Fernández Santos, Jesús. 1984. *Extramuros*. Translated by Helen R. Lane. Twentieth-Century Continental Fiction. New York: Columbia University Press.

Feyder, Linda, ed. 1992. *Shattering the Myth: Plays by Hispanic Women*. Houston: Arte Público.

Fiedler, Leslie. 1968. *The Return of the Vanishing American*. New York: Stein and Day.

Flores-Muñoz, Shirley. 1997. "Pedagogy and Resistance: Teaching the Histories of U.S. Women of Color." Ph.D. dissertation, University of California, Santa Cruz.

Forté-Escamilla, Kleya [Edna Escamill]. 1993. *Mada: An Erotic Novel*. Toronto: Sister Vision/Black Women and Women of Colour Press.

———. 1994. *The Storyteller with Nike Airs and Other Barrio Stories*. San Francisco: Aunt Lute Foundation.

Foster, David William, ed. 1999. *Chicano/Latino Homoerotic Identities*. Latin American Studies, vol. 17. New York: Garland.

Foucault, Michel. 1972. *The Archaeology of Knowledge and the Discourse on Language*. Translated by A. M. Sheridan Smith. New York: Pantheon.

———. 1990. *The History of Sexuality, an Introduction*. New York: Vintage.

———. 1994. *The Order of Things: An Archaeology of the Human Sciences*. New York: Vintage.

Franco, Jean. 1989. *Plotting Women: Gender and Representation in Mexico*. New York: Columbia University Press.

Freedman, Estelle B. 1996. "The Prison Lesbian: Race, Class, and the Construction of the Aggressive Female Homosexual, 1915–1965." *Feminist Studies* 22 (2): 397–423.

Fregoso, Rosa Linda. 1993a. *The Bronze Screen: Chicana and Chicano Film Culture*. Minneapolis: University of Minnesota Press.

———. 1993b. "Humor as Subversive De-Construction: Born in East L.A." In *The Bronze Screen: Chicana and Chicano Film Culture*, 49–64. Minneapolis: University of Minnesota Press.

———. 2001. *Lourdes Portillo: The Devil Never Sleeps and Other Films*: University of Texas Press.

Fregoso, Rosa Linda, and Angie Chabram. 1990. "Introduction: Chicana/o Cultural Representations: Reframing Alternative Critical Discourses." *Cultural Studies* 4 (3): 203–212.

French, Laurence. 1978. "The Perversion of Incarceration: A Social-Psychological Perspective." *Corrective and Social Psychiatry & Journal of Behavior Technology, Methods and Therapy* 24 (1): 16–19.

Frilot, Shari. 1996. *Black Nations/Queer Nations? Lesbian and Gay Sexualities in the African Diaspora*. New York: Third World Newsreel.

Fusco, Coco. 1995. *English Is Broken Here: Notes on Cultural Fusion in the Americas*. New York: New Press.

Gámez, Rocky. 1983a. "Doña Marciana García." In *Cuentos: Stories by Latinas*, edited by Alma Gómez, Cherríe Moraga, and Mariana Romo-Carmona, 7–15. New York: Kitchen Table/Women of Color Press.

———. 1983b. "From *The Gloria Stories*." In *Cuentos: Stories by Latinas*, edited by Alma Gómez, Cherríe Moraga, and Mariana Romo-Carmona, 138–146. New York: Kitchen Table/Women of Color Press.

———. 1988. "A Baby for Adela." In *Politics of the Heart: A Lesbian Parenting Anthology*, edited by Sandra Pollack and Jeanne Vaughn, 100–110. Ithaca, NY: Firebrand Books.

———. 1989. "A Slow, Sweet Kind of Death." In *Intricate Passions*, edited by Tee Corinne, 65–74. Austin, TX: Banned Books.

———. 1990. "A Matter of Fact." In *Riding Desire*, edited by Tee Corinne, 36–43. Austin, TX: Banned Books.

García, Alma M., ed. 1997. *Chicana Feminist Thought: The Basic Historical Writings*. New York: Routledge.

García, Angela. 1994. "Yo Yo." In *Beyond Definition: New Writing from Gay and Lesbian San Francisco*, edited by Marci Blackman and Trebor Healey, 39–41. San Francisco: Manic D Press.

García-Noriega y Nieto, Lucia. 1993. *Cronos y cromos: 9 de diciembre de 1993–20 de febrero de 1994*. [México, D.F.]: Fundación Cultural Televisa.

García-Orozco, Antonia. 1999. "Chicana Lesbian Drag: The Politics of Pleasure." Paper presented at the National Association of Chicana and Chicano Studies 25th Annual Conference, San Antonio, TX.

Gaspar de Alba, Alicia. 1992a. "Excerpts from the Sapphic Diary of Sor Juana Inés de la Cruz." *Frontiers* 12 (3): 171–179.

———. 1992b. "Juana Inés." In *New Chicana/Chicano Writing 1*, edited by Charles Tatum, 1–15. Tucson: University of Arizona Press.

———. 1993a. "Facing the Mariachis." In *The Mystery of Survival and Other Stories*. Tempe, AZ: Bilingual Press/Editorial Bilingüe.

———. 1993b. "La Mariscal." In *The Mystery of Survival and Other Stories*, 41–46. Tempe, AZ: Bilingual Press/Editorial Bilingüe.

———. 1993c. *The Mystery of Survival and Other Stories*. Tempe, AZ: Bilingual Press/Editorial Bilingüe.

———. 1993d. "The Piñata Dream." In *The Mystery of Survival and Other Stories*, 53–69. Tempe, AZ: Bilingual Press/Editorial Bilingüe.

———. 1993e. "They're Just Silly Rabbits." In *The Mystery of Survival and Other Stories*, 32–40. Tempe, AZ: Bilingual Press/Editorial Bilingüe.

———. 1994a. "Cimarrona." In *In Other Words: Literature by Latinas of the United States*, edited by Roberta Fernández, 404–422. Houston: Arte Público.

————. 1994b. "Malinche's Rights." In *Currents from the Dancing River: Contemporary Latino Fiction, Nonfiction and Poetry*, edited by Ray Gonzalez, 261–266. San Diego: Harcourt Brace.

————. 1998a. *Chicano Art Inside/Outside the Master's House: Cultural Politics and the Cara Exhibition*. Austin: University of Texas Press.

————. 1998b. "The Politics of Location of the Tenth Muse of America: Interview with Sor Juana Inés De La Cruz." In *Living Chicana Theory*, edited by Carla Trujillo, 136–165. Berkeley: Third Woman Press.

————. 1999. *Sor Juana's Second Dream*. Albuquerque: University of New Mexico Press.

————, ed. 2003. *Velvet Barrios: Popular Culture and Chicana/o Sexualities*. New York: Palgrave.

Gillman, Laura, and Stacey M. Floyd-Thomas. 2001. "Con un pie a cada lado/With a Foot in Each Place: Mestizaje as Transnational Feminisms in Ana Castillo's *So Far from God*." *Meridians: Feminism, Race, Transnationalism* 2 (1): 58–75.

Gilroy, Paul. 1987. *"There Ain't No Black in the Union Jack": The Cultural Politics of Race and Nation*. Black Literature and Culture. Chicago: University of Chicago Press.

————. 1992. *The Black Atlantic: Modernity and Double Consciousness*. Cambridge, MA: Harvard University Press.

Goldsby, Jackie. 1990. "What It Means to Be Colored Me." *Out/Look* (Summer): 8–17.

————. 1993. "Queen for 307 Days: Looking B(l)ack at Vanessa Williams and the Sex Wars." In *Sisters, Sexperts, and Queers: Beyond the Lesbian Nation*, edited by Arlene Stein. New York: Plume.

Gómez, Alma, Cherríe Moraga, and Mariana Romo-Carmona, eds. 1983. *Cuentos: Stories by Latinas*. New York: Kitchen Table/Women of Color Press.

Gomez, Jewelle. 1991. *The Gilda Stories*. Ithaca, NY: Firebrand Books.

Gómez-Peña, Guillermo. 1996a. *The New World [B]Order: Prophecies, Poems & Loqueras for the End of the Century*. San Francisco: City Lights Books.

————. 1996b. "The Two Guadalupes." In *Goddess of the Americas*, edited by Ana Castillo, 178–183. New York: Riverhead Books.

Gómez-Vega, Ibis. 1991. *Send My Roots Rain*. San Francisco: Aunt Lute Foundation.

Gonzales-Berry, Erlinda, and Chuck Tatum, eds. 1996. *Recovering the U.S. Hispanic Literary Heritage*. Vol. 2. Houston: Arte Público.

González, Deena. 1990. "The Widowed Women of Santa Fe: Assessments on the Lives of an Unmarried Population, 1850–80." In *Unequal Sisters*, edited by Ellen Carol DuBois and Vicky L. Ruíz, 34–50. New York: Routledge.

————. 1991. "Malinche as Lesbian: A Reconfiguration of 500 Years of Resistance." *California Sociologist* 14 (1–2): 91–97.

————. 1993. "La Tules of Image and Reality: Euro-American Attitudes and Legend Formation on a Spanish-Mexican Frontier." In *Building with Our Hands: New Directions in Chicana Studies*, edited by Adela de la Torre and Beatríz M. Pesquera, 75–90. Berkeley: University of California Press.

————. 1998. "Speaking Secrets: Living Chicana Theory." In *Living Chicana Theory*, edited by Carla Trujillo, 46–77. Berkeley: Third Woman Press.

———. 2000. *Refusing the Favor: The Spanish-Mexican Women of Santa Fe, 1820–1880.* Oxford: Oxford University Press.

———. 2001. "'Lupe's Song': On the Origins of Mexican-Woman-Hating in the United States." In *Race in 21st-Century America,* edited by Curtis Stokes, Theresa Meléndez, and Genice Rhodes-Reed, 143–158. East Lansing: Michigan State University Press.

González, Jennifer A. 1995. "Negotiated Frontiers." In *From the West: Chicano Narrative Photography,* edited by Chon A. Noriega, 17–22. Seattle: University of Washington Press.

González, María C. 1998. "Intelletual Trajectories: Chicana Queer Theory." Paper presented at the National Association of Chicana and Chicano Studies 25th Annual Conference, México, D.F.

González, María R. 1990. "El embrión nacionalista visto a través de la obra de Sor Juana Inés de la Cruz." In *Between Borders: Essays on Mexicana/Chicana History,* edited by Adelaida Del Castillo, 239–253. Encino, CA: Floricanto Press.

González, Nancie L. 1969. *The Spanish-Americans of New Mexico: A Heritage of Pride.* Rev. and enl. ed. Albuquerque: University of New Mexico Press.

Gonzalez, Ray. 1993. Review of *So Far from God. Nation* 256 (22): 772–773.

González, Rudolfo (Corky). 1967. *I Am Joaquín / Yo soy Joaquín.* Denver: El Gallo. Reprinted in Hernández-Gutiérrez and Foster 1997, 207–222.

Green, Rayna. 1975. "The Pocahontas Perplex: The Image of Indian Women in American Culture." *Massachusetts Review* 16: 698–714.

Griswold del Castillo, Richard, Teresa McKenna, and Yvonne Yarbro-Bejarano, eds. 1991. *Chicano Art: Resistance and Affirmation.* Los Angeles: Wight Art Gallery, University of California, Los Angeles.

Guerrero, Andrés Gonzales. 1987. *A Chicano Theology.* New York: Orbis Books.

Gutierrez, Ramón. 1991a. "El Santuario de Chimayo: A Syncretic Shrine in New Mexico." In *Feasts and Celebrations in North American Ethnic Communities,* edited by Ramón A. Gutiérrez and Geneviève Fabre, 71–86. Albuquerque: University of New Mexico.

———. 1991b. *When Jesus Came, the Corn Mothers Went Away: Marriage, Sexuality and Power in New Mexico 1500–1846.* Stanford: Stanford University Press.

———. 1993. "Community, Patriarchy and Individualism: The Politics of Chicano History and the Dream of Equality." *American Quarterly* 45 (1): 44–73.

Gutiérrez, Ramón, and Genaro Padilla, eds. 1993. *Recovering the U.S. Hispanic Literary Heritage.* Vol. 1. Houston: Arte Público.

Gutiérrez-Jones, Carl. 1992. "Legislating Languages: *The Ballad of Gregorio Cortez* and the English Language Amendment." In *Chicanos and Film: Representation and Resistance,* edited by Chon A. Noriega, 195–206. Minneapolis: University of Minnesota.

———. 1995. *Rethinking Borderlands: Between Chicano Culture and Legal Discourse.* Berkeley: University of California Press.

Habell-Pallán, Michelle. 1996. "Family and Sexuality in Recent Chicano Performance: Luis Alfaro's Memory Plays." *Ollantáy Theater Journal* 5 (1): 33–42.

———. 1999. "El Vez Is 'Taking Care of Business': The Inter/National Appeal of Chicana/o Popular Music." *Cultural Studies* 13 (2): 195–210.

Habell-Pallán, Michelle, and Mary Romero, eds. 2002. *Latino/a Popular Culture*. New York: New York University Press.

Halberstam, Judith. 1998. "Transgender Butch: Butch/FTM Border Wars and the Masculine Continuum." *GLQ* 4 (2): 287–310.

Hale, C. Jacob. 1998. "Consuming the Living, Dis(Re)Membering the Dead in the Butch/FTM Borderlands." *GLQ* 4 (2): 311–48.

Hall, Radclyffe. [1928] 1981. *The Well of Loneliness*. New York: Avon.

Hammonds, Evelynn. 1994. "Black (W)Holes and the Geometry of Black Female Sexuality." *Differences* 6 (2–3): 126.

———. 1995. "Toward a Genealogy of Black Female Sexuality: The Problematic of Silence." In *Feminist Genealogies, Colonial Legacies, Democratic Futures*, edited by M. Jacqui Alexander and Chandra Talpade Mohanty, 170–180. New York: Routledge.

Haraway, Donna. 1991a. "A Cyborg Manifesto." In *Simians, Cyborgs, and Women: The Reinvention of Nature*, 149–181. New York: Routledge.

———. 1991b. "Otherwordly Conversations, Terran Topics, Local Terms." *Science as Culture* 3, pt. 1 (14): 64–98.

———. 1991c. *Simians, Cyborgs, and Women: The Reinvention of Nature*. New York: Routledge.

———. 1997. *Modest_Witness@Second_Millennium.Femaleman© _Meets_Oncomouse™: Feminism and Technoscience*. New York: Routledge.

Harris, Bertha. 1973. "The More Profound Nationality of Their Lesbianism: Lesbian Society in Paris in the 1920s." In *Amazon Expedition*, edited by Phyllis Birkby, Bertha Harris, Jill Johnston, Esther Newton, and Jane O'Wyatt, 77–88. Albion, CA: Times Change Press.

———. 1976. "Lesbians and Literature." Paper presented at the Modern Language Association.

———. 1977. "What We Mean to Say: Notes toward Defining the Nature of Lesbian Literature." *Heresies* (Fall): 5–8.

Hart, Lynda. 1994. *Fatal Women: Lesbian Sexuality and the Mark of Aggression*. Princeton, NJ: Princeton University Press.

———, ed. 1989. *Making a Spectacle: Feminist Essays on Contemporary Women's Theatre, Women and Culture*. Ann Arbor: University of Michigan Press.

Heard, Martha E. 1988. "The Theatre of Denise Chávez: Interior Landscapes with *sabor nuevomexicano*." *Americas Review* 16 (2): 83–91.

Heath, Jennifer. 1994. *Black Velvet: The Art We Love to Hate*. San Francisco: Pomegranate Artbooks.

Helguera, Jesus. 1941. *La leyenda de los volcanes*. In *Chicano Expressions: A New View in American Art*, edited by Inverna Lockpez, Tomás Ybarra Fausto, Judith Baca, and Kay Turner. New York: INTAR Latin American Gallery.

HEMBRA. 1976. *Hermanas en movimiento brotando raíces de Aztlán*. Austin: University of Texas Press.

Hernández, Ellie. 1993. "A Blind Sided View of *Margins*." *esto no tiene nombre* 2 (3): 7.

———. 1998. "Transnational Discourse in Gloria Anzaldúa's *Borderlands/La Frontera*." Paper presented at the 114th annual meeting of the Modern Language Association, San Francisco.

————. 2003. "Chronotope of Desire: Emma Pérez's *Gulf Dreams.*" In *Chicana Feminisms: A Critical Reader,* edited by Gabriela F. Arredondo, Aida Hurtado, Norma Klahn, Olga Nájera-Ramírez, and Patricia Zavella, 155–178. Durham, NC: Duke University Press.

Hernández, Ester. 1975. "La Virgen de Guadalupe defendiendo los derechos de los xicanos." In *Chicano Art: Resistance and Affirmation 1965–1985,* edited by Richard Griswold del Castillo, Teresa McKenna, and Yvonne Yarbro-Bejarano. Los Angeles: Wight Gallery, University of California, Los Angeles.

————. 1976. "Libertad." In *Chicano Art: Resistance and Affirmation 1965–1985,* edited by Richard Griswold del Castillo, Teresa McKenna, and Yvonne Yarbro-Bejarano. Los Angeles: Wight Gallery, University of California, Los Angeles.

Hernández-Gutierrez, Manuel de Jesús, and David William Foster, eds. 1997. *Literatura Chicana, 1965–1995: An Anthology in Spanish, English, and Caló.* New York: Garland.

Herrera-Sobek, María. 1986. "*La Delgadina*: Incest and Patriarchal Structure in a Spanish/Chicano Romance-Corrido." *Studies in Latin American Popular Culture* 5: 90–107.

————. 1987. "The Politics of Rape: Sexual Transgression in Chicana Fiction." *Americas Review* 15 (3–4): 171–188.

————. 1990. *The Mexican Corrido: A Feminist Analysis.* Bloomington: Indiana University Press.

————. 1991. "The Mexican/Chicano Pastorela." In *Feasts and Celebrations in North American Ethnic Communities,* edited by Ramón A. Gutiérrez and Geneviève Fabre, 47–56. Albuquerque: University of New Mexico.

————. 1998. "The Corrido as Hypertext: Undocumented Mexican Immigrant Films and the Mexican/Chicano Ballad." In *Culture across Borders: Mexican Immigration and Popular Culture,* edited by David R. Maciel and María Herrera-Sobek, 227–258. Tucson: University of Arizona.

————, ed. 1993. *Reconstructing a Chicano/a Literary Heritage.* Tucson: University of Arizona Press.

Herrera-Sobek, María, and Virginia Sánchez Korrol, eds. 1999. *Recovering the U.S. Hispanic Literary Heritage.* Vol. 3. Houston: Arte Público.

Herrera-Sobek, María, and Helena María Viramontes, eds. 1988. *Chicana Creativity and Criticism: Charting New Frontiers in American Literature.* Houston: Arte Público.

————. 1995. *Chicana (W)Rites on Word and Film.* Series in Chicana/Latina Studies. Berkeley: Third Woman Press.

————. 1996. *Chicana Creativity and Criticism: Charting New Frontiers in American Literature.* 2d ed., rev. and exp. Albuquerque: University of New Mexico Press.

Hidalgo, Hilda. 1987. "El ser yo no es un lujo." In *Compañeras: Latina Lesbians — An Anthology,* edited by Juanita [Díaz] Ramos, 72–76. New York: Latina Lesbian History Project.

Hinojosa, Claudia. 1988. "Una perspectiva lesbiana del lesbianismo." In *Fem: 10 años de periodismo feminista,* edited by Colección Mujeres en Su Tiempo, 149–153. México, D.F.: Fascículos Planeta.

Hollibaugh, Amber, and Cherríe Moraga. 1983. "What We're Rollin' around in

Bed With: Sexual Silences in Feminism." In *Powers of Desire: The Politics of Sexuality*, edited by Ann Snitow, Christine Stansell, and Sharon Thompson, 394–405. New York: Monthly Review Press.

Hollingsworth, Gerelyn. 1985. *Ex-Nuns: Women Who Have Left the Convent*. Jefferson, NC: McFarland.

Holoch, Naomi, and Joan Nestle, eds. 1990. *Women on Women: An Anthology of American Lesbian Short Fiction*. New York: Plume.

Hom, Alice Y., and Ming-Yuen S. Ma. 1993. "Premature Gestures: A Speculative Dialogue on Asian Pacific Islander Lesbian and Gay Writing." In *Critical Essays: Gay and Lesbian Writers of Color*, edited by Emmanuel S. Nelson, 21–51. New York: Haworth Press.

hooks, bell, and Julie Dash. 1992. "Dialogue between bell hooks and Julie Dash." In *Daughters of the Dust: The Making of an African American Woman's Film*, 27–67. New York: New Press.

Horno-Delgado, Asunción, Eliana Ortega, Nina M. Scott, and Nancy Saporta Sternbach, eds. 1989. *Breaking Boundaries: Latina Writings and Critical Readings*. Amherst: University of Massachusetts Press.

Hull, Gloria T., Patricia Bell Scott, and Barbara Smith, eds. 1982. *All the Women Are White, All the Blacks Are Men, but Some of Us Are Brave: Black Women's Studies*. New York: Feminist Press.

Hulme, Peter. 1986. *Colonial Encounters: Europe and the Native Caribbean, 1492–1797*. New York: Metheun.

Hurtado, Aída. 1989. "Relating to Privilege: Seduction and Rejection in the Subordination of White Women and Women of Color." *Signs* 14 (4): 833–855.

———. 1997. *The Color of Privilege*. Ann Arbor: University of Michigan Press.

———. 1998. "Sitios y Lenguas: Chicanas Theorize Feminisms." *Hypatia: A Journal of Feminist Philosophy* 13 (2): 134–161.

Islas, Arturo. 1990. *Migrant Souls*. New York: William Morrow.

Jackson, Helen Hunt. 1884. *Ramona*. New York: Grosset and Dunlap.

James, Joy, ed. 1998. *The Angela Y. Davis Reader*. Cambridge, MA: Blackwell.

Jameson, Fredric. 1981. *The Political Unconscious: Narrative as a Socially Symbolic Act*. Ithaca, NY: Cornell University Press.

Jáuregi, B. Sifuentes. 1997. "National Fantasies: Peeking into the Latin American Closet." In *Queer Representations: Reading Lives, Reading Cultures*, edited by Martin Duberman, 290–304. New York: New York University Press.

Jiménez, Karleen Pendleton. 1998. "Not Everyone Turns Pink under the Sun." Unpublished manuscript.

Jordan, June. 1992. "A New Politics of Sexuality." In *Technical Difficulties*, 187–195. New York: Pantheon.

Julien, Isaac. 1989. *Looking for Langston*. [Film] Water Bearer Films, New York.

Keating, AnaLouise. 1993. "Writing, Politics, and Las Lesberadas: Platicando Con Gloria Anzaldua." *Frontiers* 14: 105–130.

———. 2000a. *Gloria E. Anzaldúa: Interviews/Entrevistas*. New York: Routledge.

———. 2000b. "The Intimate Distance of Desire: June Jordan's Bisexual Inflections." *Journal of Lesbian Studies* 4 (2): 81–94.

———. 2002. "Towards a New Politics of Representation? Absence and Desire in Denise Chavez's *The Last of the Menu Girls*." In *We Who Love to Be Astonished: Experimental Women's Writing and Performance Poetics*, edited by Laura Hinton, Cynthia Hogue, and Rachel Blau DuPlessis, 71–80. Tuscaloosa: University of Alabama Press.

Keefe, Susan, and and Amado Padilla. 1987. *Chicano Ethnicity*. Albuquerque: University of New Mexico Press.

Keller, Yvonne C. 1997. "Pulp Passions: Lesbian Popular Fiction, 1950–1965." Ph.D. dissertation, University of California, Santa Cruz.

Kennedy, Elizabeth Lapovsky, and Madeline D. Davis. 1993. *Boots of Leather, Slippers of Gold: The History of a Lesbian Community*. New York: Penguin.

Klor de Alva, J. Jorge. 1986. "California Chicano Literature and Pre-Columbian Motifs: Foil and Fetish." *Confluencia* 1 (2): 18–26.

———. 1990. "Chicana History and Historical Significance: Some Theoretical Considerations." In *Between Borders: Essays on Mexicana/Chicana History*, edited by Adelaida R. Del Castillo, 61–86. Encino, CA: Floricanto Press.

Lamphere, Louise, Patricia Zavella, and Felipe Gonzales, with Peter B. Evans. 1993. *Sunbelt Working Mothers: Reconciling Family and Factory*. Anthropology of Contemporary Issues. Ithaca, NY: Cornell University Press.

Lanza, Carmela Delia. 1998. "Hearing the Voices: Women and Home and Ana Castillo's So Far from God." *MELUS* 23 (1): 65–79.

Leal, Luís. 1979. "The Problem of Identifying Chicano Literature." In *The Identification and Analysis of Chicano Literature*, edited by Francisco Jiménez, 2–6. New York: Bilingual Press/Editorial Bilingüe.

Levins Morales, Aurora. 2001. *Remedios: Stories of Earth and Iron from the History of Puertorriqueñas*. Boston: South End Press.

Li, Gloria Elsa. 1995. "Bernice Zamora: Interview." In *Chicana (W)Rites on Word and Film*, edited by María Herrera-Sobek and Helena María Viramontes, 283–303. Berkeley: Third Woman Press.

Limón, Graciela. 1993. *In Search of Bernabé*. Houston: Arte Público.

———. 1999. *Day of the Moon*. Houston: Arte Público.

———. 2002. *Erased Faces*. Houston: Arte Público.

Limón, José E. 1990. "La Llorona, the Third Legend of Greater Mexico: Cultural Symbols, Women, and the Political Unconscious." In *Between Borders: Essays on Mexicana/Chicana History*, edited by Adelaida R. Del Castillo, 399–432. Encino, CA: Floricanto Press.

———. 1994. *Dancing with the Devil: Society and Cultural Poetics in Mexican-American South Texas*. New Directions in Anthropological Writing. Madison: University of Wisconsin Press.

———. 1997. "Tex-Sex-Mex: American Identities, Lone Stars, and the Politics of Racialized Sexuality." *American Literary History* 9 (3): 598–616.

———. 1999. *American Encounters: Greater Mexico, the United States, and the Erotics of Culture*. Boston: Beacon Press.

Lockpez, Inverna, Tomás Ybarra-Frausto, Judith Baca, and Kay Turner. 1986. *Chicano Expressions: A New View in American Art*. Exhibition catalog. Los Angeles: Otis Art Institute of Parson School of Design; San Francisco: Museo de Arte Mexicano.

Lomas, Clara. 1993. "The Articulation of Gender in the Mexican Borderlands, 1900–1915." In *Recovering the U.S. Hispanic Literary Heritage,* edited by Ramón Gutiérrez and Genaro Padilla, 293–308. Houston: Arte Público.

Lomas Garza, Carmen. 1990. *Family Pictures/Cuadros de familia.* San Francisco: Children's Book Press.

Lopez, Alma. 1999a. "Alma Lopez." *Frontiers* 20 (1): 80–85.

———. 1999b. "Artist's Statement." Posted to artist's website www.almalopez.net. Cited by permission of Alma Lopez.

———. 2000. "Mermaids, Butterflies, and Princesses." *Aztlán* 25 (1): 189–191.

López, Josefina. 1996a. *Real Women Have Curves: A Comedy.* Woodstock, IL: Dramatic Publishing.

———. 1996b. *Simply Maria, or, the American Dream: A One-Act Play.* Woodstock, IL: Dramatic Publishing.

López, Sonia A. 1977. "The Role of the Chicana within the Student Movement." In *Essays on La Mujer,* edited by Rosaura Sanchez and Rosa Martinez Cruz, 16–29. Los Angeles: Chicano Studies Center Publications, University of California, Los Angeles.

López, Tiffany Ana, ed. 1993. *Growing up Chicana/o.* New York: William Morrow.

Lorde, Audre. 1977. "Poetry Is Not a Luxury." *Chrysalis* 3. Reprinted in *Sister Outsider* 1984, 36–39.

———. 1978. "The Transformation of Silence into Language and Action." *Sinister Wisdom* 6: 256.

———. 1982. "Learning from the 60's." Paper presented at the Malcolm X Weekend, Harvard University.

———. 1983. *Zami: A New Spelling of My Name.* Trumansberg, NY: Crossing Press.

———. 1984a. *A Burst of Light.* Ithaca, NY: Firebrand Books.

———. 1984b. *Sister Outsider: Essays & Speeches.* Freedom, CA: Crossing Press.

Luna-Jiménez, Nanci. 1993. "Strategic Interventions: Cartographies of Discourse." Unpublished essay.

Lynch, Lee. 1990. "Cruising the Libraries." In *Lesbian Texts and Contexts,* edited by Karla Jay and Joanne Glasgow, 39–48. New York: New York University Press.

Macklin, June. 1980. "'All the Good and Bad in This World': Women, Traditional Medicine, and Mexican American Culture." In *Twice a Minority: Mexican American Women,* edited by Margarita B. Melville, 127–148. St. Louis: Mosby.

MALCS. [1983] 1993a. "MALCS Declaration." In *Chicana Critical Issues,* edited by MALCS, vii. Berkeley: Third Woman Press.

———. 1993b. "Nueva Declaracíon de MALCS." Paper presented at the MALCS Summer Institute.

MALCS, Norma Alarcón, Rafaela Castro, Deena Gonzalez, Margarita Melville, Emma Pérez, Tey Diana Rebolledo, Christine Sierra, and Adaljiza Sosa-Riddell, eds. 1993. *Chicana Critical Issues.* Chicana/Latina Studies. Berkeley: Third Woman Press.

Mallon, Florencia E. 1994. "The Promise and Dilemma of Subaltern Studies: Perspectives from Latin American History." *American Historical Review* 99 (5): 1491–1515.

María, Luz, and Ellen J. Stekert. 1992. "Santa Barraza." Paper presented at the Santa Barraza La Raza/Galeria Posada, Sacramento, CA.

Márquez, Antonio C. 1994. "The Historical Imagination in Arturo Islas's *The Rain God* and *Migrant Souls.*" *MELUS* 19 (2): 3–16.

Marrero, M. Teresa. 2003. "Out of the Fringe: Desire and Homosexuality in the 1990s Latino Theater." In *Velvet Barrios: Popular Culture and Chicana/o Sexualities,* edited by Alicia Gaspar de Alba, 283–294. New York: Palgrave/Macmillan.

Marshall, Paule. 1983. *Praise Song for the Widow.* New York: Putnam's.

Martin, Del, and Phyllis Lyon. 1991. *Lesbian/Woman.* Glide Publications Edition. Volcano, CA: Volcano Press.

Martínez, Demeteria. 1996. *Mother Tongue.* Bilingual Press/Editorial Bilingüe Edition. New York: Ballantine Books.

Martinez, Elizabeth Coonrod. 1998. "Recovering a Space for History between Imperialism and Patriarchy: Julia Alvarez's *In the Time of the Butterflies.*" *Thamyris: Mythmaking from Past to Present* 5 (2): 263–279.

Martínez-Echazábal, Lourdes. 1990. *Para una semiotica de la mulatez.* Madrid: Ediciones Jose Porrua Turanzas.

Matthews, Tede. 1992. "Bienvenidos a Jotolandia/Entre nosotros." *Out/Look* 4 (Winter): 55–61.

McCracken, Ellen. 1989. "Sandra Cisneros' *The House on Mango Street*: Community-oriented Introspection and the Demystification of Patriarchal Violence." In *Breaking Boundaries: Latina Writings and Critical Readings,* edited by Asunción Horno-Delgado, Eliana Ortega, Nina M. Scott, and Nancy Saporta Sternbach, 62–71. Amherst: University of Massachusetts Press.

McKenna, Teresa. 1991. "On Chicano Poetry and the Political Age: Corridos as Social Drama." In *Criticism in the Borderlands: Studies in Chicano Literature, Culture, and Ideology,* edited by Héctor Calderón and José David Saldívar, 181–202. Durham, NC: Duke University Press.

———. 1997. *Migrant Song: Politics and Process in Contemporary Chicano Literature.* Austin: University of Texas Press.

McLaughlin, Sheila. 1987. *She Must Be Seeing Things.* New York: First Run Features Home Video.

Medina, Dolissa. ca. 1995. *Ondas on Her Tongue* [Webpage]. [Cited 2001.] Available at www.ims40.org/sirena2/tongue.htm.

Melville, Margarita B., ed. 1980. *Twice a Minority: Mexican American Women.* St. Louis: Mosby.

Menchu, Rigoberta. 1984. *I, Rigoberta Menchu: An Indian in Guatemala.* Translated by Ann Wright. Edited by Elizabeth Burgos Debray. London: Verso.

Mercer, Kobena. 1994. *Welcome to the Jungle: New Positions in Black Cultural Studies.* New York: Routledge.

Mermann-Jozwiak, Elisabeth. 2000. "Gritos de la Frontera: Ana Castillo, Sandra Cisneros, and Postmodernism." *MELUS* 25 (2): 101–118.

Mesa-Bains, Amalia. 1991. "El Mundo Femenino: Chicana Artists of the Movement: A Commentary on Development and Production." In *Chicano Art: Resistance and Affirmation,* edited by Richard Griswold del Castillo, Teresa McKenna, and Yvonne Yarbro-Bejarano, 131–140. Los Angeles: Wight Art Gallery, University of California, Los Angeles.

Mireya, Corona. 1996. Review of *Latin Satins*. *ConMoción* 2: 13.

Mirza, Heidi Safia, ed. 1997. *Black British Feminism: A Reader*. New York: Routledge.

Mitchell, Angelyn. 2001. "Not Enough of the Past: Feminist Revisions of Slavery in Octavia E. Butler's Kindred." *MELUS* 26 (3): 51–75.

Mohanty, Chandra Talpade, Ann Russo, and Lourdes Torres, eds. 1991. *Third World Women and the Politics of Feminism*. Bloomington: Indiana University Press.

Mohr, Nicholasa. 1987. "An Awakening . . . Summer 1956." In *Woman of Her Word: Hispanic Women Write*, edited by Evangelina Vigil, 107–112. Houston: Arte Público.

Molloy, Sylvia, and Robert McKee Irwin, eds. 1998. *Hispanisms and Homosexualities*. Series Q. Durham, NC: Duke University Press.

Monroy, Douglas. 1990. " 'They Didn't Call Them "Padre" for Nothing': Patriarchy in Hispanic California." In *Between Borders: Essays on Mexicana/Chicana History*, edited by Adelaida R. Del Castillo, 433–445. Encino, CA: Floricanto Press.

Monsiváis, Carlos. 1983. "Este es el pachuco, un sujeto singular." In *A través de la frontera*, edited by Salvador Leal, 83–90. México, D.F.: Centro de Estudios Económicos y Sociales del Tercer Mundo, A.C.; Instituto de Investigaciones Esteticas, U.N.A.M.

Montejano, David. 1987. *Anglos and Mexicans in the Making of Texas, 1836–1986*. Austin: University of Austin Press.

Montes, Amelia. 1999a. " 'Es necesario mirar bien': Letter Making, Novel Writing, and American Nationhood in the Nineteenth Century." Ph.D. dissertation, University of Denver.

———. 1999b. "Rewriting the Present: Nineteenth-Century Historical Novels." In *Recovering the U.S. Hispanic Literary Heritage*, vol. 3, edited by María Herrera-Sobek and Virginia Sánchez Korrol, 16–73. Houston: Arte Público.

———. 1999c. "While Pilar Tobillo Sleeps." In *Hers 3: Brilliant New Fiction by Lesbian Writers*, edited by Terry Wolverton and Robert Drake, 9–21. New York: Faber and Faber.

———. 2002. "As If in a Photographic Instance." Unpublished manuscript.

Montoya, Delilah. 1995. "Artist's Statement." In *From the West: Chicano Narrative Photography*, edited by Chon A. Noriega, 62. Seattle: University of Washington Press.

Montoya, José. 1972. "El Louie." In *Aztlán: An Anthology of Mexican American Literature*, edited by Luis Valdez and Stan Steiner, 333–337. New York: Vintage Books.

Moore, George. 1998. "Beyond Cultural Dialogues: Identities in the Interstices of Culture in Jimmy Santiago Baca's *Martín and Meditations on the South Valley*." *Western American Literature* 33 (2): 153–177.

Moraga, Cherríe. 1982. "Played between White Hands." *off our backs* (July): n.p.

———. 1983. *Loving in the War Years: Lo que nunca pasó por sus labios*. Boston: South End Press.

————. 1986. *Giving Up the Ghost: Teatro in Two Acts*. Los Angeles: West End Press.

————. 1989. Review of *Trini. Third Woman* 157–162.

————. 1990. "La Ofrenda." *Out/Look* 10 (2): 50–55.

————. 1993. *The Last Generation*. Boston: South End Press.

————. 1994a. *Giving Up the Ghost*. In *Heroes and Saints & Other Plays*, 1–35. Boston: South End Press.

————. 1994b. *Heroes and Saints*. In *Heroes and Saints & Other Plays*, 85–149. Boston: South End Press.

————. 1994c. *Heroes and Saints & Other Plays*. Albuquerque: West End Press.

————. 1994d. *The Shadow of a Man*. In *Heroes and Saints & Other Plays*, 37–84. Boston: South End Press.

————. 1996a. "El mito azteca." In *Goddess of the Americas*, edited by Ana Castillo, 68–71. New York: Riverhead Books.

————. 1996b. *Watsonville: Some Place Not Here*. In *Latino Plays from the Southcoast Repertory*, edited by Hispanic Playwrights Project, 339–425. New York: Broadway Play Publishing.

————. 2000a. *A Mexican Medea*. In *Out of the Fringe: Contemporary Latina/Latino Theatre and Performance*, edited by Caridad Svich and María Teresa Marrero, 289–363. New York: Theatre Communications Group.

————. 2000b. *Who Killed Yolanda Saldívar?* Read at Festival of Lesbian Playwrights, Magic Theater, San Francisco, January.

————. 2001. *The Hungry Woman and Heart of the Earth*. Albuquerque: University of New Mexico Press.

————. 2002. *Watsonville and A Circle in the Dirt*. Albuquerque: University of New Mexico Press.

Moraga, Cherríe, and Gloria Anzaldúa, eds. 1983. *This Bridge Called My Back: Writings by Radical Women of Color*. Persephone Press Edition. New York: Kitchen Table/Women of Color Press.

Moraga, Cherríe, and Ana Castillo, eds. 1988. *Esta puente, mi espalda: Voces de mujeres tercermundistas en los Estados Unidos*. Translated by Ana Castillo and Norma Alarcón. San Francisco: ISM Press.

Morell, Mary. 1991. *Final Session*. San Francisco: Spinsters Book Co.

————. 1993. *Final Rest*. Minneapolis, MN: Spinsters Ink.

Morena, Naomi Littlebear. 1980. *Survivors: A Lesbian Rock Opera*. Unpublished play.

————. 1987. "The Men in Your Life." In *Compañeras: Latina Lesbians —An Anthology*, edited by Juanita [Díaz] Ramos, 129–130. New York: Latina Lesbian History Project.

————. 1988. "Coming out Queer and Brown." In *For Lesbians Only: A Separatist Anthology*, 345–347. London: Onlywomen Press.

Moreno, Renee. 1994. *The Holy Tree*. Videocassette.

Morgan, Claire [Patricia Highsmith]. 1952. *The Price of Salt*.

Morley, David, and Kuan-Hsing Chen, eds. 1996. *Stuart Hall: Critical Dialogues in Cultural Studies*. New York: Routledge.

Mörner, Magnus. 1967. *Race Mixture in the History of Latin America*. Boston: Little, Brown.

Morrison, Toni. 1973. *Sula*. New York, Knopf.

———. 1989. *Beloved*. New York: Plume.

Muñoz, Carlos, Jr. 1989. *Youth, Identity, Power: The Chicano Movement*. Haymarket Series. London: Verso.

Muñoz, José Esteban. 1999. *Disidentifications: Queers of Color and the Performance of Politics*. Minneapolis: University of Minnesota Press.

Murray, Yxta Maya. 1998. *Locas*. New York: Grove Press.

Muska, Susan, and Greta Olgasdottir. 1998. *Brandon Teena Story*. [Film] Marketed and distributed by New Video, New York.

Nava, Gregory. 1994. *My Family/Mi familia*. [Film] New Line Home Video, New York.

———. 1997. *Selena*. [Film] Warner Studios.

Nava, Michael. 1986. *The Little Death*. Los Angeles: Alyson Publications.

———. 1988. *Goldenboy*. Boston: Alyson Publications.

———. 1991. *How Town*. New York: Ballantine Books.

———. 1992. *The Hidden Law*. New York: HarperCollins.

———. 1996. *The Death of Friends*. New York: Putnam.

———. 1997. *The Burning Plain*. New York: Putnam.

Negrón-Muntaner, Frances. 1997. "Jennifer's Butt." *Aztlán* 22 (2): 181–194.

———. 2000. "Feeling Pretty: *West Side Story* and Puerto Rican Identity Discourses." *Social Text* 18 (2): 83–106.

Nelson, Emmanuel S., ed. 1993. *Critical Essays: Gay and Lesbian Writers of Color*. New York: Haworth Press.

Nestle, Joan, ed. 1992. *The Persistent Desire: A Femme-Butch Reader*. Boston: Alyson Publications.

Noriega, Chon A., ed. 1995. *From the West: Chicano Narrative Photography*. Seattle: University of Washington Press.

Norris, Linda. 1974. "Comparison of Two Groups in a Southern State Women's Prison: Homosexual Behavior versus Non-Homosexual Behavior." *Psychological Reports* 34 (1): 75–78.

O'Grady, Lorraine. 1992. "Olympia's Maid: Reclaiming Black Female Subjectivity." *Afterimage* 20 (1): 14–17.

O'Shea, Kathleen. 1999. *Women and the Death Penalty in the United States, 1900–1998*. Westport, CT: Praeger.

———. 2000. *Women on the Row: Revelations from Both Sides of the Bars*. Ithaca, NY: Firebrand Books.

Obejas, Achy. 1994. *We Came All the Way from Cuba So You Could Dress Like This?* Pittsburgh: Cleis Press.

———. 1996. *Memory Mambo*. San Francisco: Cleis Press.

———. 2001. *Days of Awe*. New York: Ballantine Books.

Ocampo, Esperanza. 1993. "La Virgen de Guadalupe: Transformative Symbol of Mexican Identity and Hope." In *Chicano Cultural Studies Research Cluster*. Working Paper Series. Santa Cruz: Center for Cultural Studies, University of California, Santa Cruz.

Okja Keller, Nora. 1998. *Comfort Women*. New York: Penguin.

Olguín, B. V. 1997. "Tattoos, Abjection, and the Political Unconscious: Toward a Semiotics of the Pinto Visual Vernacular." *Cultural Critique* 37: 159–213.

Olivares, Julián. 1987. "Sandra Cisneros' *The House on Mango Street,* and the Poetics of Space." *Americas Review* 15 (3–4): 160–170.

Omi, Michael, and Howard Winant. 1986. *Racial Formation in the United States from the 1960s to the 1980s.* Critical Social Thought. New York: Routledge.

Omosupe, Ekua. 1991. "Black/Lesbian/Bulldagger." *Differences* 3 (2): 101–111.

Orozco, Cynthia E. 1986. "Sexism in Chicano Studies and the Community." In *Chicana Voices,* edited by Theresa Cordoba, 11–18. Austin: Center for Mexican American Studies, University of Texas.

Orozco, Sylvia. 1978. "Las Mujeres: Chicana Artists Come into Their Own." *Moving On* 2: 14–16.

Ortiz, Ricardo L. 1992. "Rechy, Isherwood, and the Numbers Game." In *El poder hispano: Actas del V Congres de Culturas Hispanas de los Estados Unidos,* edited by Alberto Moncada Lorenzo, Carmen Flys Junquera, and José Antonio Gurpegui Palacios, 507–518. Alcalá, Spain: Universidad de Alcalá, Centro de Estudios Norteamericanos, Servicio de Publicaciones.

———. 1993. "Sexuality Degree Zero: Pleasure and Power in the Novels of John Rechy, Arturo Islas, and Michael Nava." In *Critical Essays: Gay and Lesbian Writers of Color,* edited by Emmanuel S. Nelson, 111–126. New York: Haworth Press.

———. 1998. "L.A. Women: Jim Morrison with John Rechy." *Literature and Psychology* 41 (Fall): 41–77.

Ortiz Taylor, Sheila. 1982. *Faultline.* Tallahassee, FL: Naiad Press.

———. 1985. *Spring Forward/Fall Back.* Tallahassee, FL: Naiad Press.

———. 1990. *Southbound.* Tallahassee, FL: Naiad Press.

———. 1998. *Coachella.* Albuquerque: University of New Mexico Press.

———. 2002. "Extranjera." Unpublished manuscript.

Ortiz Taylor, Sheila, and Sandra Ortiz Taylor. 1996. *Imaginary Parents: A Family Autobiography.* Albuquerque: University of New Mexico Press.

Otero, Rosalie. 1988a. "Amelia." In *Voces: An Anthology of Nuevo Mexicano Writers,* edited by Rudolfo Anaya, 7–18. Albuquerque: El Norte.

———. 1988b. "The Closet." In *Las mujeres hablan: An Anthology of Nuevo Mexicana Writers,* edited by Tey Diana Rebolledo, Erlinda Gonzales-Berry, and Teresa Márquez, 40–51. Albuquerque: El Norte.

Owens, Louis. 2002. "'The Very Essence of Our Lives': Leslie Silko's Webs of Identity." In *Leslie Marmon Silko's Ceremony: A Casebook,* edited by Allan Chavkin, 91–115. Oxford: Oxford University Press.

Padilla, Felix M. 1985. *Latino Ethnic Consciousness: The Case of Mexican Americans and Puerto Ricans in Chicago.* Notre Dame, IN: University of Notre Dame Press.

Padilla, Genaro M. 1993. *My History, Not Yours: The Formation of Mexican American Autobiography.* Wisconsin Studies in American Autobiography. Madison: University of Wisconsin Press.

Palacios, Monica. 1990a. "Introduction to La Llorona Loca: The Other Side." In *Lesbian Bedtime Stories 2,* edited by Terry Woodrow, 173. Willits, CA: Tough Dove Press.

———. 1990b. "La Llorona Loca: The Other Side." In *Lesbian Bedtime Stories 2*, edited by Terry Woodrow, 174–177. Willits, CA: Tough Dove Press.

———. 1991. "Personality Fabulosa." *Out/Look* 4 (2): 32–37.

———. 1993. "Taquería Tease." *VIVA Arts Quarterly* 3 (Summer): n.p.

———. 1998. "Tomboy." In *Living Chicana Theory*, edited by Carla Trujillo, 306–309. Berkeley: Third Woman Press.

———. 2000. *Greetings from a Queer Señorita*. In *Out of the Fringe: Contemporary Latina/Latino Theatre and Performance*, edited by Caridad Svich and María Teresa Marrero, 365–392. New York: Theatre Communications Group.

Paredes, Américo. 1958. *"With His Pistol in His Hand": A Border Ballad and Its Hero*. Austin: University of Texas Press.

———. 1990. *George Washington Gómez*. Houston: Arte Público.

Paredes, Raymond. 1981. "Mexican American Authors and the American Dream." *MELUS* 8 (4): 71–80.

Parker, Pat. 1978. *Movement in Black: The Collected Poetry of Pat Parker 1961–1978*. Ithaca, NY: Firebrand Books.

Paz, Octavio. 1961. *The Labyrinth of Solitude: Life and Thought in Mexico*. New York: Grove Press.

———. 1988. *Sor Juana, or, the Traps of Faith*. Translated by Margaret Sayers Peden. Seix Barral Edition. Cambridge, MA: Belknap Press.

Peña, Manuel H. 1982. "Folksong and Social Change: Two Corridos as Interpretive Sources." *Aztlán* 13 (1–2): 12–42.

———. 1992. "Música fronteriza: Border Music." *Aztlán* 21 (1–2): 191–225.

Pendleton Jiménez, Karleen. 1998. "Not Everyone Turns Pink under the Sun." Unpublished manuscript.

———. 1999. "The Lake at the End of the Wash." In *Hers3: Brilliant New Fiction by Lesbian Writers*, edited by Terry Wolverton and Robert Drake, 177–181. New York: Faber and Faber.

Pérez, Domino Renée. 2002. "Caminando con La Llorona: Traditional and Contemporary Narratives." In *Chicana Traditions: Continuity and Change*, edited by Norma Cantú and Olga Nájera-Ramírez, 100–113. Urbana: University of Illinois Press.

———. 2003. "Lost in the Cinematic Landscape: Chicanas as Lloronas in Contemporary Film." In *Velvet Barrios: Popular Culture and Chicana/o Sexualities*, edited by Alicia Gaspar de Alba, 215–228. New York: Palgrave.

Pérez, Emma. 1991a. "Gulf Dreams." In *Chicana Lesbians: The Girls Our Mothers Warned Us About*, edited by Carla Trujillo, 96–108. Berkeley: Third Woman Press.

———. 1991b. "Sexuality and Discourse: Notes from a Chicana Survivor." In *Chicana Lesbians: The Girls Our Mothers Warned Us About*, edited by Carla Trujillo, 159–184. Berkeley: Third Woman Press.

———. 1994. "Irigaray's Female Symbolic in the Making of Chicana Lesbian *Sitios y Lenguas*." In *The Lesbian Postmodern*, edited by Laura Doan, 104–117. New York: Columbia University Press.

———. 1995. "Selena's Sisters." *Lesbian Review of Books* 2 (1): 4.

———. 1996. *Gulf Dreams*. Berkeley: Third Woman Press.

————. 1999. *The Decolonial Imaginary: Writing Chicanas into History.* Theories of Representation and Difference. Bloomington: Indiana University Press.

————. 2003. "Forgetting the Alamo, or, Blood Memory." Unpublished manuscript.

Pérez, Gail. 2002. [1998]. "Ana Castillo as Santera: Reconstructiong Popular Religoius Praxis." In *A Reader in Latina Feminist Theology: Religion and Justice,* edited by María Pilar Aquino, Daisy L. Machado, and Jeanette Rodriguez, 53–79. Austin: University of Texas Press.

Pérez, Laura Elisa. 1998. "Spirit Glyphs: Reimaging Art and Artist in the Work of Chicana Tlamatinime." *Modern Fiction Studies* 44 (1): 36–76.

————. 1999. "*El Desorden*: Nationalism and Chicana/o Aesthetics." In *Between Woman and Nation,* edited by Ann Kaplan and Norma Alarcón, 19–46. Durham, NC: Duke University Press.

Pérez-Torres, Rafael. 1994. "The Ambiguous Outlaw: John Rechy and Complicitious." In *Fictions of Masculinity: Crossing Cultures, Crossing Sexualities,* 204–225. New York: New York University Press.

————. 1995. *Movements in Chicano Poetry: Against Myths, against Margins.* Cambridge Studies in American Literature and Culture, vol. 88. Cambridge: Cambridge University Press.

————. 1996. "Feathering the Serpent: Chicano Mythic 'Memory.'" In *Memory and Cultural Politics: New Approaches to American Ethnic Literatures,* edited by Amritjit Singh, Joseph T. Skerrett Jr., and Robert E. Hogan, 291–319. Boston: Northeastern University Press.

————. 1998. "Chicano Ethnicity, Cultural Hybridity and the Mestizo Voice." *American Literature* 70 (1): 153–176.

Peri Rossi, Cristina. 1991. *Fantasías eroticas.* Biblioteca Erotica. Madrid: Temas de Hoy.

Perry, Mary Elizabeth. 1999. "From Convent to Battlefield: Cross-Dressing and Gendering the Self in the New World of Imperial Spain." In *Queer Iberia: Sexualities, Cultures, and Crossings from the Middle Ages to the Renaissance,* edited by Josiah Blackmore and Gregory S. Hutcheson, 394–419. Durham, NC: Duke University Press.

Pesquera, Beatríz M., and Denise M. Segura. 1993. "There Is No Going Back: Chicanas and Feminism." In *Chicana Critical Issues,* edited by MALCS, 95–116. Berkeley: Third Woman Press.

Picco, Liz Raptis. 1993. "En nuestras mentes (a Defense of *Margins*)." *esto no tiene nombre* 2 (3): 5.

El Plan Espiritual de Aztlán. In *Documents of the Chicano Struggle,* 4–6. New York: Pathfinder Press.

"The Plan of Delano." In *Aztlán: An Anthology of Mexican American Literature,* edited by Luis Valdez and Stan Steiner. New York: Alfred A. Knopf.

Portillo, Lourdes. 1998. *Corpus: A Selena Home Movie.* [Film] Xochitl Films, San Francisco.

Portillo [Trambley], Estela. 1976. [1971]. *Day of the Swallows.* In *Contemporary Chicano Theater,* edited by Roberto J. Garza, 206–245. Notre Dame, IN: University of Notre Dame Press.

Portillo Trambley, Estela. 1983. *Sor Juana and Other Plays*. Ypsilanti, MI: Bilingual Press/Editorial Bilingüe.

———. 1986. *Trini*. Binghamton, NY: Bilingual Press/Editorial Bilingüe.

———. 1993. *Rain the Scorpions and Other Stories*. Binghamton, NY: Bilingual Press/ Editorial Bilingüe.

Pratt, Mary Louise. 1992. *Imperial Eyes: Travel Writing and Transculturation*. London: Routledge.

———. 1993. "'Yo soy La Malinche': Chicana Writers and the Poetics of Ethnonationlism." In *Twentieth-Century Poetry: From Text to Context*, edited by Peter Verdonk, 171–187. New York: Routledge.

Propper, Alice M. 1982. "Make-Believe Families and Homosexuality among Imprisoned Girls." *Criminology* 20 (1): 127–138.

Quintana, Alvina. 1990. "Politics, Representation and the Emergence of a Chicana Aesthethic." *Cultural Studies* 4, no. 3 (October): 257–263.

———. 1991. "Ana Castillo's *The Mixquiahuala Letters*: The Novelist as Ethnographer." In *Criticism in the Borderlands: Studies in Chicano Literature, Culture, and Ideology*, edited by Héctor Calderón and José David Saldívar, 72–83. Durham, NC: Duke University Press.

———. 1996. *Home Girls: Chicana Literary Voices*. Philadelphia: Temple University Press.

Quintana Ranck, Katherine. 1982. *Portrait of Doña Elena*. Berkeley: Tonatiuh-Quinto Sol International. Originally published as *Grito del Sol* 6, nos. 3–4 (1981), "A Tonatiuh Romance."

Raber, Erin. 1998. "'La peór de todas': Chicana/Mexicana Lesbian Activism." Paper presented at the National Association of Chicana and Chicano Studies 25th Annual Conference, México, D.F.

Radcliffe, Sarah, and Sallie Westwood. 1996. *Remaking the Nation: Place, Identity and Politics in Latin America*. London: Routledge.

Ramos, Gloria. 1989. "Rush Hour Bunny." In *In a Different Light*, edited by Carolyn Weathers and Jenny Wrenn, 83–90. Los Angeles: Clothespin Fever Press.

Ramos, Juanita [Díaz], ed. 1994. *Compañeras: Latina Lesbians—An Anthology*. Latina Lesbian History Project Edition. New York: Routledge.

Rebolledo, Tey Diana. 1987. "Tradition and Mythology: Signatures of Landscape in Chicana Literature." In *The Desert Is No Lady*, edited by Vera Norwood and Janice Monk, 96–124. New Haven, CT: Yale University Press.

———. 1993. "'¿Y dónde estaban las mujeres?': In Pursuit of an Hispana Literary and Historical Heritage in Colonial New Mexico, 1580–1840." In *Reconstructing a Chicano/a Literary Heritage*, edited by María Herrera-Sobek, 140–157. Tucson: University of Arizona Press.

———. 1995. *Women Singing in the Snow: A Cultural Analysis of Chicana Literature*. Tucson: University of Arizona Press.

Rebolledo, Tey Diana, Erlinda Gonzales-Berry, and Teresa Márquez, eds. 1988. *Las mujeres hablan: An Anthology of Nuevo Mexicana Writers*. Albuquerque: El Norte.

Rebolledo, Tey Diana, and Eliana S. Rivero, eds. 1993. *Infinite Divisions: An Anthology of Chicana Literature*. Tucson: University of Arizona Press.

Rechy, John. 1963. *City of Night*. New York: Grove Press.

————. 1991. *The Miraculous Day of Amalia Gómez*. New York: Arcade.

Retter, Yolanda. 1997. "Lesbian Spaces in Los Angeles, 1970–90." In *Queers in Space: Communities, Public Places, Sites of Resistance,* edited by Gordon Brent Ingram, Anne-Marie Bouthillette, and Yolanda Retter, 325–337. Seattle: Bay Press.

————. 1998. "On the Side of Angels: Lesbian Activism in Los Angeles, 1970–1990." Ph.D. dissertation, University of New Mexico.

Revard, Carter. 1998. "Walking among the Stars." In *Family Matters, Tribal Affairs,* 3–26. Tucson: University of Arizona.

Rich, Adrienne. [1979] 1983. "Compulsory Heterosexuality and Lesbian Existence." In *Powers of Desire: The Politics of Sexuality,* edited by Ann Snitow, Christine Stansell, and Sharon Thompson, 177–205. New York: Monthly Review Press.

————. 1986. "Notes toward a Politics of Location." In *Blood, Bread, and Poetry: Selected Prose, 1979–85,* 210–231. New York: Norton.

Riggs, Marlon, prod. and dir. 1989. *Tongues Untied.* [Video]. 55 min. Frameline, San Francisco.

Rivera, Tomás. 1987. *. . . Y no se lo tragó la tierra.* Translated by Evangelina Vigil-Piñon. Houston: Arte Público.

Rivera-Valdés, Sonia. 1989. "Las historias prohibidas de Marta Veneranda." *Third Woman* 4: 90–98.

Riviere, Joan. 1987. [1929]. "Womanliness as a Masquerade." In *Formations of Fantasy,* edited by Victor Burgin, James Donald, and Caren Kaplan, 35–44. New York: Routledge.

Rodriguez, Ana Patricia. 2001. "Refugees of the South: Central Americans in the U.S. Latino Imaginary." *American Literature* 73 (2): 387–412.

Rodriguez, Clara, ed. 1997. *Latin Looks: Images of Latinas and Latinos in the U.S. Media.* Boulder, CO: Westview Press.

Rodriguez, Joseph A. 1998. "Becoming Latinos: Mexican Americans, Chicanos, and the Spanish Myth in the Urban Southwest." *Western Historical Quarterly* 29 (2): 165–185.

Rodriguez, Ralph E. 2000. "Chicana/o Fiction from Resistance to Contestation: The Role of Creation in Ana Castillo's *So Far from God." MELUS* 25 (2): 63–82.

Rodriguez, Randy. 1998a. "The Problem with Richard(s): Sissies and Their Fathers in *Pocho* and *Hunger of Memory.*" Paper presented at the National Association of Chicana and Chicano Studies 25th Annual Conference, México, D.F.

————. 1998b. "Queer(y)ing Richard Rodriguez: *Days of Obligation,* Camp and Neo-Con(Tra Cultural) Nationalist Politics." Paper presented at the National Association of Chicana and Chicano Studies 25th Annual Conference, Mexico, D.F.

————. 1998c. "Richard Rodriguez Reconsidered: Queering the Sissy." *Texas Studies in Literature and Language* 40 (4): 396–423.

Rodriguez, Richard. 1982. *Hunger of Memory.* New York: Bantam.

————. 1992. *Days of Obligation: An Argument with My Mexican Father.* New York: Penguin Books.

Rodriguez, Richard T. 2001. "On the Subject of Gang Photography." *Aztlán* 25 (1): 151–167.

————. 2002. "Serial Kinship: Representing La Familia in Early Chicano Publications." *Aztlán* 27 (1): 123–138.

————. 2003. "Verse of the Godfather." In *Velvet Barrios: Popular Culture and Chicana/ o Sexualities*, edited by Alicia Gaspar de Alba, 107–124. New York: Palgrave.

Rodriguez, W. Phil. 1998. *"Ojos que no ven/Eyes That Fail to See*: Translating the AIDS Body via Telenovela." Paper presented at the New Directions in Chicana/ Chicano Studies conference, University of California, Los Angeles.

Rogers, Carole Garibaldi. 1996. *Poverty, Chastity, and Change: Lives of Contemporary American Nuns*. Twayne's Oral History Series. New York: Twayne.

Román, David. 1997. "Latino Performance and Identity." *Aztlán* 22 (2): 151–167.

Romero, Lora. 1993. "'When Something Goes Queer': Familiarity, Formalism, and Minority Intellectuals in the 1980s." *Yale Journal of Criticism* 6, no. 1 (Spring): 121–142.

Romero, Mary. 1992. *Maid in the U.S.A.* Perspectives on Gender. New York: Routledge.

Romo-Carmona, Mariana. 1997. *Living at Night*. Duluth, MN: Spinsters Ink.

Rosaldo, Renato. 1989. *Culture and Truth: The Remaking of Social Analysis*. Boston: Beacon Press.

————. 1991. "Fables of the Fallen Guy." In *Criticism in the Borderlands: Studies in Chicano Literature, Culture, and Ideology*, edited by Héctor Calderón and José David Saldívar, 84–93. Durham, NC: Duke University Press.

Rubio-Goldsmith, Raquel. 1990. "Oral History: Considerations and Problems for Its Use in the History of Mexicanas in the United States." In *Between Borders: Essays on Mexicana/Chicana History*, edited by Adelaida R. Del Castillo, 161–173. Encino, CA: Floricanto Press.

Ruíz de Burton, María Amparo. 1995. *Who Would Have Thought It?* Recovering the U.S. Hispanic Literary Heritage. Houston: Arte Público.

————. 1997. *The Squatter and the Don*. Recovering the U.S. Hispanic Literary Heritage. Houston: Arte Público.

Ruíz, Vicki L. 1987. *Cannery Women/Cannery Lives: Mexican Women, Unionization, and the California Food Processing Industry, 1930–1950*. 1st ed. Albuquerque: University of New Mexico Press.

————. 1999. *From out of the Shadows: Mexican American Women in Twentieth-Century America*. Oxford: Oxford University Press.

Sagarin, Edward. 1976. "Prison Homosexuality and Its Effect on Post-Prison Sexual Behavior." *Psychiatry* 39 (3): 245–257.

Said, Edward. 1979. *Orientalism*. New York: Random House.

Saldaña-Portillo, Josefina. 2001. "Who's the Indian in Aztlán? Re-Writing Mestizaje, Indianism, and Chicanismo from the Lacandón." In *The Latin American Subaltern Studies Reader*, edited by Ileana Rodríguez, 402–423. Durham, NC: Duke University Press.

Saldívar, José David. 1991. *The Dialectics of Our America: Genealogy, Cultural Critique, and Literary History*. Post-Contemporary Interventions. Durham, NC: Duke University Press.

————. 1997. *Border Matters: Remapping American Cultural Studies*. American Crossroads. Berkeley: University of California Press.

Saldívar, Ramón. 1990. *Chicano Narrative: The Dialectics of Difference*. Wisconsin Project on American Writers. Madison: University of Wisconsin Press.

Saldívar-Hull, Sonia. 1991. "Feminism on the Border: From Gender Politics to Geopolitics." In *Criticism in the Borderlands: Studies in Chicano Literature, Culture, and Ideology*, edited by Héctor Calderón and José David Saldívar, 203–220. Durham, NC: Duke University Press.

——. 2000. *Feminism on the Border: Chicana Gender Politics and Literature*. Berkeley: University of California Press.

Sánchez, George J. 1993. *Becoming Mexican American: Ethnicity, Culture and Identity in Chicano Los Angeles, 1900–1945*. New York: Oxford University Press.

Sanchez, Marta E. 1990. "Arturo Islas' *The Rain God*: An Alternative Tradition." *American Literature* 62 (2): 284–304.

Sánchez, Rosaura. 1990. "The History of Chicanas: A Proposal for a Materialist Perspective." In *Between Borders: Essays on Mexicana/Chicana History*, edited by Adelaida R. Del Castillo, 1–30. Encino, CA: Floricanto Press.

——. 1993. "Nineteenth-Century Californio Narratives: The Hubert H. Bancroft Collection." In *Recovering the U.S. Hispanic Literary Heritage*, edited by Ramón Gutiérrez and Genaro Padilla, 279–292. Houston: Arte Público.

Sánchez, Rosaura, and Rosa Martinez Cruz, eds. 1977. *Essays on La Mujer*. Los Angeles: Chicano Studies Center Publications, University of California, Los Angeles.

Sánchez-Scott, Milpa. 1988. *Roosters*. New York: Dramatist's Play Service.

Sand, Jordan. 1999. "Historians and Public Memory in Japan: The 'Comfort Women' Controversy." *History and Memory* 11 (2): 117–152.

Sandoval, Anna. 1995. "No dejen que se escapen: Modes of Repression and Modes of Resistance in Chicana and Mexicana Literature." Ph.D. dissertation, University of California, Santa Cruz.

Sandoval, Chéla. 1991. "U.S. Third World Feminism: The Theory and Method of Oppositional Consciousness in the Postmodern World." *Genders* 10 (Spring): 1–24.

——. 1992. "U.S. Third World Feminism." In *The Oxford Companion to Women's Writing in the United States*, edited by Cathy N. Davidson, Linda Wagner-Martin, and Elizabeth Ammons, 880–882. New York: Oxford University Press.

——. 2000. *Methodology of the Oppressed*. Minneapolis: University of Minnesota Press.

SanGiovanni, Lucinda. 1978. *Ex-Nuns: A Study of Emergent Role Passage*. Modern Sociology. Norwood, NJ: Ablex.

Saporta Sternbach, Nancy. 1989. "'A Deep Racial Memory of Love': The Chicana Feminism of Cherríe Moraga." In *Breaking Boundaries: Latina Writings and Critical Readings*, edited by Asunción Horno-Delgado, Eliana Ortega, Nina M. Scott, and Nancy Saporta Sternbach, 48–61. Amherst: University of Massachusetts Press.

Scott, Carla F. 1993. "The Hottentot Effect: The Crisis of Black Lesbian Representation." Ph.D. qualifying essay in History of Consciousness, University of California, Santa Cruz.

Serros, Michele. 1993. *Chicana Falsa*. Culver City, CA: Lalo Press.

Shea, Renee H. 1999. "'The Hunger to Tell': Edwidge Danticat and *The Farming of*

Bones." Macomere: Journal of the Association of Caribbean Women Writers and Scholars 2: 12–22.

Shemak, April. 2002. "Re-Membering Hispaniola: Edwidge Danticat's *The Farming of Bones."* *Modern Fiction Studies* 48: 83–112.

Shohat, Ella. 1991. "Imaging Terra Incognita." *Public Culture* 3 (2): 41–70.

Silko, Leslie Marmon. 1996. "The Border Patrol State." In *Yellow Woman and a Beauty of the Spirit: Essays on Native American Life Today,* 115–123. New York: Simon & Schuster.

Silver, Jon, Joe Dees, Annette Oropeza, and José Luis Orozco. 1989. *Watsonville on Strike.* [Documentary] Migrant Media Productions, Watsonville, CA.

Sirias, Silvio, and Richard McGarry. 2000. "Rebellion and Tradition in Ana Castillo's *So Far from God* and Sylvia Lopez-Medina's *Cantora."* *MELUS* 25 (2): 83–100.

Smith, Barbara. 1982. "Toward a Black Feminist Criticism." In *All the Women Are White, All the Blacks Are Men, but Some of Us Are Brave: Black Women's Studies,* edited by Gloria T. Hull, Patricia Bell Scott, and Barbara Smith, 157–175. New York: Feminist Press.

Snitow, Ann, Christine Stansell, and Sharon Thompson, eds. 1983. *Powers of Desire: The Politics of Sexuality.* New Feminist Library. New York: Monthly Review Press.

Sosa-Riddell, Adaljiza. 1973. "Como duele." *El Grito* 7 (1): 61.

Sperling Cockroft, Eva, and Holly Barnet-Sanchez, eds. 1990. *Signs from the Heart: California Chicano Murals.* Albuquerque: Socal and Public Art Resource Center and University of New Mexico Press.

Spivak, Gayatri Chakravorty. 1988. "Can the Subaltern Speak?" In *Marxism and the Interpretation of Culture,* edited by Cary Nelson and Lawrence Grossberg, 271–313. Urbana: University of Illinois Press.

Steinberg, Stephen. 1989. *The Ethnic Myth: Race, Ethnicity, and Class in America.* Boston: Beacon Press.

Stevens, John L. 1969. *Incidents of Travel in Central America, Chiapas, and Yucatán.* Vols. 1–2. New York: Dover.

Stevens, Maurice. 1996. "Public (Re)Memory, Vindicating Narratives, and Troubling Beginnings: Toward a Cultural Postcolonial Psychoanalytical Theory." In *Fanon: A Critical Reader,* edited by Lewis R. Gordon, T. Denean Sharpley-Whiting, and Renée T. White, 203–219. Oxford: Blackwell.

Stoller, Nancy E. 1998. *Lessons from the Damned: Queers, Whores, and Junkies Respond to AIDS.* New York: Routledge.

Tafolla, Carmen. 1989. "Federico y Elfiria." *Third Woman* 4: 105–111.

Takagi, Dana. 1994. "Maiden Voyage: Excursion into Sexuality and Identity Politics in Asian America." *Amerasia Journal* 20 (1): 1–18.

Tatum, Charles M., ed. 1992. *New Chicana/Chicano Writing 1.* Tucson: University of Arizon Press.

Tavizonee-Salas, Sean [Aureliano DeSoto]. 1993. "The Sum of All Fears: The Conceptualization of Gay Distopia in Richard Rodriguez's 'Late Victorians'." Paper presented at Queer Sites, New College & Trinity College, University of Toronto.

Tedlock, Dennis, trans. and annot. 1996. *Popul Vuh*, New York. Simon & Schuster.
Terrill, Joey, 1994. *La historia de amor*. VIVA Lesbian and Gay Latino Artists, Los Angeles.
Torres, Lourdes. 1991. "The Construction of the Self in U.S. Latina Autobiographies." In *Third World Women and the Politics of Feminism*, edited by Chandra Talapade Mohanty, Ann Russo, and Lourdes Torres, 271–287. Bloomington: Indiana University Press.
———. 2003. "Violence, Desire, and Transformative Remembering in Emma Pérez's *Gulf Dreams*." In *Tortilleras: Hispanic and Latina Lesbian Expression*, edited by Lourdes Torres and Inmaculada Pertusa-Seva, 228–239. Latin American/Latino Studies. Philadelphia: Temple University Press.
Torres, Lourdes, and Inmaculada Pertusa-Seva, eds. 2003. *Tortilleras: Hispanic and Latina Lesbian Expression*. Latin American/Latino Studies. Philadelphia: Temple University Press.
Tropicana, Carmelita, and Uzi Parnes. 1998. "The Conquest of Mexico as Seen through the Eyes of Hernán Cortés's Horse." *Aztlán* 23 (1): 129–132.
Troyano, Alina. 2000a. *I, Carmelita Tropicana: Performing between Cultures*. Edited by Chon A. Noriega. Boston: Beacon Press.
———. 2000b. "Sor Juana: The Nightmare." In *I, Carmelita Tropicana: Performing between Cultures*, 123–136. New York: Beacon Press.
Troyano, Ela. 1994. *Carmelita Tropicana: Your Kunst Is Your Waffen*. [Film] First Run/Icarus Films, New York.
Trujillo, Carla. 1991a. "Chicana Lesbians: Fear and Loathing in the Chicano Community." In *Chicana Lesbians*, edited by Carla Trujillo, 186–194. Berkeley: Third Woman Press.
———, ed. 1991b. *Chicana Lesbians: The Girls Our Mothers Warned Us About*. Berkeley: Third Woman Press.
———. 1998. "La Virgen de Guadalupe and Her Reconstruction in Chicana Lesbian Desire." In *Living Chicana Theory*, edited by Carla Trujillo, 214–231. Berkeley: Third Woman Press.
———. 2003. *What Night Brings*. Willamantic, CT: Curbstone Press.
Turner, Kay. 1986. "Home Altars and the Arts of Devotion." In *Chicano Expressions: A New View in American Art*, edited by Inverna Lockpez, Tomás Ybarra-Frausto, Judith Baca, and Kay Turner, 40–48. New York: INTAR Latin American Gallery.
Valdez, Luis. 1968. *La conquista de México*. In *Early Works*, 53–65. Houston: Arte Público.
———. 1969. *I Am Joaquín*. [Film] 1 hr., 22 min. El Centro Campesino Cultural, San Juan Bautista, CA.
———. 1976. *Los Vendidos*. In *Contemporary Chicano Theatre*, edited by Roberto J. Garza, 15–27. Notre Dame, IN: University of Notre Dame Press.
———. 1981. *Zoot Suit*. [Film] 1 hr., 44 min. MCA Universal Home Video, Universal City, CA.
———, prod. and dir. 1986. *La Bamba*. [Film] 1 hr., 43 min. Columbia Pictures, Burbank, CA.

————. [1981] 1987. *Corridos.* [Television production] 58 min. KQED, San Francisco.

————. 1989. *The Shrunken Head of Pancho Villa.* In *Necessary Theater,* edited by Jorge Huerta, 153–207. Houston: Arte Público.

Vance, Carole S., ed. 1984. *Pleasure and Danger: Exploring Female Sexuality.* Boston: Routledge & Kegan Paul.

Vargas, Deborah R. 2002a. "Bidi Bidi Bom Bom: Selena and Tejano Music in the Making of Tejas." In *Latino/a Popular Culture,* edited by Michelle Habell-Pallán and Mary Romero, 117–126. New York: New York University Press.

————. 2002b. "Cruzando Frontejas: Mapping Selena's Tejano Music 'Crossover.'" In *Chicana Traditions: Continuity and Change,* edited by Norma Cantú and Olga Nájera-Ramírez, 224–236. Urbana: University of Illinois Press.

Vargas, Kathy. 1995. "Artist's Statement." In *From the West: Chicano Narrative Photography,* edited by Chon A. Noriega, 73. Seattle: University of Washington Press.

Vargas, Margarita. 1990. "Lo apolineo y lo dionisiaco hacia una semiotica en *Sor Juana y The Day of the Swallows* de Estela Portillo Trambley." *Gestos: Teoria y Practica del Teatro Hispanico* 5 (9): 91–98.

Vasconcelos, José. 1966. *La raza cosmica: Misión de la raza iberoamericana.* Colección Austral. México, D.F.: Espasa-Calpe Mexicana.

————. [1929] 1979. *La raza cosmica/The Cosmic Race: A Bilingual Edition.* Translated by Didier T. Jaén. Pensamiento Mexicano. Los Angeles: Department of Chicano Studies, California State University.

Vaz, Kim M., Mary Filippo, Deborah G. Plant, and Toni Thomas. 1992. *Spirit Murder: Stopping the Violent Deaths of Black Women*: Tampa: University of South Florida.

Velasco, Sherry. 2000. *The Lieutenant Nun: Transgenderism, Lesbian Desire, and Catalina de Erauso.* Austin: University of Texas Press.

————. 2003. "Interracial Lesbian Erotics in Early Modern Spain: Catalina de Erauso and Elana/o de Céspedes." In *Tortilleras: Hispanic and Latina Lesbian Expression,* edited by Lourdes Torres and Inmaculada Pertusa-Seva, 213–227. Philadelphia: Temple University Press.

Vélez, Isabel. 1996. "Crossing 'El Rio': Migrations and Sexual Identity." Paper presented at the National Association of Chicana and Chicano Studies 23d Annual Conference, Chicago.

Veyna, Angelina F. 1993. "'It Is My Last Wish That . . .': A Look at Colonial Nuevo Mexicanas through Their Testaments." In *Building with Our Hands: New Directions in Chicana Studies,* edited by Adela de la Torre and Beatríz M. Pesquera, 91–108. Berkeley: University of California Press.

Vigil, Evangelina, ed. 1987. *Woman of Her Word: Hispanic Women Write.* Houston: Arte Público.

Villanueva, Alma Luz. 1994a. "El Alma/The Soul, Three." In *Weeping Woman: La Llorona and Other Stories,* 151–156. Tempe, AZ: Bilingual Press/Editorial Bilingüe.

————. 1994b. *Naked Ladies.* Tempe, AZ: Bilingual Review Press/Editorial Bilingüe.

————. 1994c. *Weeping Woman: La Llorona and Other Stories.* Tempe, AZ: Bilingual Press/Editorial Bilingüe.

Villanueva, Tino. 1993. *Scene from the Movie "Giant."* Willimantic, CT: Curbstone Press.

Villareal, José Antonio. 1970. *Pocho.* New York: Anchor Books.

Villaseñor, Victor. 1991. *Rain of Gold.* Houston: Arte Público.

————. 1997. *Wild Steps of Heaven.* New York: Delta.

Viramontes, Helena María. 1985a. "The Cariboo Cafe." In *The Moths and Other Stories* 65–80. Houston: Arte Público.

————. 1985b. *The Moths and Other Stories.* Houston: Arte Público.

————. 1987. "Miss Clairol." *Americas Review* 15 (3–4): 101–105.

————. 1996. *Under the Feet of Jesus.* New York: E. P. Dutton.

Warner, Michael. 1993. "Introduction." In *Fear of a Queer Planet: Queer Politics and Social Theory,* edited by Michael Warner, vii–xxxi. Minneapolis: University of Minnesota Press.

Weber, Devra Anne. 1990. "Mexican Women on Strike: Memory, History, and Oral Narratives." In *Between Borders: Essays on Mexicana/Chicana History,* edited by Adelaida R. Del Castillo, 174–200. Encino, CA: Floricanto Press.

Wheatwind, Marie-Elise. 1994a. Review of *Last Generation. Women's Review of Books* 11 (4): 22.

————. 1994b. Review of *Naked Ladies. Women's Review of Books* 11 (8): 25.

White, Hayden. 1973. *Metahistory: The Historical Imagination in Nineteenth-Century Europe.* Baltimore: Johns Hopkins University Press.

————. 1982. "The Politics of Historical Interpretation: Discipline and De-Sublimation." *Critical Inquiry* 9: 113–137.

Widén, Robert. 1991. *Aztlán es una fabula.* Cover illustration, *The Miraculous Day of Amalia Gómez.* New York: Arcade.

Woodrow, Terry, ed. 1989. *Lesbian Bedtime Stories.* Willits, CA: Tough Dove Books.

————. ed. 1990. *Lesbian Bedtime Stories 2.* Willits, CA: Tough Dove Books.

Woolf, Virginia. 1938. *Three Guineas.* London: Hogarth Press.

————. 1984. *A Room of One's Own.* New York: Harcourt Brace Jovanovich.

Yarbro-Bejarano, Yvonne. 1985. "Chicana's Experience in Collective Theatre: Ideology and Form." *Women & Performance* 2 (2): 45–58.

————. 1986a. "Cherríe Moraga's *Giving Up the Ghost*: The Representation of Female Desire." *Third Woman* 3 (1–2): 113–120.

————. 1986b. "The Female Subject in Chicano Theatre: Sexuality, 'Race,' and Class." *Theatre Journal* 38 (4): 389–407.

————. 1987. "Chicana Literature from a Chicana Feminist Perspective." *Americas Review* 15 (3–4): 139–145.

————. 1991. "De-Constructing the Lesbian Body: Cherríe Moraga's *Loving in the War Years.*" In *Chicana Lesbians: The Girls Our Mothers Warned Us About,* edited by Carla Trujillo, 143–155. Berkeley: Third Woman Press.

————. 1993a. "Cherrie Moraga's *Shadow of a Man.*" In *Feminist Performances,* edited by Lynn Hart and Peggy Phelan, 85–104. Ann Arbor: University of Michigan Press.

————. 1993b. "Turning It Around: Chicana Art Critic Yvonne Yarbro-Bejarano

Discusses the Insider/Outsider Visions of Ester Hernández and Yolanda López." *Crossroads* 31 (May): 15, 17.

———. 1994. "Gloria Anzaldúa's *Borderlands/La Frontera*: Cultural Studies, 'Difference,' and the Non-Unitary Subject." *Cultural Critique* 28 (Fall): 5–28.

———. 1995a. "Expanding the Categories of Race and Sexuality in Lesbian and Gay Studies." In *Professions of Desire: Lesbian and Gay Studies in Literature*, edited by George E. Haggerty and Bonnie Zimmerman, 124–135. New York: Modern Language Association of America.

———. 1995b. "The Lesbian Body in Latina Cultural Production." In *¿Entiendes?* edited by Emilie L. Bergman and Paul Julian Smith, 181–197. Durham, NC: Duke University Press.

———. 1997. "Crossing the Border with Chavela Vargas: A Chicana Femme's Tribute." In *Sex and Sexuality in Latin America*, edited by Daniel Balderstorm and Donna Guy, 33–43. New York: New York University Press.

———. 1998. "Laying It Bare: The Queer/Colored Body in Photography by Laura Aguilar." In *Living Chicana Theory*, edited by Carla Trujillo, 277–305. Berkeley: Third Woman Press.

———. 2000. "Traveling Transgressions: *Cubanidad* in Performances by Carmelita Tropicana and Marga Gómez." In *Reading and Writing the Ambiente: Queer Sexualities in Latino, Latin American and Spanish Culture*, edited by Susana Chávez-Silverman and Librada Hernández, 200–217. Madison: University of Wisconsin Press.

———. 2001a. "'The Miracle People': Heroes and Saints and Contemporary Chicano Theatre." In *The Wounded Heart: Writings on Cherríe Moraga*, 64–81. Austin: University of Texas Press.

———. 2001b. *The Wounded Heart: Writings on Cherríe Moraga*. Chicana Matters. Austin: University of Texas Press.

Ybarra-Frausto, Tomás. 1986. "Grafica/Urban Iconography." In *Chicano Expressions: A New View in American Art*, edited by Inverna Lockpez, Tomás Ybarra-Frausto, Judith Baca, and Kay Turner, 21–27. New York: INTAR Latin American Gallery.

Yung, Judy. 1995. *Unbound Feet: A Social History of Chinese Women in San Francisco.* Berkeley: University of California Press.

Yvevacha. 1992. "Could We Have Done More?" *esto no tiene nombre* 1 (4): 21.

Zavella, Patricia. 1987. *Women's Work and Chicano Families: Cannery Workers of the Santa Clara Valley.* Ithaca, NY: Cornell University Press.

———. 1989. "The Problematic Relationship of Feminism and Chicana Studies." *Women's Studies* 17 (1–2): 25–36.

———. 1991. "Mujeres in Factories: Race and Class Perspectives on Women, Class, and Family." In *Gender at the Crossroads of Knowledge*, edited by Micaela di Leonardo, 312–336. Berkeley: University of California Press.

———. 1992. "Feminist Insider Dilemmas: Constructing Identity with 'Chicana' Informants." *Frontiers* 13 (3): 53–76.

———. 1997. "Playing with Fire: The Gendered Construction of Chicano/Mexicana Sexuality." In *The Gender/Sexuality Reader: Culture, History, Political Economy*, edited by Roger N. Lancaster and Micaela di Leonardo, 392–408. New York: Routledge.

Zimmerman, Bonnie. 1990. *The Safe Sea of Women: Lesbian Fiction, 1969–1989.* New York: Beacon.

———. 1993a. "Perverse Reading: The Lesbian Appropriation of Literature." In *Sexual Practice, Textual Theory: Lesbian Cultural Criticism,* edited by Susan J. Wolfe and Penelope Stanley, 135–149. Cambridge, MA: Blackwell.

———. 1993b. "What Has Never Been: An Overview of Lesbian Feminist Criticism." In *Sexual Practice, Textual Theory: Lesbian Cultural Criticism,* edited by Susan J. Wolfe and Penelope Stanley, 33–54. Cambridge, MA: Blackwell.

Index